Perspectives on Job Enrichment and Productivity

*Selected readings
on the theory, definition, and need, as well as
on the practice and applications of job enrichment.*

Edited and Compiled by

Waino W. Suojanen   Mackey J. McDonald
Gary L. Swallow   W. William Suojanen

Publishing Services D'
School of Busi
Georgia S
Atlant
1

Library of Congress Cataloging in Publication Data

Perspectives on job enrichment and productivity.

    1. Job satisfaction–Addresses, essays, lectures.
2. Personnel management–Addresses, essays, lectures.
3. Industrial organization–Addresses, essays,
lectures. I. Suojanen, Waino W.
HF5549.5.J63P42   658.31'42   75-31553
ISBN 0-88406-008-X

Published by

Publishing Services Division
School of Business Administration
Georgia State University
University Plaza
Atlanta, Georgia 30303 U S A

Printed and bound in the United States of America

Cover Design by Fredd Chrestman

Contents

Preface   vii

Acknowledgements   ix

Introduction   xi

PART ONE:
THEORY, DEFINITION, NEED

Chapter

1. Job Enrichment and Management Theory: 3
   An Overview
       Donald R. Hudson
       James R. Miller
       Waino W. Suojanen

2. Quality of Working Life: What Is It?   17
       Richard E. Walton

3. Job Enrichment and Organizational Change   31
       Warren S. Bollmeier, II
       Waino W. Suojanen

4. Job Enrichment: A Re-evaluation   49
       Mitchell Fein

5. Critical Factors in Job Enrichment   71
       Fred Luthans
       Edward Knod

6. Job Satisfaction: Sorting Out the Nonsense   87
   William Gomberg

7. Job Satisfaction: A Union Response   101
   William W. Winpisinger

8. The Thirteenth Dilemma   109
   Ted Mills

9. Humanizing the Work Scene   123
   Walter A. Haas, Jr.

10. "Work in America": A Review Article   131
    William E. Reif

PART TWO:
PRACTICE AND APPLICATIONS

Chapter

11. Job Enrichment: Challenge of the Seventies   147
    Roy W. Walters

12. On Ending Worker Alienation   157
    Robert Schrank

13. A Nonpartisan View of Participative Management   181
    Harold M. F. Rush

14. Return on Involvement   195
    Richard N. Arthur

15. Employe Development and the Modern Work Force   205
    Stephen H. Fuller

16. Job Enrichment at The Travelers   215
    Norman Edmonds

17. Improving Job Satisfaction in Local Governments   227
    Sam Zagoria

18. Successful Job Enrichment: A Case Example   237
    Merrill E. Douglass
    T. Stephen Johnson

19. Changing Work Organization at Volvo   247
    Pehr Gyllenhammar

20. Kaiser Aluminum's Action Guide to   257
    Job Enrichment
    Susan E. Walima

About the Editors . . .

Waino W. Suojanen is a Professor of Management in the School of Business Administration at Georgia State University; *Gary L. Swallow* is a Captain in the United States Army; *Mackey J. McDonald* is a plant manager with the Hanes Corporation; and *W. William Suojanen* is in the Sloan School of Management at Massachusetts Institute of Technology, formerly an editor on the *Sloan Management Review.*

Preface

This volume is dedicated to the proposition that job enrichment will pose an important challenge within the economic sphere of life during the last quarter of the twentieth century. Orthodox job enrichment will probably represent the major portion of this thrust during the next five or ten years. In subsequent decades, we anticipate that more experimental approaches and partial solutions will focus on sociotechnical systems and participative management. In time, we look for American management and labor to become interested in the conceptual applications of industrial democracy at the working levels of the organization.

The Editors

Acknowledgements

The final test of a book of readings is its endurability. The literature of management is replete with articles devoted to the general area of productivity and job enrichment; to read hundreds of them and to select but a score or so for inclusion in this volume has been possible only because of the cooperation of a number of people.

Those of us who did the early work in the project appear as editors. Others who helped in the refining editorial processes — Carlton Bessinger, Tom Gregory, Tim Klinger, Thomas Sims, R. Cary Bynum, and Virginia Waldrop — each deserve to be listed as editors, but we have run out of room.

We wish to thank Georgia State University and its Publishing Services Division for financial support and technical assistance. Last but not least, we are indebted to the authors and publishers who have by their permissions allowed us to construct this approach and to achieve the hoped-for balance in our perspective on the quality of work life.

The twenties and thirties were marked by an emphasis that

Introduction

Management is changing continuously. Whether from the viewpoint of the student, the practitioner, or the researcher, its state of flux is evidence of its viability — its parameters ever shifting and its projections still extending. Its disciplines are diverse; its concepts are changing, so sensitive are its doctrines to the fluidity of its component subjects. Yet many will say — and indeed be correct in so saying — that "this is the same old stuff we have heard for years, except said in a different way, or with new buzz words."

Management is the psychology of business more so than the physiology of business. Thus we, the editors, have collected readings that address the broader spectrum of those intrinsic work values known as "the quality of work life." The authors of articles in this volume have come to grips with the factors which most directly affect this very sensitive area of management; their observations, experiments, analyses, and solutions provide a framework for practical application of the dynamics of job enrichment through the most advanced concepts and systems known today.

In retrospect, we can trace the beginnings of a theory of management from the late nineteenth century when the corporation had first become the representative form of economic organization. The *theory of management* in those days was the province of the practitioner rather than the academic. Frederick W. Taylor acquired his reputation as the "Father of Scientific Management" from his work as a major technical-staff executive. Other theorists with strong roots in the workaday world made significant contributions to the literature while, at the same time, developing tools and techniques for the practicing manager. Planning, organizing, staffing, directing, and controlling came to be known as the *processes of management.*

The twenties and thirties were marked by an emphasis that

identified management engineering as the core of the discipline. More than half a century ago, the Hawthorne Studies were initiated under the sponsorship of the National Research Council, the Western Electric Company, and the Harvard Business School; their profound effect would eventually produce almost a total revolution in the theory of management. The war years of the forties and early fifties saw the maturation of the behavioral sciences approach and the emergence of matrix organization and project management. The later fifties and sixties produced the ultimate triumph of systems management—man's successful travels in space and the spectacular technology of the initial landing on the moon.

These theories evolved and came to focus within the various *schools of management.* Initially there was the classical or rational school, which argued that work or tasks can be so organized as to accomplish the objectives of the organization most effectively and efficiently. Adherents of this view feel that both organizational structure and the tools and techniques of management are the product of rational thought, based on "legitimate" authority and utilization of bureaucratic models. The rational theory assumes that behavior is economically logical, coinciding with the objectives of the organization when properly managed.

The behavioral science school states that organizations develop spontaneously and naturally when people associate with one another in the pursuit of common needs, interests, and objectives. This school traces its antecedents to the Hawthorne Studies of 1924 which we have mentioned earlier. Yet a third school developed, which has further served to integrate the literature: the systems approach to organizations. The prototype systems approach mobilizes hardware, software, and people in order to achieve large-scale objectives that are quite technologically advanced. Closely linked with this approach is operations research. (As we know it today, operations research originated during the twenties and thirties in the United Kingdom as a response to the growing threat of World War II.)

These varying approaches to management were marked by mutual antagonisms and conflicts. Each has tended to view management in terms of extremes — as a dichotomy rather than a continuum. The new management vocabulary is characterized by such terms as *achievers and nonachievers, X and Y managers, satisfiers and nonsatisfiers, hygiene factors and motivators, productivity and nonproductivity, union and nonunion; labor and management; autocratic and democratic; young and old; male and female; black and white; industry and academia,* to mention but a few.

Organizational behavior and management practices have been studied in a variety of settings ranging from the arts and crafts to sweat shops and scientific engineering, from scientific production to behavioral adaptation, from hostility and conflict to automated production. It is now becoming increasingly clear that pride in productivity and concern for craftsmanship can be achieved through such constructive devices as mini-grouping, job enrichment, humanization of participative management. And therein lies the most viable definition of the quality of **work life.**

PART ONE
Theory, Definition and Need

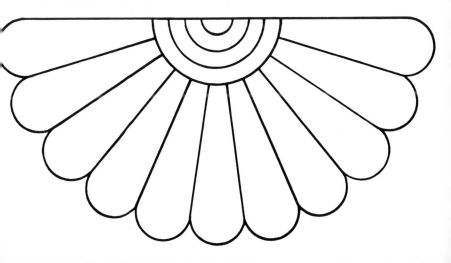

Donald R. Hudson is Associate Professor of Management, University of Miami, Miami, Florida.

James R. Miller is Associate Dean and Director of the Office of Services, School of Business Administration, Georgia State University, Atlanta, Georgia.

Waino W. Suojanen is Professor of Management, School of Business Administration, Georgia State University, Atlanta, Georgia.

1

Job Enrichment and Management Theory
An Overview

Donald R. Hudson   James R. Miller
Waino W. Suojanen

Several years ago, an advertisement by the Swedish automobile manufacturer, Saab, boldly declared that the company was departing from the traditionally accepted method of assembling automobiles. The advertisement proclaimed Saab's reason for changing its production system as follows: "Bored people build bad cars. That's why we're doing away with the assembly line." Instead of being strung out along an assembly line, workers at Saab plants are now organized into small production teams consisting of three or four workers each. During an intensive training program each worker is trained to perform each job performed by his production team. Following completion of the training program, workers within each production team have the authority to decide which jobs are to be performed by each worker in the team. Since the implementation of this new production system, Saab officials claim a significant increase in employee morale, supported by reduced absenteeism and lower turnover rates.

The basis for Saab's action is difficult to understand in terms of traditional American concepts of the motivation of factory workers. Here, workers in the automobile industry have consistently received higher pay and better fringe benefits than factory workers in many other industries. According to traditional beliefs, economic needs are the primary motivational factor and, therefore, good pay and high fringe benefits should provide sufficient incentive for workers to produce good cars. The monotony of the assembly line should be more than offset by the economic rewards. In spite of these economic incentives, poor workmanship and even deliberate acts of sabotage continue to occur on a rather wide scale in the automobile industry. In the United States, a few progressive organizations have recognized the fallacy of concentrating upon the economic needs of workers as the sole motivator. These have responded by changes in organization structure and decision-making processes which are more appropriate to the employee needs of the last quarter of the twentieth century.

Traditional Management Theory

Early in the development of formal organizations, an authority system emerged which assumed total responsibility for decision making. In time, this authority structure developed into the familiar pyramidal hierarchy which is commonplace in American organizations as the formal organization matured. In its most rigid form, the pyramidal hierarchy became the military command structure. This in turn is supported by two basic principles: (1) Each subordinate has one clearly defined superior from whom he receives his orders; (2) All orders must be obeyed without question. Status differentials, such as the split between the officer and the enlisted man, were developed. These defined the levels of authority within the organization and the expected behavior of a member was dictated largely by his organizational position.

In order that the goals of the organization be achieved, desired patterns of behavior have to be maintained throughout the organization. Coercive power is based on the perception by subordinates that a superior has the ability to force members to behave in a desired manner. Coercive power focuses on the needs of the worker as an economic man. The power of management to "hire and fire" at will represents almost absolute control over his economic welfare. The power of the organization to dictate behavior is legitimized by the simple fact that when the worker sold his time to the company, he also sold the right to control his behavior along with it. The organization found that its goals could be more easily attained by manipulating the economic needs of its workers. Thus, the economic needs of man are accepted as the most significant motivational factor.

Fordism and Taylorism

Mass production was introduced by Henry Ford into American industry in 1913. "Fordism" combined two 19th century innovations—interchangeable parts and specialization of labor—with early 20th century management practices. Current American management practice continues to view the worker as a poorly designed multipurpose machine tool motivated by lower level biological and safety needs, and completely standardized as to ability, strength and perseverance. The work environment is characterized by simplified job content, close control by management and staff and repetitive body actions determined in advance by motion and time study. Industrial and production engineers provide the creative and innovative thrust of designing the assembly system and managers take care of any exceptions which may occur.

Beginning some years prior to 1913, Frederick W. Taylor had begun to promote Scientific Management as the optimal planning and control system for the industrial age. In common with Henry Ford, Taylor based his approach on the assumption that industrial workers are motivated by a fear of hunger and deprivation, and will do all they can to avoid these undesirable conditions. Given these basic fears, human beings are strongly motivated to seek increased economic rewards within the organization. Therefore, a worker will strive to make as much money as possible, although limitations of time, capacity and ability will ultimately control how much he can earn. Through the use of Scientific Management, individual jobs can be completely redesigned to overcome human limitations. This permits workers to produce more and to earn more. Although Taylor's research into the design of work resulted in numerous improvements in the physical layout of industries, his ideas concerning human behavior served only to perpetuate the previous misconceptions of the functional theory of management.

The classical theory of motivation (from which both Henry Ford and Frederick W. Taylor drew their ideas about human behavior), generally assumes that man is lazy and irresponsible and has to be closely supervised. Although the worker desires money and will work in order to obtain it, he will attempt to do as little as possible in return for his wages. In order to counter this inherent laziness, the organization must exercise close direction and control over the working action of the employee. This theory completely denies the existence of self-motivation.

The Hawthorne Studies

It was only when the results of the Hawthorne studies of Western Electric Company were published that the major shortcomings of functional theory became apparent. In keeping with the functional assumptions of classical theory, management at the Hawthorne plant had sought to increase production by improving the economic rewards available to the workers. Researchers discovered that neither economic incentives nor work design appeared to have any relationship to productivity. Instead, the concept of the worker as a Social Man emerged—one who was seeking satisfaction through membership in a stable work group. This was quite in contrast to the earlier assumption that the worker was an isolated individual within the organization. He now appeared as a social being who interacted meaningfully with his fellow workers and satisfied certain of his needs in the job environment.

The Hawthorne studies demonstrated the existence and the importance of an informal organization within the context of the broader formal organization. Four general functions of peer group informal organization have since been identified.

1. The group provides its members with certain satisfactions which they need in order to function effectively. These satisfactions, such as emotional support, cannot be supplied by the larger organization.

2. The group provides for the horizontal flow of information, which opens up the process of communication.

3. The group often restricts output, thus protecting its members from arbitrary performance standards.

4. In a technical capacity, the group provides "engineers" from below by making those corrections which are necessary in order to get the work done.

If the goals of the organization are to be achieved, all members should direct their efforts to the accomplishment of these objectives. When inconsistencies arise between the objectives of the organization and the needs of the mature personality, the end result frequently is conflict between the informal system and the formal organization. This pattern of conflict can take numerous forms, ranging from work slowdowns to acts of sabotage.

One of the results of the protest decade of the 1960s was the awareness that much had changed in the intervening century. In the world of work, this disaffection may not have been as pronounced as it was in the world of youth, but it was strong enough nonetheless to make management stand up and take notice. While work content had been reduced to the point that many jobs had become dull and tiring—even destructive to the worker's esteem and to his need for self-actualization, the educational level of the worker had continued to climb upward. Concepts of job structure that were appropriate to first-generation immigrants resulted in resentment and low productivity and sloppy workmanship when applied to their grandchildren.

Approaches to the Improvement of the Quality of Work Life

As a result of the protest movement, although considerably muted by the deepening of the economic depression, a number of fundamental approaches to the improvement of the quality of work life have been discussed during the last ten years. This can be classified into five different areas of interest. Listed alphabetically, they are:

1. Industrial democracy
2. Job enrichment
3. Organizational development
4. Participative management
5. Sociotechnical systems

Within the traditional pyramidal organization, workers are frequently placed in job situations which demand only limited utilization of their abilities. Work becomes increasingly more routinized and monotonous at the lower levels of the organization. Workers become increasingly repressed, inhibited and frustrated as they find themselves unable to achieve need fulfillment through their work activities. This causes the undesirable behavioral patterns previously mentioned such as absenteeism, low productivity, and poor workmanship. The characteristic response on the part of management when this occurs is to tighten its control over the workers. All this does is to make matters worse. Hostility increases when management tightens the screws and workers become even more resistant to organizational pressure. If the worker is to support the goals of the organization, he must accept those goals as being both significant as well as so designed that they serve as a means for his own personal need attainment. When workers are integrated into small production teams such as those discussed in some of the selections in this volume, supportive relationships can be developed and maintained which increase each worker's sense of personal worth and importance. Each worker within a socio-technical system is motivated both by a sense of the importance of his job and through participation with his fellow workers in striving to achieve mutually desired goals.

If we omit organizational development, the other four approaches can be listed on a continuum ranging from the most probable to the least probable in terms of their adoption in American industry. If we do this, they will appear on the continuum as follows:

Orthodox Job Enrichment	Socio-Technical Systems	Participative Management	Industrial Democracy

This volume examines the various aspects of job enrichment. For that reason, there is little profit in discussing orthodox job enrichment at length in an introductory chapter. Suffice it to say that job enrichment has been accepted and tried and it works. It represents a solid first step in the direction of improving the quality of work life.

It is easier to visualize the relationships shown on the continuum if we refer to Figure 1 and Figure 2.

Suojanen's Authority Model

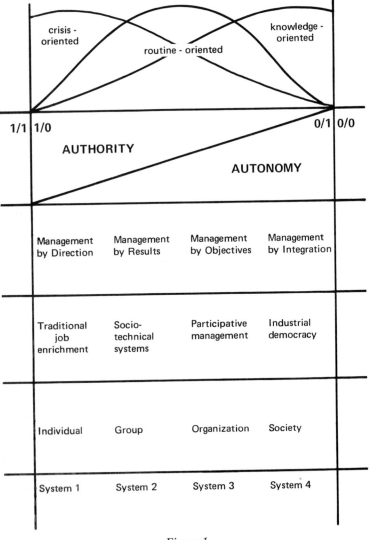

Figure 1

In *The Dynamics of Mangement*, published in 1966, Suojanen presented a first version of the model in Figure 1. Because of limitation of space, we do not propose to discuss all aspects of Figure 1 here except to point out that *traditional job enrichment* appears on the left side of the model. Vertically, it corresponds with a high degree of *authority*, *Management by Direction* (MBD), an emphasis on the *individual* worker and is comparable to *System 1* in the Likert scale.

The reader will note that Figure 2 is an extension of Figure 1. As indicated, Management by Direction focuses on crisis-oriented situations, is boss-centered, and describes the framework within which most American organizations operate.

Sociotechnical Systems

Sociotechnical systems go a step further than orthodox job enrichment. Research findings indicate that workers who are allowed to participate in making decisions that affect them become committed to them and tend to carry them out far more effectively than when decisions are dictated from above. This tends to hold true even when the decisions that are adopted are not completely supported by the work teams. To invite participation by subordinates is still considered heretical by most American managers, until the benefits of such interaction could clearly be demonstrated. For example, group decision making at the technological level generally results in a greater number of alternative solutions to a problem. It also can provide first-hand technical expertise in dealing with actual operational problems.

Although the use of production teams and group decision making concerning technology have been shown to be beneficial factors in improving worker morale, American organizations remain reluctant to move as far as Volvo and Saab have moved in the direction of group determination of sociotechnical systems.

The location of sociotechnical systems on the continuum can be located by reference to Figures 1 and 2. If we drop our plumb-line down from Management by Results (MBR), it goes through Sociotechnical System in the next lower panel and so on through Group and System 2 on the Likert scale. Referring to Figure 2, we can see that MBR moves from the Authoritative to the Democratic style of leadership and calls for a degree of worker involvement in decision making that remains difficult for American managers to accept.

Participative Management

During the past quarter century, many volumes of articles and books have been written extolling the virtues of participative

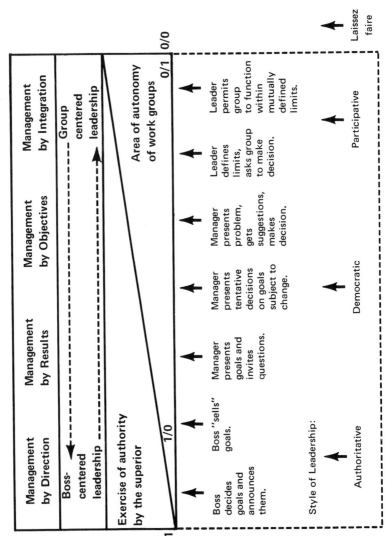

Continuum of Leadership Behavior

Figure 2

management. In a philosophical and futuristic sense we are in agreement with participative management. Much of our own writing and practice have been directed in this vein.

Management practitioners, in their discussions with college professors, often indicate that they believe in participative management. Many of them believe that Theory Y assumptions (that people are able and responsible) make much more sense that the Theory X assumptions (that people are lazy and irresponsible and have to be closely supervised). As Argyris puts it, the "espoused theory" of American managers tends to fall into the right side of the model portrayed in Figures 1 and 2.

In their own organizations, however, American management practitioners behave quite differently. If their espoused theory is Theory Y, then, despite protestations to the contrary, their "theory-in-use" is Theory X. When one examines the behavior of senior managers in American organizations very carefully, this discrepancy between espoused theory and theory-in-use is easily understood. American organizations reward behavior that accomplishes results and most managers are loathe to operate in an environment as unstructured as that propounded by professors when discussing participative management. The dismal experience of Non-Linear Systems with participative management comes to mind as perhaps the outstanding example of this.

American management has always been more ready to move toward participative management to thwart the white-collar woes than it has been to counter the blue-collar blues. There are exceptions, such as Donnelly Mirrors, Inc. which is discussed in this volume, but, twenty-five years later, all these exceptions do is prove the rule. The Federal Government has, in recent years, placed a great deal of emphasis on participative management in the form of Management by Objectives (MBO). Analysis, however, indicates that MBO at the federal level is group-focused rather than organization-pervasive. If this is the case, then MBO is but a variant of sociotechnical systems at the white-collar level rather than being truly democratic and participative (refer again to Figures 1 and 2).

Industrial Democracy

The Scandinavian countries—Denmark, Finland, Iceland, Norway, and Sweden—are much farther down the road to participative management and industrial democracy than we are in the United States. The Saab and Volvo experiences represent an industrial philosophy in which management and unions cooperate with government both extensively and intensively. This cooperation reaches from the highest policy levels right to the shop floor.

Many Scandinavian organizations have action committees of

management and shop stewards at the plant level. Their objective is action to involve workers in a wholehearted program with the immediate objective of improving the quality of work life at the operating level of the organization. The general thrust is to provide workers with more autonomy and greater control over their working activity. Workers meet in groups and make decisions such as whether they need a supervisor, who is to perform what job, and what changes in technology would add to increased productivity. These responsibilities include setting vaction schedules and determining days off as well as actually hiring new workers. Ultimately the work team provides its own supervision, seeking assistance from management only when it is needed.

A few well-publicized examples of industrial democracy in practice can be found in the United States. Among the best known of these is Donnelly Mirrors located in Holland, Michigan. A study on the Donnelly Experience is presented in this volume so we will not repeat it here.

A relatively recent experiment in industrial democracy was started in 1972 in Bolivar, Tennessee. The parties to the agreement are Harman International Industries and the United Automobile Workers. Interestingly enough, Harman makes automotive mirrors —the same product that is manufactured by Donnelly.

In contrast to Donnelly, the Bolivar plant of Harman is unionized. The top leadership of the UAW is very much interested in the Bolivar experiment because the plant is an old one. The UAW supposedly feels that unless job enrichment can be applied in existing work environments, it does not have much future. The union also may want to consider the Bolivar experience as a bargaining lever if it ultimately turns out to be successful.

In Bolivar an eight-member joint plant committee is used to develop the policy for the experiment. There are four members each from management and labor. Reporting to the joint committee are the core groups which consist of a supervisor and worker. The core groups, under the guidance of a professional, make the kinds of initiatives discussed in "Return on Involvement" as well as those characteristic of the Scandinavian programs.

The core groups work in teams. They supervise themselves, change the technology as appropriate, and they rotate jobs among the membership. During the three years since the inception of the experiment, progress reportedly has been slow. It appears that local union officials have viewed the project with skepticism. Workers have been reluctant to commit themselves to new-fangled concepts of participative management.

Both top management and top union leadership seem to be solidly behind the experiment. Numerous outside organizations have provided funding and are studying the project carefully. Only time will tell whether this experiment will be successful.

Union Attitudes

American labor unions have traditionally been suspicious of job enrichment as a device of management to delude workers into thinking that they have gained a measure of victory at the bargaining table. They feel that management is offering the intangible and sometimes cost-reducing features of job enrichment to avoid expending hard-cost monies in wage increases, fringe benefits, work-week reductions and the like. Participation in corporate management or even in departmental management decision making is denounced as a sell-out of union loyalty. Under closer analysis, the main objection would appear to be fear of the loss of union power if battle lines between worker and management become less clearly drawn. The union viewpoint is, however, represented among the valid perspectives that must be considered, as in the articles by AFL-CIO Machinists' spokesman William Winpisinger, or federation advocate Gomberg.

Conclusion

All of these varying approaches to management in the past were marked by mutual antagonisms and conflicts. Each viewed management in terms of extremes—as a dichotomy rather than a continuum. The new vocabulary developed included terms such as: achievers and nonachievers; X and Y managers; satisfiers and nonsatisfiers; hygiene factors and motivators; productivity and nonproductivity; union and nonunion; labor and management; autocratic and democratic; young and old; male and female; black and white; and industry and academia.

Organizational behavior and management practices have been studied in a variety of settings ranging from the arts and crafts through sweat shops and scientific engineering; from scientific production to behavioral adaptation; from hostility and conflict to automated production. It is now becoming increasingly clear that pride in productivity and concern for craftsmanship can once again be achieved by such constructs as small groups, job enrichment, humanization of work, and quality of worklife.

The various approaches to management discussed here have been conceptualized in Figure 3. It illustrates the internal pressures of employees, unions, and management and the external pressures that impinge on the organization from society, the environment, the government, and the international sector. As suggested by the model, there are both positive and negative theories surrounding the topics covered. Similarly, as indicated in the model, organizations have had both favorable and unfavorable experiences with the tools and techniques described herein. If we grant that productivity must be increased and quality improved if

Model of Productivity Improvement Environment

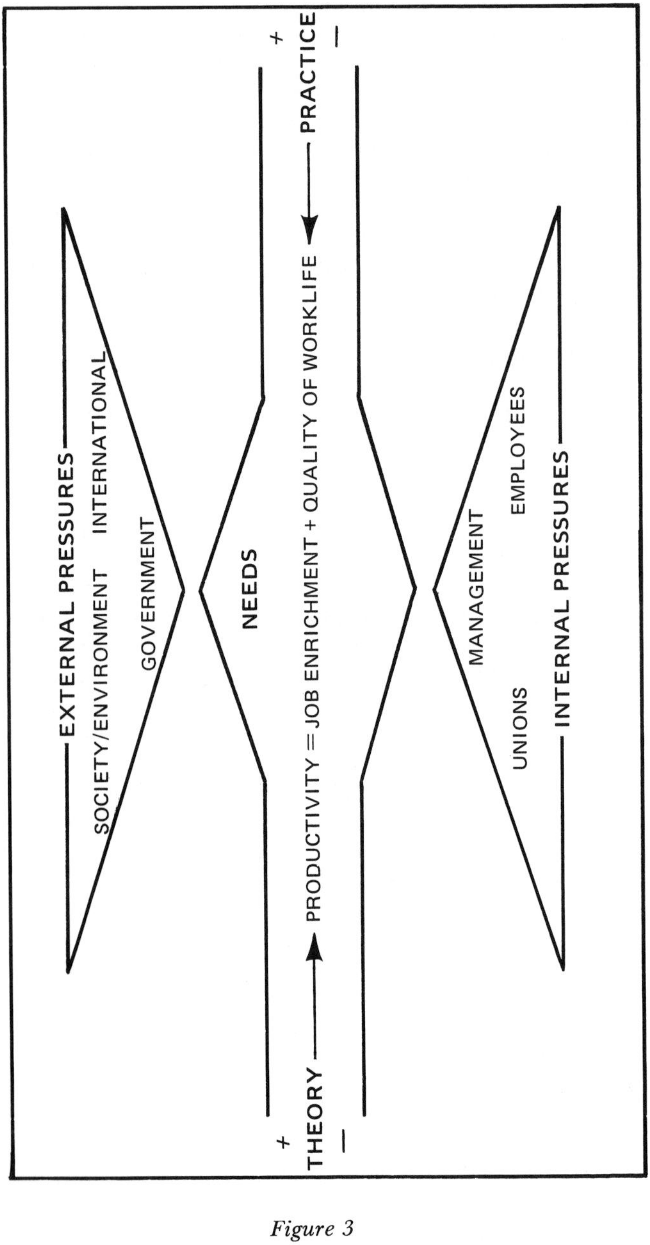

Figure 3

man is to survive in an age of scarcity, then the equation Productivity = Job Enrichment and Quality of Worklife, shown in the center of the model, becomes even more relevant in the future.

In conclusion, the improvement of the quality of worklife can be approached from the viewpoint of a number of the behavioral sciences, technologies, and disciplines. The most important point to bear in mind is that the quality of worklife in one organization will show a wide variance from even that of a neighboring competitor. For this reason, it is important to remember that there are no grand "isms" which will solve all problems in perpetuity. Rather, the critical point is that experiments and partial solutions must continue for quite some time so that both management and labor can learn to work together.

Union-management relations in the United States, when contrasted to the situation in the Scandinavian countries, are still in a very primitive state. The Harman experiment stands out as a notable exception, but at this time there is little one can say other than that progress is slow. American workers, on the whole, view almost any change toward MBI as an attempt to speed up production by making them work harder.

Some years ago, an attempt was made to apply MBI to the Non-Linear Systems organization. The pace was rapid and the scale was total. After five years of trying, the experiment was declared a failure and the company returned to the previous philosophy and structure—that described by the left end of Figures 1 and 2. Given this experience, it is important to reiterate once again that traditional job enrichment offers the best hope of success in the immediate future. MBD and MBR will be around for a good many years just as will boss-centered leadership. To be realistic is to recognize that theory which is not yet applicable is not bad — but rather that its time has not yet come. That is the message we hope is conveyed by the perspectives in this volume.

Richard E. Walton is Director, Division of Research, Graduate School of Business Administration, Harvard University.

2
Quality of Working Life: What Is It?

Richard E. Walton

Introduction

In recent years the phrase "quality of life" has been used with increasing frequency to describe certain environmental and humanistic values neglected by industrialized societies in favor of technological advancement, industrial productivity, and economic growth. Within business organizations, attention has been focused on the "quality of human experience in the work place." At the same time many firms have questioned their viability in increasingly competitive world markets. These dual concerns have created a growing interest in the possibilities of redesigning the nature of work. Many current organizational experiments seek to improve both productivity for the organization and the quality of working life for its members.

Although the broad productivity criterion contains some dilemmas, such as short-run versus long-run effectiveness, this criterion is relatively straightforward when compared with the concept of the quality of working life. How should the quality of working life be conceptualized, and how can it be measured? What are the appropriate criteria, and how are they interrelated? How is each related to productivity? Are these criteria uniformly salient for all employee groups? These questions are central to both research on the quality of the human experience in work organizations and action programs which seek to improve that experience.

The phrase "quality of working life" suggests comprehensiveness. The concept embraces, but is broader than, the aims of a long series of legislative acts that began in the early twentieth century. These acts include child labor laws, the Fair Labor Standards Act which established the eight-hour day and the forty-hour week, and workmen's compensation laws which have protected the job-injured employee and have eliminated many hazardous working conditions.

The concept is also broader than the aims of the unionization movement which made rapid progress in the 1930s and the 1940s, when emphasis was placed on job security, due process at the work place, and economic gains for the worker. It is broader than the notion proposed by psychologists in the 1950s that a positive relationship existed between morale and productivity and that improved human relations would lead to the enhancement of both. Finally the concept is broader than any of the attempts at reform in the 1960s, such as the drive for equal employment opportunity and the numerous job enrichment schemes.

The concept of the quality of working life in the 1970s nevertheless must include the values that were at the heart of these earlier reform movements. It also must include recently emphasized human needs and aspirations, such as the desire for a socially responsive employer.

Criteria for the Quality of Work Life

Eight major conceptual categories are now proposed, ranging from adequate and fair compensation for work to the social relevance of work; they provide a framework for analyzing the salient features of the quality of working life.

1. *Adequate and Fair Compensation*

The typical impetus for employment is earning a living. How well that aim is achieved fundamentally affects the quality of working life. More than any of the other criteria, adequacy of compensation is a relative concept. There simply is no consensus on objective or subjective standards for judging the adequacy of compensation.

Fairness in compensation, on the other hand, has various operational meanings. Job evaluation specifies relationships between pay and factors such as training required, job responsibility, and noxiousness of working conditions. By other approaches, supply and demand for particular skills or community averages determine the fair level of compensation. Another standard of fairness relates to ability to pay; more profitable firms should pay more. A variant of this standard is that when changes in work rules increase productivity of employees, it is only fair that the economic fruits of productivity be shared with the employees involved. Occasionally the application of one standard of fairness produces a pattern of compensation that is judged unfair by another standard.

The adequacy and fairness of pay are partly ideological questions. For example a twenty to one ratio between the pay of the top executive and the hourly worker of a firm may have been accepted in the recent past, but it may be regarded as too large in the future.

Although accepted operational measures are not available to judge the adequacy and the fairness of work compensation, both factors are important determinants of the quality of working life.

Adequate income: Does the income from full-time work meet socially determined standards of sufficiency or the subjective standard of the recipient?

Fair compensation: Does the pay received for certain work bear an appropriate relationship to the pay received for other work?

2. Safe and Healthy Working Conditions

It is widely accepted in our society that workers should not be exposed to physical conditions or hourly arrangements that are unduly hazardous or detrimental to their health. Legislation, union action, and employer concern have resulted in continually rising standards of satisfactory working conditions. Aspects of these improvements include: reasonable hours enforced by a standardized normal work period beyond which premium pay is required; physical working conditions that minimize risk of illness and injury; age limits imposed when work is potentially destructive to the welfare of persons below (or above) a certain age.

It is possible that in the future, more stringent standards will be imposed where health is less the issue than comfort; the goal will be to minimize odors, noises, or visual annoyances. On the other hand, the general improvement in the quality of working conditions and the earlier maturation of youth may lead to a relaxation of age limits in some areas of work.

3. Immediate Opportunity to Use and Develop Human Capacities

The industrial revolution and a simplistic extension of its underlying logic have taken much of the meaning out of work. Work has tended to be fractionated, deskilled, and tightly controlled. The planning of work has been separated from its implementation. These tendencies have progressed in varying degrees from one job to the next; therefore jobs differ in how much they enable employees to use and develop their skills and knowledge. Some of the job qualities necessary for this development follow:

Autonomy: Does the work permit substantial autonomy and self-control relative to external controls?

Multiple skills: Does the work allow one to exercise a wide range of skills and abilities rather than merely repeat the same narrow skill?

Information and perspective: Is one allowed to obtain meaningful information about the total work process and the results of his own action, so that he can appreciate the relevance and consequences of his actions?

Whole tasks: Does one's work embrace a whole task or is it some fragment of a meaningful task?

Planning: Does one's work include planning as well as implementation of activities?

These aspects of the job affect the ego involvement, self-esteem, and challenge obtained for the work itself.

4. *Future Opportunity for Continued Growth and Security*

Here the focus shifts from the job to career opportunities. Although the opportunity for self-improvement through education and hard work has been considered an American birthright, the typical industrial job can now be completely learned within a few weeks or a few years, after which the blue-collar worker has reached nearly the peak of his earnings and can look forward to only minor improvements.

Promotion of blue-collar workers to supervisory and managerial positions is often foreclosed by formal educational prerequisites. Engineers and other professionals tend to peak somewhat later, but they often confront an additional source of discouragement, the obsolescence of their knowledge and skills. When these professionals reach their middle thirties, their earnings begin to level off. Frequently by this time their knowledge has been exploited and their specialties deepened, but no provision for continued education or broadened capabilities has been made. There is little prospect for advancement in salaries and promotions. This period coincides with a stage of life where professionals are likely to be reevaluating their commitments to careers, families, and avocations. The result is that many lose interest in their professional work, no longer invest in their career pursuits, and increase the sterility of their work lives. Thus attention needs to be given to the following aspects of working life:

Development: The extent to which one's current activities (work assignments and educational pursuits) contribute to maintaining and expanding one's capabilities rather than leading to obsolescence.

Prospective application: The expectation to use expanded or newly acquired knowledge and skills in future work assignments.

Advancement opportunities: The availability of opportunities to advance in organizational or career terms recognized by peers, family members, or associates.

Security: Employment or income security associated with one's work.

5. Social Integration in the Work Organization

The preceding categories relate to the worker's immediate and long-range opportunities of expressing and developing individual abilities. Since work and career are typically pursued within the framework of social organizations, the nature of personal relationships become another important dimension of the quality of working life. Whether the worker has a satisfying identity and experiences self-esteem will be influenced by the following attributes in the climate of his work place:

Freedom from prejudice: Acceptance of the worker for work-related traits, skills, abilities, and potential without regard to race, sex, creed, and national origin, or to life styles and physical appearance.

Egalitarianism: The absence of stratification in work organizations in terms of status symbols and/or steep hierarchical structures.

Mobility: The existence of upward mobility as reflected, for example, by the percentage of employees at any level who potentially could qualify for higher levels.

Supportive primary groups: Membership in face-to-face work groups marked by patterns of reciprocal help, socio-emotional support, and affirmation of the uniqueness of each individual.

Community: The sense of community in work organizations that extends beyond face-to-face work groups.

Interpersonal openness: The way members of the work organization relate to one another their ideas and feelings.

6. Constitutionalism in the Work Organization

A member of a work organization is affected by many decisions that are made on his behalf or about his status in the organization. What rights does he have, and how can he protect his rights? The labor unions have brought constitutionalism to the work place to protect employees from arbitrary or capricious actions by employers. In a few unions workers now enjoy some of these same rights vis-a-vis the union authority structure itself; mechanisms exist whereby a member may appeal, ultimately to an impartial judge, certain union actions that affect the member. In unorganized employment, there are wide variations in the extent to which the organizational culture respects personal privacy, tolerates dissent, adheres to high standards of equity in distributing organizational rewards, and provides for due process in work-related matters. The following aspects of constitutionalism are key elements in providing higher quality to working life:

Privacy: The right to personal privacy; for example, withholding from the employer information about the worker's off-the-job behavior or about actions of members of his family.

Free speech: The right to dissent openly from the views of superiors in the organization without fear of reprisal.

Equity: The right to equitable treatment in all matters including the employee compensation scheme, symbolic rewards, and job security.

Due process: Governance by the "rule of law" rather than the rule of men in such matters as equal opportunity in all aspects of the job, privacy, and dissent, including procedures for due process and access to appeals.

7. Work and the Total Life Space

An individual's work experience can have positive or negative effects on other spheres of his life, such as his relations with his family. Prolonged periods of working overtime can have a serious effect on family life. If frequent transfers are required, there are psychological and social costs when families are uprooted from their networks of friends, acquaintances, and local affiliations. The relationship of work to the total life space is best expressed by the concept of balance. The balanced role of work is defined by work schedules, career demands, and travel requirements that do not take up leisure and family time on a regular basis. Likewise balance refers to advancement and promotion that do not require repeated geographical moves.

The application of this criterion is often debatable. When a person invests enormous time and energy in work at the expense of family, it is unclear whether this pattern is a cause or symptom of deficiencies in the family situation. Sometimes the employing organization is imposing demands that seriously affect the employee's ability to perform other life roles, such as spouse or parent. In other cases, however, these demands are largely self-imposed to escape the responsibilities and strains of family roles. If work did not absorb this time and energy, the person would shift his attention to other pursuits outside the family, such as hobbies or civic activities.

8. The Social Relevance of Work Life

The socially beneficial roles of the employing organization and the socially injurious effects of its activities increasingly have become salient issues for employees. Does the worker perceive the organization to be socially responsible in its products, waste disposal, marketing techniques, employment practices, relations to underdeveloped countries, participation in political campaigns, etc.? Organizations which are seen to be acting in a socially irresponsible manner will cause increasing numbers of employees to depreciate the value of their work and careers, which in turn affects worker self-esteem.

Perspectives on the Quality of Working Life Criteria

The scheme of eight conceptual categories outlined above invites several types of analyses, including how each quality of life attribute is related to the others in practice; how each relates to productivity; how some criteria currently are especially salient for one employee group but not for others; and why there are changes over time.

Interrelationships among Quality of Work Life Criteria

There are complex relationships among the eight conceptual

categories. Several pairs tend to be positively correlated; for example, the quality of the immediate work challenge not only affects current job satisfaction but also offsets the tendency toward skill obsolescence. Other pairs contain apparent inconsistencies; for example, heavy emphasis on the rule of law in work organizations may promote impersonality and impede some forms of social integration. The elaborate rules governing job rights, which provide job security and prevent arbitrary treatment by superiors, have limited the flexibility to make work more challenging. The high involvement of employees which results from such job attributes as autonomy, whole task responsibility, and membership in a cohesive face-to-face group occasionally works against a balance between work and other life roles.

The question arises whether there are inherent trade-off relationships among some of these qualities of working life which necessitate a decline in one quality in order to improve another. Perhaps this is not the case, since these relationships are not immutably set. For example it may be that new mechanisms or changes in cultural attitudes can provide constitutionalism without encouraging impersonal relations and rigidity in roles and responsibilities.

Relationship of Criteria to Productivity

How do changes in each of these aspects of working life affect the productivity and long-run effectiveness of the employing organization? General positive or negative correlations between productivity and changes in the quality of a particular dimension of work life cannot be proposed; the relationship depends to some extent upon the particular employee's awareness of deficiencies. Productivity also seems to have a curvilinear relationship to most work-life dimensions. Two general criteria are examined below.

Considering the potential levels of productivity for any given class of work and group of employees, there is probably some optimal level of opportunity to use and develop capacities; this opportunity level is created by the autonomy, multiplicity of skills required, work information, and planning responsibility existing in the work situation. It is also recognized that increasing autonomy, multiplicity of skills, etc., does not have a linear effect on the quality of the work experience. Since employee satisfaction and self-esteem are derived from this aspect of work, there is some optimal amount of opportunity to use and develop one's capacities. Figure 1 illustrates these points, showing the quality of work experience continuing to rise with increases in "opportunity" after the maximum effects on productivity have been realized. The particular slopes of the curves and the relationship between the quality of work life and productivity curves would vary from one work setting to another. Current interest in redesigning work in order to increase the opportunity for employees to utilize and develop their capacities nevertheless indicates a widely held assumption that the employee groups involved are now somewhere to the left of the optimal point on both of these curves.

The curves portraying the direct effects of "constitutionalism" on productivity and on the quality of work life probably have a relatively small region of coincidence between them as

Figure 1

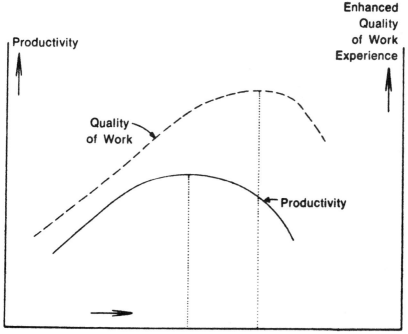

Opportunity to Use and Develop Capacities

shown in Figure 2. It can be hypothesized that situations characterized by only minimum rights depress productivity as well as quality of working life because of the consequences of insecurity, anxiety, and employee resentment on performance. Beyond some point, however, additional forms and degrees of "constitutionalism" continue to improve quality, but at a price to productivity. At a still higher level of constitutionalism, the marginal effect on quality is zero or negligible.

Figure 2

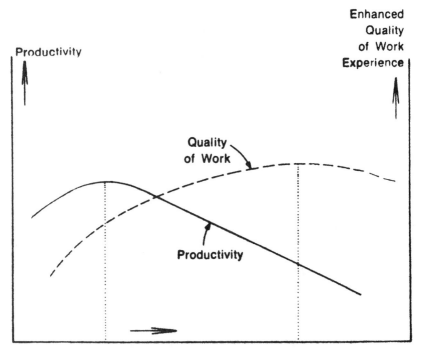

Constitutionalism in the Work Place

Deficiencies Affecting Different Employee Groups

Currently various employee groups experience different deficiencies in the quality of their work lives. The variety of existing problems is illustrated in the following situations.

Inadequate compensation is a major reason for unrest among agricultural workers and hospital employees.

A priority need has developed to provide blue- and white-collar factory workers with more autonomy, challenge, and satisfying social contact. Improvement along these dimensions of quality of work life requires innovative design in the content of work, sequence of work assignments, job hierarchies, and information and reward systems.

The lack of constitutionalism has suddenly become a recognized deficiency in the quality of work life for a number of groups of nonunionized professional employees. Engineers are laid off according to criteria different from those which they had understood determined their job security. Faculty members despair at the lack of due process in decisions affecting tenure. Primary teachers in nonunion school systems often have no recourse when they are fired for certain activities off the job. Recent growth in unionization among teachers and university professors probably results more from concerns about this aspect of work life than from concerns about the level of compensation.

A number of young doctors and lawyers have recently demanded that their employing organizations adopt policies and practices more responsive to certain acute social problems. Some engineers and scientists express similar opinions, while others become increasingly concerned about technical obsolescence. Even stockbrokers, advertising agency executives, and business managers whose work lives score high on most of the criteria listed make the news by dropping out of the career "rat race" to redress the imbalance which exists between work and other aspects of their lives.

The Diversity of Human Preferences

Regardless of how one approaches the issue of the quality of working life, one must acknowledge the diversity of human preferences—diversity in culture, social class, family rearing, education, and personality. Society is becoming more conscious of the quality of work life at a time when there is a growing heterogeneity in life styles in America. Differences in subcultures and life styles are accompanied by different definitions of what constitutes a high quality of working life. The young person with a college degree who elects to work as an auto mechanic, a taxi driver, or a mail carrier is saying something significant about his or her preferred pattern of working life. Of two employees equally skilled in performing basic elements of their work, one may prefer autonomy and the other detailed instruction. Similarly one may prefer to be closely integrated into a work team and the other relatively unencumbered by work relations.

How can these differing preferences be accommodated? Diversity within a single work unit may be realized by tailoring individual work assignments to fit individual preferences. Within an organization, diversity can be achieved by organizing work differently from one work unit to the next and allowing employees to select the pattern of work life they prefer. Finally diversity among organizations can be attained if each organization develops a unique and internally consistent pattern of work life while providing persons in the job market with information for choosing an organization that is suitable for them. Employees are thus encouraged to exercise a free and informed choice that takes into account some of the more subtle aspects of the quality of work life.

Forces Altering the Salience of Criteria over Time

Conditions of work are important because the employees involved have certain expectations about them. These conditions take on more meaning by assessing how different employees perceive their organizations along these dimensions. Each person has subjective standards of adequacy.

Why do changes occur in employees' expectations about organizational conditions? There are two different types of change and two corresponding causes for change. First, expectations are steadily changing for many of the quality criteria listed above. The evolving needs and desires reflect some basic, and not readily reversible, trends in American and Canadian societies: the rising level of education; the rising level of wealth and security; the decreased emphasis given by churches, schools, and families to obedience and authority; the decline in achievement motivation; and the shifting emphasis from individualism to social commitment.

Second, a sharp rise in expectations can be observed as a result of some focused stimuli. If change agents or the news media call attention to the plight of a certain group, its members are likely to become more aware of the oppressive conditions, more dissatisfied, and more likely to manifest negative feelings in aggressive behavioral symptoms. Examples of minor improvements then further raise expectations. This scenario of tendencies is illustrated by the blacks' expressions of dissatisfaction in the 1950s and women's discontent late in the 1960s.

Change in the Future

This examination of the causes of change suggests future developments which may occur as attitudes about the quality of working life change. There will be a period of one or two decades during which changes in organizational conditions will occur at a slower pace than that of rising employee expectations. This situation will create a trend toward more employee alienation. At the same time, the positive feedback cycle will occur more frequently, and publicized incidents of aggressively expressed alienation (for example, sit-ins) will raise the consciousness, expectations, and alienation of others. As a result, there will be rashes or epidemics of such incidents in work organizations.

These pessimistic trends are not inevitable. To deal with the problems of change, technologists, managers, union officials, and social scientists must be willing to give high priority to the redesign of work. Through such efforts, the quality of working life can be enhanced, and the expectations of workers on all levels can be understood and satisfied.

Warren S. Bollmeier II is Captain, United States Air Force, Dobbins Air Force Base, Marietta, Georgia.

Waino W. Suojanen is Professor of Management, School of Business Administration, Georgia State University, Atlanta, Georgia.

This article is reprinted from the May-June 1974 issue of **Atlanta Economic Review,** *pp. 16-22.*

3
Job Enrichment and Organizational Change

Warren S. Bollmeier, II
Waino W. Suojanen

The coming of the post-industrial society has made it possible for most people to satisfy biological and safety needs to such an extent that these hygiene or maintenance factors have lost much of the motivating force that they used to have, and indeed still have, for those who grew to adulthood during the Great Depression and the wars that followed it. In recent years, as the post-World War II generation has grown to adulthood, the satisfaction of such higher level needs as self-actualization, esteem, and the attainment of autonomy has become ever more important.

Much to-do has been made in recent years about the decline in the importance of the "work" ethic—even to the point that the term itself was changed from "Protestant" or "Puritan" ethic to "work" ethic. Those who continue to worrry about the decline in the motivational effects of the work ethic tend to forget that workers expect much more from their jobs than high wages or salaries. The Economic Man of the Scientific Management school, therefore, if not now dead, is at least headed toward extinction by the end of the century.

Autonomous, self-actualizing man seeks meaning and satisfaction in work through Gestalt—the wholeness of a task or job. He does not want to feel he is a mere part of a process. He desires a greater sense of craftsmanship and more flexibility in his working hours.[1] He wants his work to be more human. Many blue-collar workers are exhibiting a growing restlessness in situations where the work is dehumanized due to harsh and authoritarian discipline.[2] They often give vent to their feelings through absenteeism and turnover, shoddy work, and even sabotage. The net result, from management's viewpoint, is lower productivity with deteriorating quality, increasing costs, and a disgruntled labor force.

We must point out that the worker needs both a human work environment *and* a meaningful job structure. Otherwise one may have the case of the happy, "satisfied" worker, coupled with a "country club" environment that results in low productivity.

In recent years, evidence has emerged that a partial solution to the problem of the quality of worklife lies in giving the worker more responsibility and autonomy through job enlargement and job enrichment.[3] Job enlargement is based on horizontal loading, while job enrichment utilizes vertical loading. When a job is enlarged, a number of tasks of a similar nature are combined into one job, where previously there were several jobs. By contrast, a job enrichment program implies a complete work unit, or module, in which the worker or work group is held responsible (and also accountable) for all of the decisions and tasks regarding a job or an objective.

By utilizing various job enrichment techniques, firms have increased productivity, lowered employee absenteeism and turnover, improved efficiency and quality, and enhanced their employee relations.[4] Large firms, such as AT&T, and smaller firms such as Cryovac have successfully experimented with job enrichment programs.[5] Unfortunately, not all firms have had success.[6] The well-known story of Lordstown shows just how seriously the situation can sometimes deteriorate.[7]

One principal reason why job enrichment programs fail is that management continues to operate under Theory X assumptions and an authoritarian organization structure at a time when Theory Y assumptions and a much more flexible organizational design are needed. In this article we plan to present a tentative model which will attempt to relate the elements of job enrichment theory to an over-all process of organizational change, which we call ODO (over-all development of the organization). We feel that this model identifies the relevant elements of ODO and will prove useful to any organization which commits itself to improving the quality of work life.

The reader should bear in mind that the model presents only cause and effect relationships with no attempt to quantify them in any manner. This is why we refer to them as factors rather than as variables. [What we refer to as "primary moderating factors" are often call "intervening variables" in the literature.] A variable typically can be quantified and controlled. The model does not assert that changes in any of the three kinds of factors will result in any sort of controlled situation. Rather, it explains the relationships among the three sets of factors—organizational change, enrichment, and moderating. The three sets of factors included in the model are as follows:

○ Primary organizational change factors.
   —Planning and goal setting
   —Managerial style
   —Decision making
   —Communication and information channels
   —Authority structure
   —Control and audit
   —Job structure
○ Primary job enrichment factors.
   —Individual responsibility
   —Job structure
   —Feedback and control
   —Participation in decision making
   —Participation in goal setting
   —Nesting
○ Primary moderating factors.
   —Technology
   —Managerial attitudes
   —Organized labor
   —Individual attitudes toward peers
   —Individual attitudes toward superiors
   —Maintenance factors
   —Individual attitudes toward work
   —Trust relationships
   —Individual goals
   —Personnel policies

The Model

In this section we shall present the model. Our discussion covers the general interaction of the factors, a detailed analysis of the interaction of the enrichment factors on the organizational change factors, the contribution of the moderating factors along with enrichment factor feedback, and an evaluation of the model.

Interaction of the Factors

A diagram of the model is shown in Exhibit 1. There are three sets of factors: the primary organizational change factors; the primary job enrichment factors; the primary moderating factors.

The six enrichment factors represent the changes in jobs that various organizations have documented. These factors have a

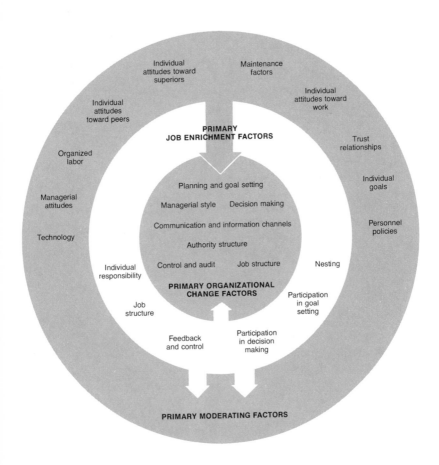

direct effect on the organizational change factors.

The moderating factors are so named because they moderate the effects of the enrichment factors. Of course, these moderating factors influence organizational change independently of job enrichment; but to study those effects is beyond the scope of this article.

The model also considers the effects of job enrichment on the moderating factors. These effects are, in essence, feedback from job enrichment to the moderating factors, which in turn affect organizational change directly. The feedback can have a reinforcing (positive) or adverse (negative) effect.

Organizational Change Factors

Let us define each organizational change factor more precisely in terms of existing, or desired, conditions. The first condition listed for each factor is the least desirable, the second, more desirable, and so on. The last condition is viewed as the "final" state implied by job enrichment. Given this, organizational change is assumed to consist of the following seven factors.

1. *Planning and goal setting*
    a. Done by managers (no individual participation)
    b. Some individual feedback (managers retain authority)
    c. Individual participates (managers retain authority)
    d. Management by objective—combined effort of manager and individual or team
    e. Management by integration—individual or team has authority for certain well-defined areas including setting of performance goals

2. *Managerial style*
    a. Exploitative authoritarian—no confidence or trust in subordinates
    b. Benevolent authoritarian—condescending confidence and trust in subordinates
    c. Participative—substantial confidence and trust in fellow employees, superior still wishes to remain in control
    d. Democratic—complete confidence and trust in all matters

3. *Decision making*
    a. All decisions made at higher levels
    b. Individual exercises authority to complete task subject to manager's supervision
    c. As job is enriched, individual or team becomes a "profit center"
    d. Individual or team makes all decisions regarding job, including buying equipment, personnel actions, discipline, with manager serving as resource person

4. *Communication and information channels*
    a. The questions flow down and the answers flow up—no freedom of discussion
    b. Superior sometimes gets ideas and opinions of subordinates—very limited freedom of discussion
    c. Subordinates feel rather free to discuss their ideas and opinions with superior—superior tries to make constructive use of them
    d. Free flow of communications and information among

colleagues—colleagues discuss matters with complete freedom and usually decide as a group

5. *Authority structure*
    a. Manager exercises all authority (Theory X)
    b. Manager delegates authority to complete specific tasks, but intervenes as he sees necessary
    c. Manager delegates all authority to complete the task (Theory Y)
    d. The organization releases authority to individual or team to control the complete job environment

6. *Control and audit*
    a. Separate inspection, costing, and audit staff functions
    b. Team provides direct feedback for foregoing functions, but has no authority
    c. Individual or team performs all inspection and audit functions—system allows for feedback as quickly as possible for evaluation of standards and performance

7. *Job structure*
    a. Specific task, narrowly defined
    b. Enlarged job, horizontal loading; may include tasks previously done by several persons
    c. Enriched job, a complete work module
    d. Nesting, combining several enriched jobs into a team structure

Effects of Enrichment Factors

Each enrichment factor has a primary effect on one or more of the organizational change factors and may have secondary effects on the remaining factors. The discussion for each enrichment factor will concentrate on the primary effects. First, however, the enrichment factors are defined more precisely as follows:

1. *Individual responsibility*—The individual or team is given all requisite authority to complete given work or tasks. Ideally, they may also possess authority to make decisions and set goals for the total work environment (work module).

2. *Job structure*—The enriched job consists of a complete work module. The work module (as previously defined) may be developed by including tasks previously done by other persons before or after the job, plus adding the elements of control and self-audit to encompass the complete job.

3. *Feedback and control*—The enriched job includes an accurate and responsive feedback system, whereby the individual or work group can readily evaluate all standards and performance goals.

4. *Participation in decision making*—The individual or team

makes decisions not only directly associated with the job, but also regarding employees, maintenance, equipment, and so forth.

5. *Participation in goal setting*—The individual or work group not only sets the task performance goals, but also participates in the overall planning of the organization. These individuals and teams may help in setting goals in such areas as research and development and marketing.

6. *Nesting*—The development of the enrichment program in any organization may lead to the combination (or nesting) of related enriched jobs.

The Effects of Increasing Individual Responsibility: When a job is enriched by giving the individual or team more responsibility, the primary effects are felt in managerial style, authority structure, and job structure.

O *Managerial style.* The more a job is enriched, the more a democratic approach is in order. Supervision is replaced by resource management. When the job is fully enriched, as in the case of the work module, the manager becomes a resource person or adviser to the individual or work group. He is the linking pin from the team to the higher levels of management. Not all persons currently in positions of first-line supervisors will be able to handle the job of resource manager or will even want to do so. In any given situation, education and training programs may be required so that managerial styles are changed.

O *Authority structure.* Closely related to changes in managerial style, the authority structure becomes highly decentralized with job enrichment. The resource manager has much less operational authority than the typical first line supervisor. Ideally, the team exercises total control over the work environment. This authority must stay with the team; the resource manager cannot subvert the team's authority or the system will break down.[8]

O *Job structure.* Enriching a job may require a complete job restructuring in order to give the individual or the team more authority. For example, tasks that were previously done by other persons may be incorporated into a job. Where a worker previously turned the same six screws on an assembly line all day long, he may now assemble an entire component.

The Effects of Changing Job Structure: When work is enriched through a restructuring of the job itself, the primary effects are felt in managerial style, the authority structure, and the overall organizational job structure.

O *Managerial style.* The managerial style must adapt to the particular type of work. Ideally, it will be as general and unrestrictive as possible. In the case of an extremely complicated process, the work should be organized in such a way that each team has access to the resource manager. Where the work is less complex, the resource manager may be an adviser to several such teams.

○ *Authority structure.* Each work team will have increased authority over more tasks simply by virtue of the restructuring of the work itself. Authority is delegated to the team because it is at this level that the most relevant and applicable knowledge is available. Furthermore, all authority for restructured work should be formally delegated.

○ *Job structure.* When a number of jobs are restructured, a major change in the overall organizational work structure may be in order. For example, the jobs of a number of unneeded supervisors must be restructured or eliminated. There may also be a need for different parts of the work force to operate with varying organizational structures. For example, a part of a plant or office may utilize individual modules while the rest of the organization may utilize teams. Such a structure may be necessitated by processes which limit the number of tasks a person can perform. Note here the effect of technology as a moderating factor.

The Effects of Feedback and Control: When a job is enriched, on-time feedback and control must be provided for the individual or work team so that standards and performance can be evaluated and corrected as quickly as possible. The organizational change factors affected in the process are managerial style, communication and information systems, and control and audit.

○ *Managerial style.* The resource manager should be viewed as a staff adviser insofar as the installation and maintenance of the feedback and control system is concerned. In this case, the individual or team, rather than the resource manager, is responsible for evaluating performance. The manager still reports results to top management, but he does not set individual goals. His task is to motivate the individual and teams and, of course, to assist them in developing a workable feedback system.

○ *Communication and information channels.* Among the principal duties of the resource manager in a job enrichment program is that of motivating individuals and teams and maintaining and improving both information dissemination and communication. This is important because the quality of worklife tends to improve as participants begin to develop the problem-solving and decision-making competence which until recently has been viewed as a managerial prerogative.

○ *Control and audit.* In job enrichment, control and audit functions move from the line and the staff to the work groups. In other words, by setting team goals and evaluating their own performance standards, the team plans and controls much of its working action with the resource manager assisting in an advisory capacity. The resource manager also serves as the linking pin between the work group and staff officials. To the maximum extent possible, these staffs should be advisory in nature. For example, if the team wants to control costs on a standard cost system, the staff can be of assistance. However, it may be necessary to experiment with other partial solutions before attaining an "ideal" state.

The individual or team should perform as many of the inspection and quality control functions as possible. Wherever feasible, the team or responsible members should be held accountable to the consumer on any complaints about quality, including answering correspondence and telephone calls.

The Effects of Increasing Individual and Team Participation in Decision Making: When the quality of worklife is improved, the individual or team is often delegated authority to make decisions which affect organizational change primarily in managerial style, decision making, and the authority structure.

○ *Managerial style.* The resource manager delegates most, if not all, of his traditional authority as supervisor to make decisions about jobs or clusters of jobs to the individual or team concerned. In a sense, the manager's job then changes to more of a staff than a line position. He may, for example, suggest various team approaches to decision making under the "key man" concept.

○ *Decision making.* Job enrichment implies that all authority for decisions regarding the way work is performed is delegated to the individual or team that does the work. The team may be viewed as a profit center which moves toward a position of increased autonomy as its performance may merit. Ideally, the team will make decisions concerning the total work environment, such as replacement of machinery, selection and training of new workers, discipline of team members, and working conditions.

○ *Authority structure.* The team is delegated authority commensurate with its responsibility and attendant on the decisions that are to be made. Senior management, the resource manager, and the individual or team should come to a mutual agreement as to what decisions are to be made at each level of the organization. These delegations of authority should be reviewed periodically, in order to encourage as much decentralization as possible. This approach makes it possible for both resource managers and senior managers to devote more time to planning, particularly of the long-range type.

The Effects of Increasing Individual or Team Participation in Planning and Goal Setting: Job enrichment decentralizes the decision-making authority for planning and goal setting. This affects job structure (as previously discussed), the system of authority, and overall organizational planning.

This area has not yet been fully explored in real world experiments. The team, or work module, should be furnished with all relevant information about the products or the services that they provide to clientele. To the maximum extent possible, they should be involved in organizational planning and strategy for marketing, distribution, and finance. Similarly, if they are involved in the production-planning process, they will be better prepared to help meet market demand, to time the purchases of new equipment, and to meet special orders. Furthermore, the modern-day work force can provide invaluable assistance in the problem-solving process.

In any case, there should be a mutual agreement between the work groups and management as to the responsibilities to be exercised by both sides in planning and goal setting.

The Effects of Nesting: The next logical step following individual job enrichment is to combine related enriched jobs. This primarily affects managerial style and the authority structure. An example illustrates how this is done, as follows:

□ Suppose ABC Company sells 3 different brands of widgets. The sales representatives for each brand are located in one large office. Furthermore, the representatives are organized into 5 districts by brands so that there is a total of 15 salesmen. There are also 5 secretaries, 10 clerk-typists, 5 district managers, and 1 division manager. Each of these 5 groups is located in an area of its own, separate from the division manager and his secretary. Much of the paperwork is farmed out to the 10 "at large" clerk-typists who are located in their own separate area. This rerouting often causes delays in the processing of paperwork.

Let us assume that the jobs of the salesmen, the secretaries, and the clerk-typists are enriched. The territory structure is retained, but now each salesman sells all 3 brands within his territory. This means that the number of salesmen will remain at 15, each with a vertically loaded job. In time, the jobs of the 5 district managers can be eliminated as the salesmen themselves take over more of the planning and control. The division manager will become the resource person of this segment of the organization and will continue to be assisted by an administrative assistant instead of a secretary.

Under the nesting concept, 5 clerk-typist positions will be eliminated, and the remaining 5 will be transferred to the work teams with each position being vertically loaded and upgraded to a secretarial job. After the job enrichment program has been completely implemented, there will be 1 work team consisting of the division (resource) manager and his administrative assistant and 5 marketing teams each composed of 3 salesmen and 2 secretaries. This will eliminate 10 positions, those of the 5 district managers and the 5 clerk-typists, so that 27 people will do the work previously performed by 37.

Effects of Moderating Factors

The moderating factors can affect organizational change independently of the other factors; but, for our purposes, only the factors which tend to moderate (reinforce or inhibit) the effects of job enrichment are considered. Our discussion also includes the feedback from the enrichment factors on the moderating factors. The 10 moderating factors relevant in the model are listed here, with the questions or conditions important to job enrichment.

1. *Technology*

a. The degree to which tasks depend on, or are limited by, complex machinery or processes.

b. In a manufacturing process, the degree to which tasks can be combined or subdivided.

c. Intervening costs of replacing machinery in order to re-structure a job.

d. The extent to which machinery can relieve people from burdensome or monotonous work.

2. *Managerial attitudes*

a. The extent to which a Theory X or Y approach pervades the organization.

b. The extent to which present management will release operational authority and encourage better communication and information flows.

c. The extent to which the present managers will assume, or be retrained in, the role of the resource manager.

3. *Organized labor*

a. Opinions about salary versus wages as methods of compensation.

b. Opinions about team efforts versus individual piecework.

c. Views concerning greater individual responsibility.

d. Views on more participation in decision-making and goal-setting.

4. *Individual attitudes toward peers*

a. Unfriendly, strictly a competitive orientation.

b. Some exchange, but key ideas and exhange held back in a group environment.

c. Free flow of ideas, full development of the team concept.

5. *Individual attitudes toward superiors*

a. Theory 1/x—views the manager very much as the Theory X approach views the worker. He does only what is required of him, does not provide feedback unless coerced, tries to "beat" the system, and resents status differentials.

b. Theory 1/y—views manager as vital link between individual and organizational goals. Goes out of way to assist manager and to provide feedback, respects the authority of management.

c. Enriched Theory 1/y—views the resource person as a peer, but accepts his or her knowledge and managerial skills. Facilitates knowledge and attitude flows in all directions.

6. *Maintenance factors*
a. Wages and fringe benefits.
b. Working conditions (including safety factors).
c. Salary and incentive plans.
d. Profit-sharing plans.

7. *Individual attitudes toward work*
a. Views work as necessary evil, has an innate dislike for work, and sees no redeeming value in it.
b. Enjoys work of repetitive nature, but assumes no responsibility for more than simple tasks.
c. Seeks more complex, personally satisfying jobs, but still sees differential between work and leisure.
d. Craftsmanship, seeks job as self-fulfilling and self-actualizing; may not see the distinction between work and leisure.

8. *Trust relationships*
a. Built on fear and unfamiliarity.
b. Built on some disclosure, mostly one way, from top to bottom.
c. Built on mutual disclosure and reciprocity in all directions.

9. *Individual goals*
a. Sets no personal goals.
b. Sets personal goals but does not extend these to work tasks.
c. Sets high personal performance goals but does not integrate these fully with organizational goals.
d. Full integration of high personal performance goals with concept of work module and nesting concepts.

10. *Personnel policies*
a. Classical personnel department hires only when needs arise, maintains cumbersome paper mills, supports some retraining programs.
b. Modified classical personnel department uses refined selection methods; periodic weeding out of deadwood; minimization of personnel costs; and excellent retraining programs.
c. Enrichment policy—delegation of selection, retraining, and discipline policy to work module in cooperation with resource

manager; leads to dilution of traditional personnel functions; personnel function becomes primarily staff, assisting in training and education.

In the following dicussion we shall cover each moderating factor individually. The primary effects on organizational change are outlined, including the important feedback effects from the enrichment factors to the moderating factors.

Technology. Technology primarily affects managerial style, decision making, and job structure. On the one hand, technology can free people from cumbersome tasks and make it possible for one individual or team to perform many tasks. With the introduction of a new machine, jobs may be eliminated or restructured. Changing the job structure has effects on managerial style and decision making, as previously discussed.

On the other hand, some jobs may not be restructurable because of the lack of a necessary technology. In these cases, technology has an inhibiting rather than a reinforcing effect.

Managerial Attitudes. Managerial attitudes can effect changes in managerial style, decision making, and the authority structure. If a firm is packed with "Theory X" managers, job enrichment programs are likely to fail.[9]

Feedback can come from all the enrichment factors. For example, if increased individual responsibility and job restructuring show gains in productivity, management doubts or fears regarding the workability of a general supervisory or Theory Y approach tend to be modified.

Organized Labor. The attitudes and actions of organized labor tend to affect change primarily in managerial style and job structure. Union contracts may restrict the types of tasks performed, number of hours worked, and so forth. If the union leadership views enrichment as just another way of "sweating" labor, then this attitude will tend to inhibit worker acceptance of the program. Just as is the case with management, the feedback from the workers may serve to arrest the fears or anxieties of the union. If the job enrichment program has the blessing of union leadership, a major hurdle has been overcome.

Individual Attitudes Toward Peers. The attitudes a worker has toward his peers may result in changes in the communication and information systems, the authority structure, and the control and audit functions. If workers are competitive and individualistic, lateral communication tends to be stifled, the authority structure may be sabotaged, and control and self-audit may be impossible.

Without teamwork and communication, job enrichment programs are doomed to failure.

Individual Attitudes Toward Superiors. The attitudes a person has toward his superior may cause changes in managerial attitudes, communication and information systems, and the authority structure. If the individual worker is not receptive to a Theory Y approach, then job enrichment may not work in his case.

Feedback may come from all the enrichment factors. If job enrichment is successful, the individual or team may adapt well to general supervision. As people grow and adapt to the advisory role of the resource manager, the realization that he is an adviser rather than a "straw boss" can cause phenomenal changes in individual attitudes.

Maintenance Factors. If the basic needs of participants are not satisfied, the concept of job enrichment tends to suffer. In other words, substandard pay and fringe benefits tend to reduce worker motivation. The maintenance factors serve to satisfy the lower level need of the individual, whereas job enrichment hopefully serves to help him achieve the higher level needs.

Individual Attitudes Toward Work. An individual's attitudes toward work cause changes primarily in managerial style, authority structure, and job design. If the individual lacks a work ethic and refuses to assume responsibility, it will be hard to enrich his job and to establish the necessary managerial relationships.

Feedback improves as members grow by virture of increased responsibility and participation in decision making. When the participant is provided the opportunity to control his working actions, he responds by seeking more responsibility.

Trust Relationships. Mutual trust between the teams and the resource manager, and also within the teams, is necessary if a job enrichment program is to succeed. Feedback from all of the enrichment factors can serve to reinforce trust relationships.

Individual Goals. The attitudes of members toward goals will effect changes primarily in planning and goal setting, managerial style, and job structure. If both participants and teams are motivated to set and attain high performance goals, job enrichment will work more effectively. The logical step here is to involve them in the overall organizational planning. Feedback can come from all the enrichment factors and serve to reinforce growth toward increasing responsibility.

Personnel Policies. Existing personnel policies can restrict the planning and implementation of job enrichment programs. Certain traditional functions, such as selection and discipline, must be delegated to the team, under the advice and counsel of the resource manager. Feedback from the restructuring of the organization can cause permanent changes in the personnel functions. It is likely that the personnel function will ultimately become a staff function responsible for record keeping, education, and training.

Summary

We feel that the model developed in this article has a number of uses for any organization planning for, or developing, an improved quality of worklife program. We recognize that the model is by no means complete, but we do feel that it provides an early step in the development of the theory of work improvement and job enrichment. As such it may be viewed as an essential component of an integrative theory of management.

The approach developed here provides a useful frame of reference to use when reading about the experience of organizations which are implementing quality of worklife programs. The reader should bear in mind that work improvement programs are governed by the logic of the situation; what improves quality and increases production in one situation may prove to be a disaster in some other. The important point is to think in terms of experiments and partial solutions rather than in terms of the "isms" of macrophiliac theorizing.

Recent years have been witness to a renaissance in behavior modification theories and their application to the schoolroom and the workplace. Behavior modification techniques, along with drug therapy, electrical stimulation of the brain, and psychosurgery, deny the freedom and dignity of man. Quality of worklife programs move in the opposite direction of humanistic psychology and all that this implies in terms of satisfying esteem, autonomy, and self-actualization needs. This is quite in contrast to the situation a quarter century ago when behavioral scientists were moving toward a Theory Y frame of reference and practitioners were avowing the enduring and omnipresent relevance of a Theory X orientation.

We concede that there are and should be limits to any work improvement program. To proceed too far is to threaten the integrity of the primary job enrichment factors. This would result in a return to the concepts of hierarchy, authority, and centralization. Job enrichment should be viewed rather as falling into a continuum or a spectrum. This is a topic which is too lengthy to discuss here but has been treated in a number of other contexts.[10]

We close with a quotation from an editorial in *The New York Times* which puts the issue elegantly:

"The Chrysler accord is a pacesetter in what will undoubtedly be the major motif of industrial relations in the nineteen-seventies: a movement away from the sterility of the traditional 'battle for the buck' to union involvement in joint efforts with management to 'humanize' factory life. Modest as are the initial breakthroughs toward a cooperative voice in experiments in job enrichment, employee option on working overtime and mutual responsibility for enforcing plant health and safety standards, they are nevertheless patterns that will quickly spread through much of basic industry.

"They do not amount to co-determination on the European model, nor do they strip management of its needed and proper rights to manage. But they do represent valuable steps toward greater industrial democracy in a period when millions of younger workers are displaying restiveness under the constraints of uninspiring, repetitive jobs and are demanding freedom for fuller lives outside the work place. Reduction of in-plant friction and enlistment of employee creativity in redesigning production processes can mean significant gains in productivity as well as in worker satisfaction."[11]

---

1. "Elements of Meaningful Work," *Personnel Journal*, March 1972, p. 208.

2. J. Goodling, "Blue-Collar Blues on the Assembly Line," *Fortune*, July 1970, p. 69.

3. "Job Enrichment: A Case Study," *Burrough's Clearing House*, March 1972, p. 30; J.E. Powers, "Job Enrichment—How One Company Overcame Obstacles," *Personnel*, May 1972, p. 18; and R.N. Ford, "Job Enrichment Lessons From AT&T," *Harvard Business Review*, January-February 1973, p. 96.

4. J.F. Donnelly, "Increasing Productivity by Involving People in Their Jobs," *Personnel Administration*, September 1971, p. 8; and R.W. Walters, "The Rewards of Job Enrichment," *Supervisory Management*, January 1973, p. 39.

5. Powers, "Job Enrichment" and Ford, "Job Enrichment Lessons."

6. Goodling, "Blue-Collar Blues"; D. Sirota and A.D. Wolfson, "Job Enrichment: What are the Obstacles?" *Personnel*, May 1972, p. 8; "The Spreading Lordstown Syndrome," *Business Week*, March 4, 1972, p. 69; and J. Goodling, "It Pays to Wake Up the Blue Collar Workers," *Fortune*, September 1970, p. 133.

7. "GM Sets Teamwork Against Boredom," *Industrial Week*, January 15, 1973, p. 57.

8. Sirota and Wolfson, "Job Enrichment."

9. Ibid.

10. Waino W. Suojanen, "Evolution, Ethology and Organization," *Southern Journal of Business*, October 1970, p. 107; idem, "The Management of Creativity," *California Management Review*, Fall 1971, p. 17; and idem, "Motivation and Leadership," *Modern Office Management and Administrative Services*, edited by Carl Heyel (New York, McGraw-Hill, 1972), chap. 8, pp. 14-27.

11. "New Model at Chrysler," *The New York Times*, September 19, 1973.

Mitchell Fein is a consulting industrial engineer.

This article is reprinted from the Winter 1974 issue of **Sloan Management Review,** *pp. 69-88.*

4
Job Enrichment: A Re-evaluation

Mitchell Fein

Introduction

The quality of working life, work humanization, job enrichment, restructure of work, and other such concerns are increasingly the subject of discussions and articles in the management literature and the press. A vocal school of social scientists is pressing government officials, legislators, and management to give serious attention to the signs of unrest in industry. Their proposals are summarized in *Work in America,* a study written for the Department of Health, Education, and Welfare.[1]

To a large extent this article disagrees with the findings of that study. In the first part of the article, the theory of job enrichment is examined in detail. It is suggested that job enrichment does not work as well as has been claimed. The second part of the article develops a more balanced framework for thinking about worker motivation and job enrichment.

The Theory Behind Job Enrichment

According to the study *Work in America,* the primary cause of the dissatisfaction of white and blue-collar workers is the nature of their work. ". . . significant numbers of American workers are dissatisfied with the quality of their working lives. Dull, repetitive, seemingly meaningless tasks, offering little challenge or autonomy, are causing discontent among workers at all occupational levels."[2] The study reports that the discontent of women, minorities, blue-collar workers, youth, and older adults would be considerably less if these Americans had an active voice in decisions at the work place that most directly affect their lives. "The redesign of jobs is the keystone of this report, . . ."; work must be made more meaningful to the workers.[3] The presumption is that blue-collar employees will work harder if their jobs are enriched or expanded to give them greater control over the order of their work or its content, or to allow them more freedom from direct supervision. Far too many variations on the theme of job enrichment have appeared in the last ten years to attempt to describe even a small proportion of them. The following discussion therefore assumes that the reader is familiar with the basic ideas of job enrichment.

Do the Studies Support the Theory?

Claims for the success and usefulness of job enrichment are based primarily on a number of job enrichment case histories and studies conducted over the past ten years. These studies attempt to prove that workers really want job enrichment. However, when they are examined closely, it is found that:

1. What actually occurred in the cases was often quite different from what was reported to have occurred.
2. Most of the cases were conducted with hand-picked employees, who were usually working in areas or plants isolated from the main operations and thus did not represent a cross section of the working population. Practically all experiments have been in nonunion plants.
3. Only a handful of job enrichment cases have been reported in the past ten years, despite the claims of gains obtained for employees and management through job changes.
4. In *all* instances the experiments were initiated by management, never by workers or unions.

A review of some of the more prominent studies illustrates these points.

Survey of Working Conditions[4]

This large scale study of workers' attitudes toward work and working conditions, conducted for the Department of Labor by the Survey Research Center at the University of Michigan, is cited in numerous articles and is a mainstay of the HEW study. When examined closely, however, several errors are revealed which cast serious doubt upon the validity of its conclusions.

In the study, the workers polled were asked to rank twenty-five aspects of work in order of importance to them. They ranked interesting work first; pay, fifth; and job security, seventh. The researchers neglected, however, to indicate that these rankings averaged together the survey results for all levels of workers, from managers and professionals to low skilled workers. The researchers created a composite image that they called a "worker." The study, however, was based on a cross section of the United States work force rather than just lower-level workers.

When separated into the basic occupational categories and analyzed separately, the data show that blue-collar workers rank pay and job security higher than interesting work. Interesting work was ranked so high in SRC's results because the responses of managers, professionals, and skilled people were averaged with the responses of lower-level workers.[5]

It seems reasonable to suspect that the attitudes of managers and professionals toward their jobs might be different from those of factory workers, and that there also might be differences between skilled and unskilled workers' attitudes within occupational groupings. When the data were compiled by SRC, each subject's occupation was identified, but the results presented in the final report were lumped together for all subjects.

The new data obtained by reanalyzing the SRC data by occupational categories is supported by a large scale study that was conducted abroad. In the first phase of a study covering 60,000 people in more than fifty countries (excluding the Communist bloc), Sirota and Greenwood found that there was considerable similarity in the goals of employees around the world and that the largest and most striking differences are between jobs rather than between countries. Most interestingly, the security needs of people in lower-skilled jobs were found to be highest.[6] The final phase of the study is even more illuminating because the data include the full range of occupations, from managers to unskilled workers, reported separately by seven occupational groups. Unskilled workers in manufacturing plants abroad ranked their needs in this order: physical conditions first, security second, earnings third, and benefits fourth. A factor labeled "interesting work" was not included, but there were several which in total encompass this factor. These were ranked far below the workers' top four needs.[7]

General Foods-Topeka

General Foods-Topeka has been widely cited to show how, when jobs are enriched according to organization development principals, productivity and employee satisfaction will rise. However, Walton's reporting of this case omits critical information which greatly affects the interpretation of what actually occurred and why.[8]

Walton attributes the success of the Topeka plant to the "... autonomous work groups . . . integrated support functions . . . challenging job assignments . . . job mobility and rewards for learning . . . facilitative leadership . . . managerial decision making for operations . . . self-government for the plant community . . . congruent physical and social context . . . learning and evolution . . . " which were established for the employees.[9] He does not mention that the sixty-three Topeka employees are a group of very special people who were carefully selected from 700 applicants in five screening interviews. The fourth screening was an hour long personal interview, and the fifth was a four-hour session that included a complex two-hour personality test.[10]

General Foods-Topeka is a controlled experiment in a small plant with conditions set up to achieve desired results. The employees are not a cross section of the larger employee population, or even of Topeka. The plant and its operations are not typical of those in industry today. The results obtained are valid only for this one plant. What are other managers to do? Should they screen out nine of ten possible candidates and hire only from the select group that remains? What happens to the other nine who were not selected?

If the investigators had shown how they converted a plant bursting with labor problems into one where management and employees told glowingly of their accomplishments, the study would truly merit the praise it has received. Instead they turned their backs on the company's parent plant in Kankakee, which has many of the problems of big city plants. Even worse, they tantalize management with the prospect that, in building a new plant with new equipment, carefully selected employees, and no union, productivity will be higher.

Many managers have dreamed of relocating their plants in the wheat fields or the hills to escape from the big city syndrome. Is this Walton's message to managers in his article, "How to Counter Alienation in the Plant?"[11]

Writers who extol the GF-Topeka case do not understand that what makes this plant so unique is not only the management style but the workers themselves, who were hand-picked. These are highly motivated workers who were isolated from the mainstream of workers and now are free to do their work in their own way. One wonders how these hand-picked workers would produce without any changes at all in management practices.

Procter & Gamble

Procter & Gamble is cited by Jenkins. "Without doubt the most radical organizational changes made on a practical, day-to-day basis in the United States have taken place at Procter & Gamble, one of America's largest companies, well known for its hardboiled, aggressive management practices."[12]

What generally is not mentioned in any of the laudatory articles about P&G's organizational development practices is that P&G is an unusual company with a history of concern for its employees that is matched by few other firms in this country. In 1923 William C. Procter, then president of the company, recognized that the workers' problems were caused in large part by seasonal employment, and he established genuine job security. He guaranteed forty-eight weeks of employment a year. P&G has a long history of good wages and working conditions; they also have pioneered in old age pensions and profit sharing. Since P&G has a good reputation among workers, its plants attract some of the best workers in their areas. In seeking the reasons for P&G's success, one must not overlook their excellent bread and butter policies, among the best in the nation. Would their organizational development and job enrichment practices work without such policies?

Other Studies on Job Enrichment

Texas Instruments: The intensive job enrichment efforts of Texas Instruments management is unequalled in this country. Since 1952 the TI management has tried diligently to gain acceptance of its enrichment program by its workers. In 1968 the management announced that its goal was to involve 16 percent of its employees in job enrichment. Their data show that the actual involvement was 10.5 percent.[13] This is far from the huge success claimed in the numerous articles describing the program.

Polaroid Corporation: Experiments involve only job rotation, not job enrichment. Foulkes reports that from 1959 to 1962, 114 employees out of 2000 were involved in changing their jobs.[14] Although management had guaranteed that employees could change their jobs and be assured of a return to their original jobs if they wished, less than 6 percent of the employees actually became involved. It does not appear that the employees favored the plan or that it was broadly successful.

Texas Instruments Cleaning and Janitorial Employees: The version of this report in *Work in America* states that when Texas Instruments took over the cleaning work formerly done by an outside contracting firm, the employees were " . . . given a voice in planning, problem solving, and goal setting for their own jobs . . . the team (had the) responsibility to act independently to devise its own strategies, plans, and schedules to meet the objective . . . the cleanliness level rating improved from 65 percent to 85 percent, personnel . . . dropped from 120 to 71, and quarterly turnover dropped from 100 percent to 9.8 percent . . . cost savings for the entire site averaged $103,000 per annum."[15]

What was not reported by the study was that the outside contractor's employees received only $1.40 per hour. When TI took over the program, the starting pay was raised to $1.94 per hour for the first shift, with $.10 extra added for the second shift and $.20 extra added for the third. The janitorial employees were given good insurance programs, profit sharing, paid vacations, sick leave, a good cafeteria, and working conditions similar to those of other employees at Texas Insturments. *Work in America* does not mention that in raising the pay by 46 percent and adding benefits worth one-third of their pay, TI was able to recruit better qualified employees. Yet the study insists on attributing the improved performance to job enrichment. The omission of this pay data is strange, since the data appear prominently in the report from which the HEW task force obtained the case material.[16]

American Telephone and Telegraph: Space does not permit a discussion of the various cases reported by Robert Ford.[17] To a large degree, he redesigned jobs at AT&T which had been ineffectively set up in the first place. To label such changes "job enrichment" is to render the phrase meaningless.

The Scandinavian Experience: Work in America suggests that worker initiative is inhibited by a lack of democracy at the work place. The study points to Europe and especially to the Scandinavian countries as examples of productivity gains through democracy in the plants.[18] The assumption is that European experience in industrial relations is directly transferable to this country. In fact, it may not be. Nat Goldfinger, Research Director of the AFL-CIO, believes ". . . that industrial democracy was not needed in America: 'The issue is irrelevant here. I would suspect that most of the issues that are bugging Europeans are taken care of here in collective bargaining.' "[19]

The study of worker participation councils covering fifty different countries cited earlier supports this position. It shows clearly that this movement is the European workers' way of institutionalizing union plant locals and of establishing collective bargaining on the plant floor. It is not a new form of worker democracy as described by the behaviorists.[20]

The examples discussed above are only a sampling of the job enrichment studies. Many more could be cited, but most of them are subject to criticisms already voiced. Only lack of space prevents a fuller discussion.

Job Enrichment or Common Sense?

Admittedly there are some cases where jobs have actually been productively enriched. Much more common, however, is the masquerading of common sense as job enrichment. Many studies have simply involved the elimination of an obviously bothersome problem, which hardly warrants the use of the term job enrichment. This paper is not directed toward the common sense applications of job enrichment. Rather this analysis is aimed at the broader claims of job enrichment success.

Limits to Job Enrichment

One reason that job enrichment has not been widely implemented is that there are many factors operating within the work place to constrain its applicability. Several of these factors are discussed below.

Technology

The structure of jobs in American industry today is dictated largely by the technology employed in the production process. The size of the parts used, the equipment required for the operations, and the volume of production are all important determinants. When the blacksmith of a century ago shaped a piece of metal, his only capital equipment was a forge. He was the operator and the forge press. Today there are even large, specialized machines for parts which are viewed under a microscope. Much of the job redesign called for by proponents of job enrichment neglects the contraints imposed by technology.

There are few decisions on what to do in mass production. A piece is put into a press and hit. Two pieces or fifty are assembled in a given manner, simply because the pieces do not fit together in another way. In typing a letter or keypunching, the operators strike certain keys, not just any they wish. Even in the highly praised experimental Volvo plant where a small team assembles an engine, the workers have no choice in the selection of parts to be installed, and they must assemble the parts in a given sequence. While they may rotate their jobs within the group and thus obtain variety, this is not job enrichment or autonomy but job rotation.

In most instances it is impossible to add to jobs decision making of the kind that job enrichment theorists call for, simply because of the technology of the work. The job shops which produce only a small number of an item can provide true decision making for many of its employees, but these shops have not attracted the attention of job enrichers. They are worried about the mass production plants where work has been grossly simplified.

Another view of the technological constraints on job enrichment is offered by workers themselves. A full page article in a union newspaper recently denounced attempts by General Electric to combine the tasks of a thirty-two operator line producing steam irons into a single work station, with a headline: "Makes no difference how you slice it, it's still monotony and more speed up." Jim Matles, an officer of the United Electrical Workers, derides management's efforts, pointing out that, "As monotonous as that job was on that continuous assembly line, they were able to perform it practically without having to keep their minds on the job . . . they could talk to each other. On the new assembly line, however, the repetitiveness of the job was there just as much, but . . . they no longer could do it without being compelled to keep their minds on the job." Another union leader in the plant said, "I've finally been able to show [management] that the more repetitive or rhythmic the job, the less unhappy the worker. On jobs where the rhythm is broken and unrepetitive, the employees are unhappy and must constantly fight these jobs [rather] than do them by natural reflex."[21]

It is not intended that technological constraints be thought of as structural barriers to job enrichment. In the long run technology can be changed. Workers and managers are by no means forever locked into the present means of production. At the very least, however, proponents of job enrichment have neglected badly the immediate problems posed by technology. At their worst they have intentionally ignored them. The purpose of this section is to restore a more balanced perspective to the relationship of technology to job enrichment.

Cost

Giving workers job rotation opportunities or combining jobs can increase costs. This occurred recently at the General Motors Corporation Truck and Coach Division. Early this year they initiated an experiment using teams of workers to assemble motor homes. *Business Week* reported that, "Six-member teams assembled the body while three-member teams put the chassis together. The move was an attempt to curb assembly line doldrums and motivate workers. Last month, the experiment was curtailed. The complexity of assembly proved too difficult for a team approach, which was too slow to meet GM's production standards."[22]

Increased costs from combining jobs and in job rotation also occurred in a case reported by Louis E. Davis, a prominent advocate of job redesign. He made studies to compare the levels of output obtained with a mechanically-paced conveyor line, a line with no pacing, and a line with individuals performing all of the jobs as a "one-man line." Using the average output of the nine-operator paced line as 100 percent, Davis found that the same non-paced line operated at 89 percent, and the "one-man line" operated at 94.0 percent. Translated into unit costs, the non-paced line cost 12.4 percent more and the individual line 6.4 percent more than the conventional paced line.[2 3] Suppose that the workers liked the non-pacing or the built up job better (although this did not happen to be true). Would the consumer be willing to pay the additional cost?

Relative Levels of Skill

The possibility of making enriching changes in jobs increases with the skill level of the jobs. However, relatively few jobs have a high skill content, and relatively few workers occupy these jobs. If widespread benefits are derived from job enrichment, these are most needed for workers in the low level jobs, where boredom presumably is highest. The work of skilled workers already has challenge and interest built into the jobs, requiring judgment, ingenuity and initiative. Adding job enrichment responsibilities in some cases may only be gilding the lily. What are managers to do with low-skilled workers who make up the great majority of the work force? That is the essence of the problem confronting managers. When tested in the plant, enrichment programs do not operate as predicted. They usually can be applied only to the wrong people, to those who do not need them because their jobs potentially provide the necessary enrichment.

Work Group Norms

Studies from around the world, including the communist countries, demonstrate that the concepts of McGregor and Herzberg regarding workers' need to find fulfillment through work hold only for those workers who *choose* to find fulfillment through their work. Contrary to the more popular belief, the vast majority of workers seek fulfillment outside their work.[2 4] After almost twenty years of active research in job enrichment, it is clear that only a minority of workers is attracted to it. These workers are mostly in the skilled jobs or on their way up. However the social pressure in the plant from the workers who are not involved in job enrichment sets the plant climate, and they apparently oppose job changes. The effect of this opposition is minimal on the active minority, because they find their enrichment by moving up to the skilled jobs where they have greater freedom to exercise their initiative. Obviously, the isolation of small groups of workers is not possible in the real world industry. In the main plant, the pervasive social climate controls what goes on, and job enrichment may not be permitted to work.

Contrasting Employer and Employee Goals

Proponents of job enrichment often forget that management and workers are not motivated in the same direction; they have different goals, aspirations, and needs. The fact of life which workers see clearly, but which often is obscured to others, is that *if workers do anything to raise productivity, some of them will be penalized.*

Job enrichment predicts that increased job satisfaction will increase motivation and raise productivity. However workers know that if they increase production, reduce delays and waiting time, reduce crew sizes or cooperate in any way, less overtime will be available, some employees will be displaced, and the plant will require fewer employees. The remaining workers will receive few financial benefits. What employee will voluntarily raise his production output, only to be penalized for his diligence?

This phenomenon does not occur with "exempt" employees, the executives, administrators, professionals, and salesmen. Have you ever heard of a manager who worked himself out of a job by superior performance? Have you ever heard of a salesman whose security was threatened because he sold too much or an engineer who caused the layoff of other engineers because he was too creative? These employees usually can anticipate rewards for their creativity and effectiveness.

When workers excel and raise productivity, the company benefits and management is pleased, but the workers usually do not benefit. On the contrary, in the short term their economic interests may be threatened; some suffer loss of income. When exempt employees are more effective, they cover themselves with glory; their economic security is enhanced not threatened. Ironically, the relationship between workers and management actually provides workers with the incentive not to cooperate in productivity improvement. Most companies offer their employees the opportunity to reduce their earnings and job security as they raise productivity. Management does not, of course, intend such results, but the system often operates that way in this country.

A recent study by the Harris organization, conducted for the National Commission on Productivity, provides support for this contention.

> Nearly 7 in 10 feel that stockholders and management would benefit a lot from increased productivity, compared with scarcely more that 1 in 3 who see the same gains for the country as a whole.

The term 'increased productivity' does not have a positive connotation for most people who work for a living.

A majority believes the statement 'companies benefit from increased productivity at the expense of workers.' Hourly workers believe this by 80-14 percent.[25]

Is it any wonder that workers are alienated from their work? Would company executives improve the effectiveness of their work if they believed it would not benefit them, and more, that it would reduce their income and even cause their layoff?[26]

Do Managers Support the Theory?

If job enrichment were the panacea it is so often claimed to be, then somewhere in this country some aggressive, farsighted manager should have been able, in the past ten years, to have made it operational on a large scale basis. The claims that large productivity gains will be made through job redesign should have spurred many companies to implement it. Yet there are few successful examples. Given this lack of acceptance, it is reasonable to assume that managers do not support job enrichment.

Do the Workers Support the Theory?

Those advocating that work should be redesigned start with the premise that such changes are socially desirable and beneficial to workers. Curiously, however, these investigators are not supported in their claims by many workers or unions. There is a sharp difference of opinion between what workers say they want and what proponents of job enrichment say workers should want.[27]

Workers' opinions on the enrichment of jobs are expressed by William W. Winpisinger, Vice-President of the Machinist Union.

In my years as a union representative and officer I've negotiated for a lot of membership demands. I've been instructed to negotiate on wages . . . noise . . . seniority clauses; fought for health and welfare plans . . . and everything else you find in a modern labor-management contract. But never once have I carried into negotiations a membership mandate to seek job enrichment. In fact, quite to the contrary, working people want management to leave their jobs alone.[28]

The question of job enrichment and boredom on the job was discussed at last year's United Auto Workers convention and significantly was not made an issue in the following auto negotiations. Leonard Woodcock, President of the UAW, was sharply critical of the HEW report and a number of its suggestions. "Mr.

Woodcock was very outspoken in his denunciation of government officials, academic writers and intellectuals who contend that boredom and monotony are the big problems among assembly workers. He said 'a lot of academic writers . . . are writing a lot of nonsense' . . . [he] expressed resentment over a recent government report on work as 'elitist' in its approach, describing assembly line workers as if they were 'subhumans.' "[29]

A similar attitude on the part of European workers is reported by Basil Whiting of the Ford Foundation. He visited Europe to study their job enrichment efforts " . . . in terms of the experiments on job redesign: By and large all these experiments were initiated by management. We found no cases where they were initiated by unions and other forces in society."[30]

Despite the urgings for increased participation by workers, Strauss and Rosenstein also found that workers all over the world have failed to respond: " 'Participation' is one of the most overworked words of the decade. Along with 'meaningful' and 'involvement' it appears in a variety of forms and context." "Participation in many cases has been introduced from the top down as symbolic solutions to ideological contradictions," especially in the countries with strong socialist parties.[31] "In general the impetus for participation has come more from intellectuals, propagandists and politicians (sometimes all three combined) than it has from the rank-and-file workers who were supposed to do the participating."[32] There is obviously a lack of worker interest in participation despite claims by intellectuals that the work place is dehumanizing.

A More Balanced Approach to Worker Motivation and Job Enrichment

Studying satisfied and dissatisfied workers, job enrichment theory contends that the intrinsic nature of the work performed is the main cause of the differences between them. The job enrichment theorists propose to change the work of the dissatisfied workers to more closely resemble the work performed by the satisfied workers. There is, however, a large "if" to this approach. What if the nature of the work is not what primarily satisfies all satisfied workers? Restructuring the work and creating work involvement opportunities may ignite a small flame under some people, but to what extent is the nature of the work the determinant of a person's drive? *The simple truth is that there are no data which show that restructuring and enriching jobs will raise the will to work.*

The essential assumption of job enrichment theory is that the nature of the work performed determines to a large extent worker satisfaction or dissatisfaction. It is argued here that this is not always so. *The intrinsic nature of the work is only one factor among many that affect worker satisfaction.* Moreover, the available evidence suggests that its influence is very often subordinate to that of several other variables: pay, job security, and job rules. The inconclusive performance of job enrichment to date stems largely from those programs that have neglected to consider these factors.

A useful starting point in understanding how workers feel about their jobs is to look at how they choose their jobs. A "natural selection" model of job choice proves very fruitful in examining this process.

A "Natural Selection" Model of Job Choice

There is greater selection by workers of jobs than is supposed. The selection process in factories and offices often occurs without conscious direction by either workers or management. The data for white and blue-collar jobs show that there is tremendous turnover in the initial employment period, which drops sharply with time on the job. Apparently what happens is that a worker begins a new job, tries it out for several days or weeks, and decides whether the work suits his needs and desires. Impressions about a job are a composite of many factors: pay, proximity to home, the nature of the work, working conditions, the attitude of supervision, congeniality of fellow workers, past employment history of the company, job security, physical demands, opportunities for advancement, and many other related factors. A worker's choice of job is made in a combination of ways, through evaluating various trade-offs. Working conditions may be bad, but if pay and job security are high, the job may be tolerable. There are numerous combinations of factors which in total influence a worker's disposition to stay on the job or not.

There is dual screening which culls out those who will be dissatisfied with the work. The worker in the first instance decides whether to stay on the job, and management then has the opportunity to determine whether to keep him beyond the trial period. The combination of the worker's choice to remain and management's decision that the worker is acceptable initially screens out workers who might find the work dissatisfying.

Intrinsic and Extrinsic Job Characteristics

As a result of this selection process, workers are able to exert much control over the nature of the work which they finally accept. They can leave jobs that they do not like and only accept jobs which they find rewarding. The major constraint on the variety of work available to them is the intrinsic nature of the work itself. However, if there are no intrinsically rewarding jobs but a worker still must support his family, he will have to take an intrinsically unsatisfactory job.

Unlike the intrinsic nature of the work that he accepts, the worker has much less control over the extrinsic characteristics of his job. There may be many different kinds of jobs for which he is qualified, but most of them will pay about the same maximum salary or wage. Similarly, there will be few options regarding the different kinds of job security and work rule combinations which he can find. The suggested hypothesis is that the influence of extrinsic factors, particularly pay, job security, and work rules, on worker satisfaction has been obscured and neglected by job enrichment. Undoubtedly some workers are distressed by the highly routinized work that they may be performing, but to what extent is dissatisfaction caused by the intrinsic nature of their work? What proportion is caused by their insufficient pay? Would workers have a greater interest in the work if their living standards were raised and they could see their jobs as contributing to a good life?

Individual Differences in Job Preference

Work that one person views as interesting or satisfying may appear boring and dissatisfying to another. There are significant differences among workers, and their needs vary. Some workers prefer to work by rote without having to be bothered with decisions. Some workers prefer more complicated work. It is really a matter of individual preference.

There would undoubtedly be far greater dissatisfaction with work if those on the jobs were not free to make changes and selections in the work they do. Some prefer to remain in highly repetitive, low skill jobs even when they have an opportunity to advance to higher skill jobs through job bidding. A minority of workers strives to move into the skilled jobs such as machinists, maintenance mechanics, set-up men, group leaders, utility men, and other such positions where there is considerable autonomy in the work performed.

The continued evaluation of workers by management and the mobility available to workers to obtain jobs which suit them best refine the selection process. A year or two after entering a plant, most workers are on jobs or job progressions which suit them or which they find tolerable. Those who are no longer on the job have been "selected" out, either by themselves or by management. Given the distinction between intrinsic and extrinsic job characteristics and the greater degree of control which workers exert over the former, those who are left on the job after the selection process can be expected to be relatively more satisfied with the nature of their work than with their pay, job security, or work rules. In fact this prediction proves to be correct.

Workers' Attitudes Toward Their Work

Work in America cites a Gallup Poll which found that 80 to 90 percent of American workers are satisfied with their jobs.[33] A more recent poll found that from 82 to 91 percent of blue and white-collar workers like their work. The workers were asked, "If there were one thing you could change about your job, what would it be?" Astonishingly, very few workers said that they would make their job "less boring" or "more interesting."[34]

In a recent study, David Sirota was surprised to find that the sewing operators in one plant found their work interesting. Since the work appeared to be highly repetitive, he had expected that they would say they were bored and their talents underutilized.[35] These workers' views are supported in a large scale study by Weintraub of 2535 female sewing machine operators in seventeen plants from Massachusetts to Texas. He found that "Most of the operators like the nature of their work. Of those who were staying (65%), 9 out of 10 feel that way. Even of those who would leave (35%), 7 out of 10 like their work."[36]

For the most part workers are satisfied with the nature of their work. What they find most discomforting is their pay, their job security, and many of the work rules with which they must cope. They can find their work engrossing and still express dissatisfaction because of other job related factors such as pay, working conditions, inability to advance, and so on. When a person says his work is satisfying, he implies that his work utilizes his abilities to an extent *satisfactory to him*.

Extrinsic Determinants of Worker Satisfaction

As the studies cited above indicate, most workers appear relatively more satisfied with the intrinsic nature of their jobs than with the extrinsic job factors. The major extrinsic factors are examined below.

Pay

Pay is very important in determining job satisfaction. This is hardly a novel observation, but it is one that is too often overlooked or forgotten in job enrichment programs. Sheppard and Herrick, both of whom served on the *Work in America* task force, analyzed the SRC and other data and provided a cross section of feelings by workers about their jobs. The following quotations concerning pay are from their study.[37]

"It was found that dissatisfaction with work decreases steadily as pay rises. When earnings exceed $10,000 per year, dissatisfaction drops significantly."

If we knew why this occurs, we would probably have a major part of the answer to the question of why there is dissatisfaction at the work place. There is a cause and effect relationship involved in which it is difficult to evaluate how the various factors affect the employee. The higher the social value of the work performed, the higher is the pay. The higher the skill required of the employee, the higher is his opportunity for involvement in his work. As pay rises, to what extent does the pay level produce higher satisfaction with the affluence it brings? To what extent does the interesting content of the work cause higher satisfaction?

Construction workers are the highest paid of the blue-collar workers and have unexcelled benefits. Many professionals and managers earn less than construction workers. These workers are among the last of the craftsmen who still largely work with their hands and still may own their own tools. Their satisfaction may well come from their creative work, but to what extent does their high pay influence their attitudes?

"In the managerial, professional and technical occupations only 1 in 10 were dissatisfied."

Is it the attraction of their work or their pay which affords them their satisfaction?

"Slightly less than 1 in 4 manufacturing workers were dissatisfied. The data for workers in the service occupations.and the wholesale-retail industry are about the same."

In 1971, Bureau of Labor Statistics data for blue-collar workers showed that 58.7 percent earned less than $150 per week, 24.6 percent earned from $150 to $199, and 16.8 percent earned over $200. In 1971, the BLS "lower level" budget for a family of four was $7214 per year.[38] The SRC data showed that 56.2 percent of the subjects reported having inadequate incomes. Considering the earnings statistics, it is a wonder that more workers are not dissatisfied.

Experience reveals that increasing the availability of interesting work will not compensate for a desire for increased pay, whereas increasing pay can go far to compensate for poor working conditions. This was vividly demonstrated by the workers who collect garbage in New York City. They perform their work in all kinds of weather. Their job is highly accident-ridden and is not held in high esteem by society. Ten years ago few people were interested in the job. Then the pay scale was raised to $10,500 per year with good benefits, and a long waiting line formed for the jobs. The nature of the work had not changed. It was the same dirty, heavy work, but now the pay was attractive.[39]

Job Security

A second critical component of the work environment is job security, the continuity of income. Pay must be not only sufficiently high but also fairly regular. No one can budget for a family if he is not reasonably sure of his income for some time into the future. Most people become distressed when faced with a layoff. Reduced employment affects the morale of everyone in the organization. When employment finally is stabilized and the threat of further reductions passes, fears and memories still linger.

Because it is such an important component of the work environment, *job security is an essential precondition to enhancing the will to work.* While the idea is not new that economic insecurity is a restraint on the will to work, its effect often is minimized by managers, behavioral scientists, and industrial engineers involved in productivity improvement. Job security is as vital to productivity improvement as advanced technical processes and new equipment.

What happens to feelings of identity and loyalty when employees see their increased productivity contributing to their layoff? It is hard to conceive of a manager who would cooperate in designing his own job out of existence, as might occur when several managerial jobs are combined and one person is no longer required. When managers consider their own job security, they quite expectedly have empathy for James F. Lincoln's truism: "No man will willingly work to throw himself out of his job, nor should he." Yet managers do not extend this obvious logic to their work force.

Managers must view job security not only in the social sense of how it affects workers' lives, but as absolutely essential to high levels of productivity. In the plants without job security, workers stretch out the work if they do not see sufficient work ahead of them.[40] They will not work themselves out of their jobs. When workers stretch out their jobs, though it is hidden from view, it is reflected in costs.

Managers historically have considered job security as a union demand to be bargained as are other issues. This has been a tragic error because whenever job security is lacking, labor productivity is restrained. Paradoxically, job security must be established as a demand of *management* if it hopes to increase productivity. What would happen in contract negotiations if management started off by demanding that the new contract include job protection for the employees? This radical act might encourage profound changes in employees' attitudes.

Unduly Restrictive Plant Rules

There are many other factors beside the work itself which affect workers' attitudes. In many companies workers still are considered "hands," hired by the hour with little consideration given to their needs and desires as "people." Some managers find it easier to lay workers off with four to eight hours notice than to plan production and avoid plant delays. In many plants, the plant rules, which management calls its prerogatives and guards jealously, are insulting to human sensibilities.

A worker's self-esteem is affected by how he is treated and how he rates with the others around him. Increasingly, workers want fair treatment for everyone. However, the "hands" concept still separates the white-collar from the blue-collar workers. White-collar workers are generally paid a weekly salary and often do not punch a time clock. They have more leeway in lateness and often do not lose pay when absent. Most factory workers have few of these benefits. A white-collar worker often has a telephone available and can make personal calls during the day. Factory workers have great difficulty in making calls. Receiving calls usually is reserved for extreme emergencies. When a worker has a problem, he stays out.

The penned-in feeling of workers, which is stylishly called their blues, comes in large part from their inability to take care of these daily personal problems and needs. Any job enrichment program which hopes to succeed must effectively address the problems posed to workers by plant rules. Until now very few programs have acknowledged their importance.

What Should Be Done?

Everyone will accept the idea that improvement of the quality of working life is a desirable goal. However, how should this be done? David Sirota provides a concise statement of the problem. "I can't get it through some thick skulls that [many] people may want both—that they would like to finish a day's work and feel that they had accomplished something and still get paid for it."[41] A logical approach to formulating the problem must begin with a determination of who is now dissatisfied and why and with the recognition that people have individual needs and desires.

The *Work in America* task force believes that, " . . . pay . . . is important," it must support an 'adequate' standard of living, and be perceived as equitable—but high pay alone will not lead to job (or life) satisfaction.[42] They conclude that work must provide satisfaction and must be restructured to become the *raison d'etre* of people's lives. Their statement of the problem is correct, but their conclusion that work alone must provide satisfaction is wrong. Satisfaction can come from wherever people choose. It need not be only from their work.

The blues of many workers are due less to the nature of their work and more to what their work will not bring them in their pay envelopes. Increasingly, workers also want freedom on their jobs. Some workers prefer enriched jobs with autonomy. Most workers want more freedom to act on personal things outside of their work place. Some may want the freedom to just "goof off" once in a while. In short, workers' blues are not formed solely around the work place. Blues are partly a work place reaction to non-work related problems.

Solving problems in the plants must start with the question why should workers want enriched jobs? It is readily apparent that management and the stockholders benefit from increased worker involvement which leads to reduced costs. For their part, if all the workers get is reduced hours or even layoffs, they must resist it. It is futile to expect that workers willingly will create more for management without simultaneously benefiting themselves. *The most effective productivity results will be obtained when management creates conditions which workers perceive as beneficial to them.* The changes must be genuine and substantial and in forms which eventually are turned into cash and continuity of income. Psychic rewards may look good on paper, but they are invisible in the pocketbook. If workers really wanted psychic job enrichment, management would have heard their demands loud and clear long ago.

Change must start with management taking the first steps, unilaterally and without *quid pro quo*. There must not be productivity bargaining at first. Management must provide the basic conditions which will motivate workers to raise productivity: job security, good working conditions, good pay and financial incentives. There must be a diminution of the win-lose relationship and the gradual establishment of conditions in which workers know that both they and management gain and lose together. Labor, management, and government leaders are very concerned that rising wages and costs are making goods produced in this country less competitive in the world markets. Increasingly all three parties are engaging in meaningful dialogue to address these problems[43]

There are unquestionably enormous potentials for increased productivity which workers can unleash—if they want to. The error of job enrichment is that it tries to talk workers into involvement and concern for the nature of their work when their memories and experiences have taught them that increased productivity only results in layoffs. Only management can now create conditions which will nullify the past.

Companies which are experimenting with new work methods probably will increase their efforts. As viable methods and approaches are developed, more companies will be tempted to innovate approaches suited to their own plants. The greatest progress will come in companies where workers see that management protects their welfare and where productivity gains are shared with the employees.

In the ideal approach, management should leave to workers the final choice regarding what work they find satisfying. In real life, this is what occurs anyway. Workers eschew work that they find dissatisfying or they find ways of saying loudly and clearly how they feel about such work. We should learn to trust workers' expressions of their wants. Workers will readily signal when they are ready for changes.

---

1. U.S. Department of Health, Education, and Welfare, *Work in America*. Report of a Special Task Force to the Secretary of Health, Education, and Welfare. Prepared under the Auspices of the W.E. Upjohn Institute for Employment Research (Cambridge: MIT Press, 1973).

2. Ibid., p. xv.

3. Ibid., p. xvii.

4. U.S. Department of Labor, "Survey of Working Conditions, November 1970." Prepared by the Survey Research Center of the University of Michigan (Washington, D.C.: Government Printing Office, 1971).

5. M. Fein, "The Real Needs of Blue Collar Workers," *The Conference Board Record*, February 1973, pp. 26-33.

6. D. Sirota and J.M. Greenwood, "Understand Your Overseas Work Force," *Harvard Business Review*, January-February 1971, pp. 53-60.

7. G.H. Hofstede, "The Colors of Collars," *Columbia Journal of World Business*, September-October 1972, pp. 72-80.

8. R.E. Walton, "How to Counter Alienation in the Plant," *Harvard Business Review*, November-December 1972, pp. 70-81.

9. R.E. Walton, "Work Place Alienation and the Need for Major Innovation." Paper prepared for a Special Task Force to the Secretary of Health, Education, and Welfare (for *Work in America*), May 1972, p. 9. Unpublished.

10. D.C. King, "Selecting Personnel for a Systems 4 Organization." Paper read at NTL Institute for Applied Behavioral Science Conference, 8-9 October 1971.

11. Walton, "How to Counter Alienation in the Plant."

12. D. Jenkins, "Democracy in the Factory," *The Atlantic*, April 1973, pp. 78-83.

13. M. Fein, "Motivation for Work," in *Handbook of Work, Organization and Society*, edited by R. Dubin (Chicago: Rand McNally, 1973).

14. F.K. Foulkes, *Creating More Meaningful Work* (New York: American Management Association, 1969).

15. *Work in America*, p. 100.

16. H.M.F. Rush, *Job Design for Motivation* (New York: The Conference Board, 1971), pp. 39-45.

17. R.N. Ford, *Motivation Through Work Itself* (New York: American Management Association, 1969).

18. *Work in America*, pp. 103-105.

19. D. Jenkins, *Job Power: Blue and White Collar Democracy* (New York: Doubleday, 1973), p. 315.

20. J.M. Roach, "Worker Participation: New Voices in Management," The Conference Board, Report 594, 1973.

21. J. Matles, "Humanize the Assembly Line?" *UE News*, 13 November 1972.

22. "GM Zeroes in on Employee Discontent," *Business Week*, 12 May 1973.

23. L.E. Davis and R.R. Canter, "Job Design Research," *The Journal of Industrial Engineering* 7 (1956), p. 279.

24. Fein, "Motivation for Work."

25. See the Harris Survey published in *The Record* (Bergen, New Jersey), 19 February 1973, p. A-3.

26. A most ironic turn of events has occurred in plants with supplementary unemployment benefits (SUB). Unions are asking that layoffs occur in *inverse seniority*, with the highest seniority employees going first. By inverting seniority and giving the senior employees a choice, a layoff under SUB becomes a reward, not a penalty. For working diligently and working himself out of a job, a worker is rewarded by time off with pay.

27. M. Fein, "The Myth of Job Enrichment," *The Humanist*, September–October 1973, pp. 30-32.

28. W.P. Winpisinger. Paper presented to University Labor Education Association, 5 April 1973, at Black Lake, Michigan.

29. "UAW Indicates It Will Seek to Minimize Local Plant Strikes in Talks Next Fall," *The Wall Street Journal*, 20 February 1973, p. 5.

30. U.S., Congress, Senate, Subcommittee on Employment, Manpower, and Poverty, Labor and Public Welfare Committee, *Worker Alienation, 1972*, 92d Cong., 2d sess., S. 3916, July 25 and 26, 1972.

31. G. Strauss and E. Rosenstein, "Workers Participation: A Critical View," *Industrial Relations* 9 (1970), pp. 197, 198.

32. Ibid., p. 199.

33. *Work in America*, p. 14.

34. T.C. Sorenson, "Do Americans Like Their Jobs?" *Parade*, 3 June 1973, pp. 15-16.

35. Personal communication.

36. See   E. Weintraub, "Has Job Enrichment Been Oversold?" Address to the 25th Convention of the American Institute of Industrial Engineers, May 1973. Reprinted in the technical papers of the convention. The auto workers' jobs have been cited by many writers as the extreme of monotonous and dehumanizing work. However, a recent study of auto workers in the United States, Italy, Argentina, and India by W.H. Form found that, "Most workers believe that their work integrates their lives . . . that their jobs are satisfying. Nowhere did assemblyline workers dwell upon monotony. . . . Machine work does not make workers more unhappy at any industrial stage. Nor do workers heed the lament of the intellectuals that the monotony of the job drives them mad" (W.H. Form, "Auto Workers and Their Machines: A Study of Work, Factory, and Job Satisfaction in Four Countries," *Social Forces* 52 [1973], pp. 1-15).

37. H.L. Sheppard, and N.Q. Herrick, *Where Have All The Robots Gone?* (New York: New Press, 1972).

38. U.S. Department of Labor, *Handbook of Labor Statistics 1972*. Bulletin 1735. Bureau of Labor Statistics (Washington, D.C.: Government Printing Office, 1972).

39. The average annual pay is now $12,886.

40. In a very fundamental way, work *does* expand to fill time (Parkinson's Law).

41. Panel discussion between Louis E. Davis, Mitchell Fein, and David Sirota, Annual Convention of the American Institute of Industrial Engineers, 24 May 1973.

42. *Work in America*, p. 95.

43. See, for example, the articles on the experimental negotiating agreement in the basic steel industry by I.W. Abel and R. Heath Larry, *Sloan Management Review*, Winter 1974.

Fred Luthans is Professor of Management, University of Nebraska, Lincoln, Nebraska.

Edward Knod is Assistant Professor of Management at Western Illinois University, Macomb, Illinois.

This article is reprinted from the May-June 1974 issue of Atlanta Economic Review, *pp. 6-11.*

5
Critical Factors in Job Enrichment

Fred Luthans
Edward Knod

Job Enrichment is a vitally needed new approach to human resource management. Yet, like all organizational development (OD) techniques (past, present, and future), job enrichment (JE) is certainly not the final answer. On the one hand, popular management literature extolls the virtues of JE and reports near-sensational success stories about its application. On the other hand, especially in more academically oriented literature, there exist highly critical accounts of the empirical validity and/or universality of the concepts embodied in job enrichment. Who is right? How effective is job enrichment? The practicing manager must have answers to these questions before JE can become a useful OD technique for the more effective management of human resources.

Here we shall, first, analyze the theoretical base and review the pro and con literature on job enrichment. Then we shall look at the three most critical variables in successfully implementing job enrichment: the nature of the job to be enriched; the characteristics of the employee who will work on the enriched job; and, finally, the impact that job enrichment will have on the overall organization.

In the late 1950s, Frederick Herzberg and his colleagues conducted a series of interviews with engineers and accountants in Pittsburgh, Pennsylvania. The persons in the study were asked to describe incidents in which they had experienced favorable and unfavorable feelings about their jobs. Using this critical-incident method of research, Herzberg found that certain job factors affected job satisfaction and others affected job dissatisfaction. The factors which affected job satisfaction reflected the content of jobs—that is, they were an intrinsic part of the job itself. On the other hand, factors which determined job dissatisfaction were related to job context—that is, the conditions under which the jobs were being performed. Because the content factors seemed to be effective in motivating workers, Herzberg labeled them motivators. The context factors, on the other hand, did not lead to motivation but instead could prevent dissatisfaction. Thus, borrowing from the terminology of preventive medicine, he called the context factors the hygiene factors. (See Exhibit 1 on page 74.)

Traditionally, motivational efforts have focused almost solely on the hygiene factors. More pay, better insurance plans, longer vacations, new office furniture, and other context variables were freely given out in attempts to motivate employees. Although these hygiene factors certainly did no harm, they also did not solve the human resource problems facing management.

The natural outgrowth of the two-factor theory of motivation and the search to motivate employees more effectively led to job enrichment. Herzberg proposed that by attempting to increase the motivators rather than the hygiene factors in a job situation, the job itself could become enriched. This enriched job would provide greater job satisfaction for the employee which, in turn, would motivate him to improve job performance. Job enrichment, or JE, is the name given to this approach to job design which incorporates Herzberg's motivators in an attempt to increase job satisfaction and performance. More specifically, JE can be defined as designing jobs that include a greater work content; require a higher level of knowledge and skill; give the worker more autonomy and responsibility for planning, directing and controlling his own performance; and provide the opportunity for personal and meaningful work experience.

Some writers and practitioners do not make a distinction between job enrichment and the older job enlargement concept. However, there is a growing trend to make a clear distinction between the two. Job enlargement involves horizontal job loading while job enrichment involves vertical job loading. Simply giving the employee more of the same kind of work to do—horizontal loading—will enlarge, but not enrich, the job. Robert Janson, a noted consultant on job enrichment, states, "The purpose of job enrichment is to vertically load the job providing true work motivation by improving the work itself, that is, feeding into the task additional opportunity for motivation so that the employees have the opportunity to reach their full potential."[1] However, it should be added that not all writers have adopted this distinction. Some writers continue to use the term job enlargement to refer to programs designed to vertically load jobs in order to provide motivators. This semantic problem complicates the assessment of the literature on job enrichment.

One of the problems in assessing the success or failure of job enrichment is that there is seldom a distinction made between the two-factor theory of motivation and the JE technique itself. When separated, a more meaningful and accurate assessment can be made.

Assessment of the Two-Factor Theory: N.A. King has pinpointed a major problem area facing the two-factor theory of motivation. He has identified no less than five different versions of the two-factor theory. Waters and Waters delineate these five versions as follows:

Theory I. This version states that all intrinsic variables (motivators) combined contribute more to job satisfaction than to job dissatisfaction, and that all extrinsic variables (hygienes) combined contribute more to job dissatisfaction than to satisfaction.

Theory II. All intrinsic variables combined contribute more to job satisfaction than do all extrinsic variables combined, and all extrinsic variables combined contribute more to job dissatisfaction than do all intrinsic variables combined.

Theory III. This theory states that each intrinsic variable contributes more to job satisfaction than to job dissatisfaction, and each extrinsic variable contributes more to job dissatisfaction than to job satisfaction. Theory III is a stronger version of Theory I.

Theory IV. The conditions of Theory III hold, but, in addition, each principal intrinsic variable contributes more to job satisfaction than does any extrinsic variable, and the converse for contribution to job dissatisfaction.

Theory V. Theory V states that only intrinsic variables contribute to job satisfaction, and only extrinsic variables contribute to job dissatisfaction.[2]

At first these differences may appear to be purely semantic, but a closer inspection reveals some very important differences. In this research, King concluded that Theories III, IV, and V were invalid, that Theories I and II had not been tested in studies where the subjects' defensive biases had been eliminated. Waters and Waters, on the other hand, found from their study of 141 female office workers in a state university that their data did not support any of the five versions of the two-factor theory. However, they did report two significant findings that replicated earlier conclusions:

1. Overall satisfaction is more predictable than overall dissatisfaction.

2. Intrinsic variables are generally more potent than extrinsic variables in determining both satisfaction and dissatisfaction.

Exhibit 1: Herzberg's Two Factors

Satisfiers Content Factors or Motivators	Dissatisfiers, Context Factors, or Hygiene Factors
—Achievement	—Company Policy and Administration
—Recognition	—Supervision
—Work Itself	—Working Conditions
—Responsibility	—Interpersonal Relations
—Advancement	—Salary
—Growth	—Status
	—Job Security
	—Personal Life

Overall, most researchers agree that when Herzberg's critical-incident method of research is used, the two-factor theory is supported; but when other methodologies are used, the theory is not supported. Some researchers even question this conclusion. For example, Schneider and Locke contend that Herzberg's results are not derived from the critical-incident method, but instead come from built-in biases and deficiencies in logic which occur in his incident classification system.[3] They argue that Herzberg classifies his incidents sometimes according to the event (what happened) and sometimes according to the agent (who made the incident occur), but not consistently according to either method. They then give examples of the "correct" application of the critical-incident method, and when they do, there is no support for Herzberg's theory.

Studies using different methods than Herzberg yield little, if any, support to the two-factor theory. For example, Hulin and Smith, using a correlational study, examined intrinsic and extrinsic variables measured by the Job Description Index and found no support for the two-factor theory.[4] Victor Vroom feels that the frequency with which survey respondents indicate job-content or job-context factors as sources of job satisfaction and/or dissatisfaction is purely a function of the content and context of the respondent's work roles.[5] Since Herzberg's methodology depends on this type of survey reporting, Vroom would argue that the results are predetermined by the job being analyzed.

Besides the problems inherent in the critical-incident method of research, academicians have been highly critical of Herzberg's terminology and his methods of relating the important variables in motivation. Some have argued that Herzberg erred in his treatment of the terms satisfaction and motivation. For example, Martin Wolf feels that Herzberg oversimplified and made a mistake in equating the two terms.[6] He points out that satisfaction is an end state, while motivation is a force—or drive—to achieve some end state. Others have concentrated on Herzberg's assumption that satisfaction leads to performance. For example, Porter and Lawler contend that the relationship is much more complex.[7] They maintain that the effort or motivation that an employee exerts on a task is a function of the value of the reward and the perceived effort-reward probability. Performance, while a function of this effort, also depends on the employee's abilities or traits, and his role perceptions. Satisfaction results from the extent to which the rewards received compare with the employee's perceived level of equitable rewards for his expended effort. Prominent in the Porter-Lawler model is the idea that performance leads to satisfaction, rather than that satisfaction causes performance, which is inherent in Herzberg's theory. Other researchers make a distinction between satisfiers and motivators. Wernimont, Torey, and Kapell report a survey of 775 technical employees which ranked 17 variables in the order that they affected job satisfaction and again in the order that they affected motivation or effort.[8] The respondents did not perceive the 17 variables as having the same effect on job satisfaction and motivation to work. Such results, indicating that the same variables may not always act as both satisfiers and motivators, are counter to Herzberg's contention.

Hunt and Hill point out two other possible weaknesses in the two-factor theory.[9] They maintain that the two-factor theory does not account for individual differences in motivation when applied to job performance. Furthermore, they doubt the applicability of Herzberg's model in relating individual needs to organization objectives.

The con literature on the two-factor theory seems to be overwhelming. Herzberg, at least initially, responded to the criticisms by citing an impressive number of supportive replications of his original Pittsburgh studies.[10] He reported supporting studies conducted on agricultural administrators, professional women, hospital maintenance personnel, nurses, manufacturing supervisors, food handlers, scientists, engineers, teachers, technicians, assemblers, accountants, military officers, and managers about to retire and also cited cross-cultural studies conducted in Finland, Yugoslavia, Hungary, and Russia. M. Scott Myers, after a six-year study of the motivational problems at Texas Instruments, Inc., also gave strong support to the two-factor theory.[11] However, like Myers' work, those who infer support of the two-factor theory are in reality supporting the technique derived from it, job enrichment. The assessment of the literature on job enrichment is not as bleak as is the literature concerning the theory on which JE is based.

Assessment of Job Enrichment: In addition to Herzberg's writing on JE, several others have reported large cost reductions and/or significant increases in organizational effectiveness from JE programs. In one recent article, J.C. Swart describes several business situations in which the principles of job enrichment were employed.[12] He reports an increase in worker satisfaction, reduction in turnover, lower work error rates, and increased production efficiencies.

Some of the most publicized success stories about JE have come from Robert Ford's work at AT&T. After applying JE in the Shareholder Relations Department of 120 correspondents, the termination rate dropped 27%, and a cost savings of over $550,000 was realized in a 12-month period.[13] Ford also reports that typists on enriched jobs increased orders typed and mailed on time from 27% to 100% over a 6-month period. He believes some jobs that already have motivating work modules can still be subjected to more job enrichment by allowing the workers to control the module and provide feedback of job accomplishments. Such efforts have resulted in 50% reductions in turnover.[14]

M. Scott Myers, who joins Robert Ford as a leading advocate of JE, implemented several programs during his tenure at Texas Instruments. In one of these, young women assemblers on enriched jobs reduced the average production time for navigational instruments from 138 hours to 32 hours per unit within a one-year period.[15]

Two associates of Herzberg's, W.J. Paul and K.B. Robertson, reported successful job enrichment programs conducted in England. Sales representatives, design engineers, experimental officers, draftsmen, and production and engineering foremen were the subjects of job enrichment programs at Imperial Chemical Industries, Ltd. and Imperial Metal Industries, Ltd.[16] Paul and Robertson took precautions to adhere to the rigors of scientific experimentation in their studies. They used experimental and control groups and tried to eliminate the possible influences of interfering variables. Furthermore, they tried to minimize any "Hawthorne Effect" by keeping the subjects and their first-level supervisors uninformed about the studies while they were in progress. In each instance, the group receiving the job enrichment program outperformed their colleagues who had not received the job enrichment.

Despite such success stories, job enrichment is not without problems. For example, Hulin and Blood feel that the effects of job enrichment are overstated and possibly even unfounded.[17] Others point out that job enrichment programs actually involve limited segments of the work force population, and that there is little or no evidence of job enrichment success among unskilled or low-skilled workers. However, most of the criticism of JE is based on the underlying motivational assumptions. For example, a study by Reif and Schoderbeck showed that some workers expressed a preference for jobs that might have poor job content.[18] Occasionally, even a proponent of job enrichment will admit limitations in the application of JE. For example, Ford points out that not all of his job enrichment efforts at AT&T could be called successful, and Paul, Robertson, and Herzberg—commenting on the results of the job enrichment programs at Imperial Chemical Industries—admit that not all of the workers welcomed having their jobs enriched.[19]

A Proper Perspective

The literature on JE clearly indicates both a pro and con argument can be made for its effectiveness. JE is still in its formative years. It is experiencing some difficulty, but seems certain to find its proper place within the array of available organizational development techniques. However, to date, both scholars and practitioners have tended to take an "all or nothing" approach to the merits of job enrichment. Proponents suggested that JE had universal applicability. But when this universal applicability failed to appear, the pendulum of opinion perhaps swung too far in the opposite direction. The JE technique has probably been overly criticized by its opponents.

A more accurate assessment seems to lie somewhere between the two extreme views which dominate the bulk of current opinion. Research has indicated that JE is successful on some occasions and unsuccessful on others. Rather than continuing the debate as to whether job enrichment "works" or "doesn't work," effort could be more productively directed at identifying those situations in which job enrichment is and is not effective. Such a contingency approach to job enrichment is what is needed for the future. In the rest of the article, we shall identify the critical contingencies for the successful application of job enrichment and those cases when JE may be inappropriate.

Variables for Success

Exhibit 2 summarizes the critical variables which will determine the success or failure of a job enrichment program. The nature of the job, the characteristics of the job holder, and the overall organizational impact must be considered when applying job enrichment.

The Jobs to Be Enriched: The first point to consider in analyzing what jobs to enrich is the organizational level. The majority of the successful applications of job enrichment seem to occur in jobs above the lowest work levels. Very few JE programs have involved lower level workers. The literature seems to indicate that success in JE is partly a function of the organizational level of the job being enriched. Since the greatest number of organization members are at the lower levels, its applicability decreases considerably. However, there is some evidence that companies are trying to include the lower level workers in JE programs.[20] In this study, firms using it indicated that 50% of the workers on enriched jobs were either professionals or supervisors/managers, but the other half of the workers on enriched jobs were in the hourly worker class or the office/clerical class. Very few on enriched jobs were in the technician or para-professional category. Although JE programs are primarily directed toward upper organizational levels, this study shows that some firms are attempting to enrich jobs at lower levels. However, although the lower level jobs may badly need enrichment, attempts to accomplish this end have generally been disappointing.

The second job factor to be given attention is the autonomy of the work unit. Job enrichment experts advocate selecting jobs which contain a relatively complete, autonomous work unit (module). If such a module doesn't exist, management should attempt to create one as the initial phase of an enrichment program. For example, in jobs at AT&T where the appropriate autonomous module was already in existence, Ford states that enrichment is achieved by:
□ Improving the work module (unit of work).
□ Improving the employee's control of that module.
□ Improving the feedback which signals whether or not something has been accomplished.[21]

For successful job enrichment, the work module must be capable of being vertically loaded. The result is an employee who develops a "pride of ownership"—he has his own territory or work process. The employee in an enriched work module has clearly defined responsibility and is given recognition when his unit of work is properly performed. In these enriched jobs, the employee is often allowed to follow his task from inception to completion. Furthermore, he becomes very familiar with his work unit and is in a better position to suggest improvements. According to this work-module-criterion of successful JE, rotating types of jobs or jobs which are ill-defined subtasks of larger jobs are not suitable targets for successful JE programs.

Richard C. Grote, a practitioner working with JE programs, indicates the importance of a third important job factor in JE—job control. In a recent article, he discusses two major JE programs which were conducted at United Air Lines.[22] He notes that to successfully implement JE, employees should be asked two key questions about the activities they perform:

1. What priority do you set on what you do? (How important, in your opinion, is this task?)

2. What discretion do you have on what you do? (How much control do you have over your performance of this task?)

Exhibit 2: Critical Variables for Job Enrichment

The Job(s) to be enriched

    —Organizational level

    —Autonomous work unit

    —Job control

    —Performance feedback

The Employee on the enriched job

    —Skill level

    —Personal values

    —Need for "motivators"

The Organization impact of the Job Enrichment Program

    —Approval and support

    —Costs

    —Evaluation

Grote feels that the more control the employee has over his job, the more successful will be the JE program. Related research by Walker and Marriott and Walker and Guest support such a conclusion.[23] They found that variables such as job satisfaction, absenteeism, and turnover were largely a function of job control. For example, in assembly line jobs in which the "speed of the line" was the dominant job-control factor, there was dissatisfaction, high absenteeism, and turnover. More recently, Judson Gooding, in his analysis of automotive assembly plants, indicates that workers are trapped in unenrichable jobs because the line controls the jobs.[24] While these workers may benefit from enriched jobs, the job-control factor prohibits successful implementation of a JE program.

For responsibility to be incorporated into jobs, the worker must be able to gain and maintain control of his job. As responsibility and authority grow with the enrichment process, the worker will become less dependent on his supervisor; he will find that his job success depends more on his own judgment and abilities. Jobs in which the technology dictates that a large part of control remains outside the employee's sphere of influence do not seem suited to successful JE programs. Jobs where technology controls work rates (e.g., assembly lines) or, equally a problem area, where control is retained by superiors who refuse to delegate are both poor candidates for successful JE.

A fourth important job factor is performance feedback. This feedback goes to the employee and to the overall organization. For example, if an employee's efforts result in a considerable cost savings to the organization, both the employee and management should be aware of this performance. This type of feedback gives increased recognition. In addition, knowledge of performance results presented in a timely manner allows both the employee and management to control actions which will alleviate or prevent existing or potential problems. Enrichable jobs must be able to provide this performance feedback. Jobs which do not permit this feedback appear to be poor candidates for successful JE programs.

The Employee on the Enriched Jobs: The first important employee variable for successful job enrichment is the skill level. Most successful JE programs have contained employees who were skilled, semi-skilled, or professional. For example, the occupational groups mentioned in Herzberg's studies, Texas Instruments, and AT&T, all contained skilled, semi-skilled, and technical professional employees. There is little or no evidence of successful JE among unskilled groups of employees. This employee factor relates to the organizational level job factor discussed in the preceding section. The lower jobs in most organizations are filled with unskilled types of employees. The literature indicates a higher probability of success with a JE program aimed at semi-skilled, skilled, or technical professional employees.

Personal values are a second important employee variable in successful implementation of JE. There is evidence that some employees actually prefer jobs with what JE advocates might term "poor job content." The personal values of the employee are such that he/she does not place a value on the job satisfiers built into an enriched job. JE is built around middle-class norms or values. Job enrichment assumes employee values of striving and achievement, the intrinsic value of hard work and getting ahead, and the desirability of being responsible for one's work. In other words, JE assumes employees are guided by the Protestant ethic. This is not to make a "value judgment" as to the "proper" set of values for organizational participants. Rather, the Protestant ethic values support JE primarily because the technique itself emerged from this set of values. Hence, it logically follows that the chances for a successful JE program are enhanced if the employees exhibit these values and vice versa.

Closely related to personal values are the employee's motivational needs. By definition, job enrichment seeks to increase the motivators (achievement, recognition, responsibility, advancement, and growth) in the job. If these "motivators" are not actually needs of the employee, or at least perceived as needs, then the enriched job will not lead to employee satisfaction or motivation. If, for example, employees did not have a high need for achievement (a motivator) but did have a high need for affiliation (not a motivator according to Herzberg), job enrichment would be unsuccessful because it builds on the need for achievement and not affiliation. It should be pointed out that David McClelland, who has done an extensive amount of research on the achievement motive, estimates that only about 10% of the population are high achievers. Affiliation, on the other hand, appears to be a very powerful motive for almost everyone.

Management literature is replete with examples of problems created when affiliation was stifled by dividing work groups in the interest of change, technology, or increased efficiency. Powerful group dynamics forces exist within formal and informal work groups. If the "nonmotivators," such as employees' needs for affiliation, are more intense than their needs for the "motivators," then JE will be unsuccessful and vice versa. In addition, many employees do not have the need for fulfillment on the job. Many have resigned themselves to "putting in their eight hours" and to "living" outside the job. The organization has become a very aversive situation to them. Job enrichment may be able to turn this around, but if this value is inculcated into the employee, JE will not work.

The Organizational Impact of JE: It should probably go without saying that the approval and full support of top management should be obtained prior to a JE program—or any other organization development intervention. Numerous OD programs have failed, however, because top management gave only token approval and no real support. A poor selling job and lack of understanding has also led to a lack of support from middle management. The advocates of JE—as well as other organizational development techniques such as management by objectives or team-building—consider this variable of management approval and support crucial to the success of the program. If management is unwilling to totally commit themselves to the JE program, its success becomes very difficult, if not impossible.

Another organizational variable, besides management support and approval, is cost. A job enrichment program must be viewed in much the same manner as any other investment that the organization makes. After all, JE is an investment. The organization devotes a portion of its resources to the JE program with hopes of achieving a satisfactory return on the investment.

One author advocates that enriching jobs without large expenditures is preferable to enriching jobs which require large expenditures.[25] If, for example, in order to increase an employee's control over his/her job, expensive equipment must be purchased or costly plant alterations made, any possible cost savings resulting from increased performance may be at least partially offset. This cost factor alone can prevent JE programs from being successful in jobs requiring an inflexible, costly technology such as exists in many manufacturing types of operations.

The final factor in implementing JE is its evaluation. A recent survey found that most firms currently using JE on a formal or informal basis do not systematically evaluate the program.[26] The respondents reported that they either had no evaluation procedures or did not know the criteria being used to ascertain the organizationwide effectiveness of JE. Some studies that attempt to evaluate JE merely take attitude surveys before and during the JE program. Evaluation consists of reaction to the program and changed attitudes. Besides these peripheral types of evaluation, there must be some evaluation of the impact that JE has on organizational performance. Absenteeism, turnover, quality (rejection rates), cost reductions, and organizational productivity are some of the measurable variables which should be monitored in a JE program. Failure to attempt to determine the effects of the JE program on these performance variables would defeat the long-run purpose of the program. Performance improvement is the ultimate test of job enrichment.

A Final Comment

In the late 1950s, Frederick Herzberg developed his now famous two-factor theory of motivation. From this motivational theory came job enrichment. The literature on this organizational development technique has generally taken two positions: (1) job enrichment is the solution to all management problems, or (2) job enrichment is no good because it is based on faulty assumptions and a questionable theoretical base. The practicing manager trying to assess the value of JE has been left with this "all-or-nothing" debate. A more accurate—seemingly obvious, yet overlooked— evaluation of job enrichment is that neither is it a panacea nor is it worthless. Instead, JE can be successful or not, depending on the situation. There is a need to identify those situational variables under which job enrichment has a high probability of success. Job factors (level, autonomy, control, and feedback), employee factors (skill, values, and motives), and organizational factors (support, costs, and evaluation) must be analyzed for successful implementation of job enrichment.

---

1. Robert Janson, "Job Enrichment: Challenge of the 70's," *Training and Development Journal*, June 1970, p.7.

2. See N.A. King, "A Clarification and Evaluation of the Two-factor Theory of Job Satisfaction," *Psychological Bulletin*, July 1970, p. 18; and L.K. Waters and Carrie Wherry Waters, "An Empirical Test of Five Versions of the Two-factor Theory of Job Satisfaction," *Organizational Behavior and Human Performance*, February 1972, p. 18.

3. Joseph Schneider and Edwin A. Locke, "A Critique of Herzberg's Incident Classification System and a Suggested Revision," *Organizational Behavior and Human Performance*, July 1971, p. 441.

4. C.L. Hulin and Patricia Smith, "An Empirical Investigation of Two Implications of the Two-factor Theory of Job Satisfaction," *Journal of Applied Psychology*, October 1967, p. 396.

5. Victor Vroom, *Work and Motivation* (New York, John Wiley & Sons, 1964), p. 128.

6. Martin G. Wolf, "Need Gratification Theory: A Theoretical Reformulation of Job Satisfaction/Dissatisfaction and Job Motivation," *Journal of Applied Psychology*, February 1970, p. 87.

7. Lyman W. Porter and Edward E. Lawler, III, *Managerial Attitudes and Performance* (Homewood, Illinois, Richard D. Irwin, Inc., 1968).

8. P.F. Wernimont, P. Toren, and H. Kapell, "Comparison of Sources of Personal Satisfaction and of Work Motivation," *Journal of Applied Psychology*, February 1970, p. 95.

9. J.G. Hunt and J.W. Hill, "The New Look in Motivation Theory for Organizational Research," *Human Organization*, Summer 1969, p. 100.

10. Frederick Herzberg, *Work and the Nature of Man* (Cleveland, The World Publishing Company, 1966).

11. M. Scott Myers, "Who Are Your Motivated Workers?" *Harvard Business Review*, January-February 1964, p. 73.

12. J. Carroll Swart, "The Worth of Humanistic Management," *Business Horizons*, June 1973, p. 41.

13. Reported in Janson, op. cit.

14. Robert N. Ford, "Job Enrichment Lessons From AT&T," *Harvard Business Review*, January-February 1973, p. 96.

15. Reported in Janson, op. cit.

16. W.J. Paul and K.B. Robertson, *Job Enrichment and Employee Motivation* (London, Gower Press, Ltd., 1970).

17. C.L. Hulin and M.R. Blood, "Job Enlargement, Individual Differences and Worker Responses," *Psychological Bulletin*, January 1968, p. 41.

18. William E. Reif and Peter P. Schoderbeck, "Job Enlargement: Antidote to Apathy," *Management of Personnel Quarterly*, Spring 1966, p. 16.

19. Ford, *Motivation Through the Work Itself*, op. cit., p. 188; and J. Paul, Keith B. Robertson, and Frederick Herzberg, "Job Enrichment Pays Off," *Harvard Business Review*, March-April 1969, p. 61.

20. Fred Luthans and William E. Reif, "Job Enrichment: Long on Theory, Short on Practice," *Organizational Dynamics*, Winter 1973.

21. Ford, "Job Enrichment Lessons From AT&T," op. cit.

22. Richard C. Grote, "Implementing Job Enrichment," *California Management Review*, Fall 1972, p. 16.

23. C.R. Walker and R. Marriott, "A Study of Attitudes to Factory Work," *Occupational Psychology*, vol. 25, 1951, p. 181; and C.R. Walker and R.H. Guest, *The Man on the Assembly Line* (Cambridge, Harvard University Press, 1952).

24. Judson Gooding, "Blue Collar Blues on the Assembly Line," *Fortune*, July 1970, p. 132.

25. Grote, op. cit.

26. Luthans and Reif, op. cit.

William Gomberg is Professor of Management at the Wharton School of Finance, University of Pennsylvania.

This article is reprinted (verbatim) from the June 1973 issue of the **AFL-CIO American Federationist,** *pp. 14-19.*

6
Job Satisfaction: Sorting Out the Nonsense

William Gomberg

Social scientists—alias behavioral scientists—have become pre-occupied with the worker and his alleged unhappiness. Back in November 1970 the scientists on the staff of the Survey Research Center of the University of Michigan published a study based on interviews with a large number of workers.

Neil Herrick of the U.S. Department of Labor, closely associated with the project, noted 25 aspects of work into which inquiry was made. The eight aspects of work receiving top ranking in importance follow in the sequence in which the results were arranged: interesting work; enough equipment and help to get the job done; enough information; enough authority; good pay; opportunity to develop special abilities; job security; and seeing the result of one's work.

Implying that trade unions are wont to concentrate exclusively on pay and job security, Herrick suggests that "we take the worker at his word and seriously question traditional notions regarding his needs and priorities."

This summation has been used by a widely assorted collection of behavioral scientists to conclude that the worker is concerned beyond all else with the nature of his work, the actual job description, constrained by a technology that is assumed to be fixed and that this source of frustration has been completely neglected by the trade unions, which have confined themselves to the problems of job security and job pay.

In another lengthy document, *Work in America,* they offer their services to overcome these problems: they suggest the formation of a public corporation with the following kinds of functions:

1) To compile and certify a roster of qualified consultants to assist employers with the technical problems in altering work.

2) To provide a resource to which management and labor can turn for advice and assistance.

3) To provide an environment in which researchers from various disciplines who are working on job redesign can meet with employers, unions and workers to pool their experiences and findings.

Work in America was prepared by a 10-man task force, headed by James O'Toole, a social anthropologist, for the U.S. Department of Health, Education and Welfare.

A review of these documents, their analysis of what ails the American workers, their knowledge of the role of unions in responding to workers needs and their wants, their philosophy of past experimentation and present remedial prescriptions are long overdue.

Mitchell Fein, an industrial engineer, questions the findings of the Michigan Survey Group. He notes that they have used the term "worker" to encompass managers, professionals, and the like as well as the conventional blue-collar worker.

The Survey Research Center data was reworked by Fein to separate out the blue-collar data and he found that pay, which was fifth in the university analysis, jumped to first place. My own feeling is that these first eight work aspects may be listed in most any manner. Fein could have spared himself the effort. The number of measurement points separating these characteristics is so minute that any ranking is arbitrary—they are virtually all of equal weight. The important consideration is that Herrick's conclusion betrays a superficial knowledge of what collective bargaining is all about.

Scope of Collective Bargaining

The general public, when it reads about collective bargaining, confines its attention to wages. The professional understands that the myriad of working conditions, out of which virtually all arguments arise during the course of the administration of the contract, are closely tied to the remaining seven aspects of work that head the Survey Research Center list. Grievances over promotions, lack of equipment to do the job right, lack of help and information to do the job right dominate the grievance procedure. They are the warp and woof of daily collective bargaining.

The scope of collective bargaining has been a constant tug-of-war with management. Back in 1946 President Truman called an industrial relations conference attended by the leading management and labor spokesmen. His hope was that they could come to an accommodation to avoid costly strikes. The late George W. Taylor analyzed the reasons for the foundering of the conference. One of the two principal reasons he listed for the failure of the meeting was the insistence of management that the labor movement pledge to confine itself to the immediate employer-employe relationship. Subjects like the technology of production, the methods of manufacture, the setting of production standards, the location of plants, the allocation of work all were to be respected as management prerogatives exclusively. The trade unions refused, arguing that the interests of labor were as broad as the entire production process.

When the automobile industry insisted that production standards were not a subject for bargaining, the union retained the right to strike over the question of production standards and has not hesitated to invoke this right when it felt that the workers' interest were threatened.

Back in the 1950s it took a long strike at the International Harvester Corporation before a system was devised between the company and the Auto Workers to make production standards a subject for grievances that could be resolved either by voluntary arbitration or a strike. Production standards had originally been excluded from the grievance procedure on management's insistence. But with strikes occurring repeatedly, it then became management's turn to want production standards disputes resolved by a grievance procedure. The conflict was resolved by permitting the parties to use the route of the strike or arbitration. For all practical purposes, the strike has been abandoned.

Now it is one thing for a Barbara Garson, a magazine publicist, to publish nonsense in the June 1972 *Harpers* that the Lordstown strike was a revolt of young workers against an old leadership who supinely accepted managerial tyranny over the speed of the assembly line. It is quite another to find this line of conventional nonsense in a scholarly report. Labor historian Tom Brooks has pointed out how an identical strike at the Norwood Plant of Chevrolet of much older workers at virtually the same time was ignored because it did not fit the counter culture image of the behaviorists that a new generation of youngsters were unique young rebels. A good case can be made for work improvement without involving the exaggerations of the marginal intellectual sensationalists at the fringe of every movement, thereby alienating the real rank and file.

The HEW document on work observes that all of the problems of modern job design are attributable to Frederick W. Taylor, who is accused of fractionating work and making the worker an extension of the machine with the implicit, supine consent of the labor movement.

This must be news to many unions, including the Machinists, which has had a long history of conflict in this area early in this century. And it perhaps explains the impatience of Machinists Vice President William W. Winpisinger, who has pointed out that just as job dissatisfaction in the workplace yielded to trade union solutions in the past, such dissatisfaction can be decreased to the extent that trade union solutions are applied today.

As a case in hand, Winpisinger says that "perhaps when workers first negotiated the right to bid on better shifts, overtime and promotions on the basis of length of service, they weren't thinking in terms of 'job enrichment,' but in actual practice that's what they got."

Roots of Job Enrichment

There are deep roots to Winpisinger's thinking. In 1912, a young professor, Robert Franklin Hoxie of the University of Chicago, was retained by John R. Commons of the University of Wisconsin, who had undertaken an investigation of the scientific management movement on behalf of Congress. In the manuscript published in 1915, *Scientific Management and Labor*, Hoxie listed the objections of the labor movement to scientific management. The Machinists union was then in the forefront of the federation's struggle with this innovation. With the machinists in the vanguard, the trade unionists indicted the new technique on the grounds that it:

—tends to deprive the worker of thought, initiative, achievement and joy in his work;

—tends to eliminate skilled crafts;

—is destructive of mechanical education and skill;

—tends to deprive the worker of the possibility of learning a trade;

—condemns the worker to a monotonous routine;

—dwarfs and represses the worker intellectually;

—tends to destroy the individuality and inventive genius of the workers;

—stimulates and drives the workers up to the limits of nervous and physical exhaustion and over fatigue and overstrains them;

—tends to reduce the workers to complete dependence on the employer—to the condition of industrial serfs.

"Most significant of all, scientific management puts into the hands of employers at large an immense mass of information and methods which may be used unscrupulously to the detriment of workers and offers no guarantee against the abuse of its professed principles and practices. And most important of all, it forces the workers to depend upon the employers conception of fairness and limits the democratic safeguards of the workers!"

Now for a trade union group which was fighting back in 1915 to be told now that it is reactionary invokes some justifiable impatience with job enrichment experts who are now attempting to reverse the alleged handicaps of job fractionation.

For many years the labor movement was at complete loggerheads with the scientific management movement. No small part of the reason for that conflict was the personality of Frederick W. Taylor himself. His autocratic ways hardly endeared him to the members of the labor movement. However, in 1919 Samuel Gompers, meeting together with Morris L. Cook, an engineer who understood the principles of democracy, established a new relationship between the scientific management movement and the trade unionists.

Division within Labor Movement

Morris L. Cook co-authored a book with Philip Murray in 1940 called *Organized Labor and Production* in which were laid down the fundamental principles of the participative management movement that is now being rediscovered by the sociologists. This volume was founded upon a set of principles laid down by Robert G. Valentine, a Boston social worker turned management expert, in a famous paper in 1916, "The Relationship Between Efficiency and Consent." This principle was stated as follows: "The organization of workers can be counted on to consent to all that makes for efficiency under constitutional industrial relations. They will contest the share in the management and share of the product between themselves and the consumer. For the most part, the labor agreements in operation today are looked upon by employers as a necessary evil and by the workers as steps in their reassertion of rights as consumers and having little detailed relation to production processes. The beginning of something far better than this is seen in the agreements in the garment trades wherein the manufacturers, the workers and the public are all represented as parties."

Valentine later became consultant both to the Ladies' Garment Workers union and their employers in an attempt to stabilize the setting of production rates. It was this pioneer experience that was drawn upon by the later leadership of the ILGWU when they created the first union-sponsored Industrial Engineering Department, converting industrial engineering and scientific management from a substitute and threat to collective bargaining to a tool of collective bargaining.

The division of labor does not date from Frederick W. Taylor— it goes back to Adam Smith, who wrote in the *Wealth of Nations* in 1776: "This great increase of the quantity of work which in consequence of the division of labor, the same number of people are capable of performing, is owing to three different circumstances; first, to the increase of dexterity in every particular workman; secondly, to the saving of the time which is commonly lost in passing from one species of work to another; and lastly, to the invention of a great number of machines which facilitate one man to do the work of many."

Adam Smith, when he wrote these lines, was as aware as the modern behavioralist that what specialization did to the worker as a human being exacted a social cost—the "externalities" as they are called by the modern economist. Those costs shifted by the management to others because the price does not appear in conventional accounting systems have been a subject over which trade unionists have mulled long before they were formalized by economists and ecologists.

The labor movement has spent no small part of its energy in reassigning the costs of externalities so that they no longer fall exclusively on the workers. They have pioneered sickness, health and pension programs to lighten his burden. Labor's lobby has put legislation on the books requiring the observance of a safety code in the 1970 Occupational Safety and Health Act that is unprecedented.

It, too, is aware that the division of labor, like many another phenomenon, can be carried so far that it reaches a point of diminishing returns. It is also aware that the reunification of work can be carried so far that we will have happy workers producing for customers who have been priced out of the market. Reaching an intelligent balance is an occasion for rational analysis rather than evangelistic preaching.

All workers are not the same. Many workers will take advantage of the undemanding nature of their market-oriented work to engage in reverie or in thinking about things of more importance to them than their work. The worker may find his or her primary source of satisfaction in the after hours living that his or her market-oriented work provides so that he or she is able to do what he or she is really interested in during leisure hours. When the jobs of these workers are enriched, very often the monotony of 15 repetitive jobs instead of the monotony of one job becomes a source of distraction rather than satisfaction.

The labor movement has endeavored in the past to provide opportunities to management who were seeking higher production and its members who were seeking more challenging work. Labor history is replete with labor-management experiments like the Baltimore and Ohio plan on the railroads from 1926 to the depression in which workers were able to show management aspects of management's task that the latter had overlooked.

This is only one of a long line of historic undertakings. As late as 1960 the Kaiser Steel Long Range Union-Management Plan displayed how creative workers could be who were technically oriented and were given a chance to participate jointly in the cost savings. The rediscovery of participative management by the behaviorists in the last few years is more an invention of vocabulary than occupational technique. The kind of material published by Professor Louis Davis on how different jobs will be in the post-industrial era and how they will be more demanding than our present tasks strikes me about as authentic as the observations of those seers who not long ago told us about all the upgraded jobs that were going to flow from automation. The jobs remain as trivialized as ever, and I suspect that the so-called post industrial era will carry more than its share of such trivialized work.

The trade unionists have probably done more to eliminate sub-human work by raising wages than all of the elaborate schemes of the scholars laid end to end. When employers find that they must pay high wages for what they consider sub-human, repetitive work they somehow manage to automate the job so that it is no longer performed by a human.

In fact, the higher the wage, the more likely the employer is to seek a capital substitute for the worker. For example, suppose an international road building contractor owns a trench digging machine that does the work of 100 men. He only owns one of these machines and he has contracts to dig ditches in Taiwan and in New York City. Where is he likely to use the machine? Obviously in New York City where the rate for common labor, protected by unions, is quite high rather than in Taiwan where a few cents an hour additional expended by employing more labor spares the employer the risk of investing in a machine.

Trend to Participative Management

All of the claims being made for the miraculous increases in productivity and worker satisfaction by the evangelistic behaviorists have been heard before.

Back in the 1930s a management consultant, Allan Mogensen, founded the work simplification movement. He was training workers and management in participative techniques. Workers were indoctrinated with a set of motion principles to apply to their various jobs. They took great joy in using their ingenuity to fractionate their jobs and other jobs with the same miraculous reports of increased productivity that we now get from the behaviorist for doing the opposite of the work simplification experts. This former enthusiasm ran its course.

In fact, behaviorists have invented a name for these spurts in productivity that seem to come with any kind of initial attention to long neglected workers. They call it "the Hawthorne effect" after the pioneering experiments at the Hawthorne plant of the Bell System in Chicago in the 1930s. A proper test calls for an extended longitudinal study of many of these modifications to see if they are real. Too often the initial spurt is followed by a return to "normal."

The behaviorists ask for the labor movement's commitment to a program for experimentation using their rediscovered techniques. It seems the labor movement has a right to look at past experimentation of the behaviorists and ask what kind of commitment are the behaviorists ready to give the labor movement.

M. Scott Myers, the author of "Overcoming Union Opposition to Job Enrichment," writes in the *Harvard Business Review* for May-June 1971 that "applications of the job enrichment concept, particularly in non-union work forces, have enabled managers to transform potentially hostile creativity into constructive outlets before it could be crystallized into anti-organization efforts. Moreover, job enrichment in the non-union organization is harnessing talent in a manner that gives a competitive advantage to the organization and also offers the only realistic strategy for preventing the unionization of its workforce."

The same Myers is then advertised for a seminar in Dallas in February 1973 in which he offers to give you a strategy and tactics to avoid a union and simultaneously to gain union-management cooperation if you have a union—a little something for everybody.

Another prize package of the behaviorists is the alleged miracle that took place in the Harwood Manufacturing Company when it merged with Weldon Pajama.

The Harwood "miracle" has been hailed as a unique experiment in employe participation which resulted in decisive increases in productivity and job satisfaction after the Harwood company absorbed Weldon Pajama.

We are indebted to Fein for the analysis that it was not participative management, but indeed quite authoritative management—albeit with due process, since it was a union plant.

Here is what Fein has said about Harwood:

"When Harwood purchased the Weldon Company in 1962, all sorts of traditional business problems were encountered and Harwood management moved into Weldon and restructured it in its own image. The complete case history of Weldon is described in *Management by Participation*. The foreword of the book says that it ' . . . reports an extraordinarily successful improvement of a failing organization through introduction of a new management system. An unprofitable enterprise was made profitable, and a better place to work, in the short span of two years. Many managers and students will want to know how this was done.' Harwood management made ' . . . a business decision to undertake a participative approach to the salvaging of the Weldon enterprise.'

"Though Harwood's management stated they were devoted to the participative approach to managing, nowhere in the book is there any evidence that the changeover in management practices involved appreciable participation by the employes in formulating decisions or in making changes. There was no restructuring of jobs or job enrichment. Nor is there any mention that Weldon's workers participated to any appreciable extent in creating improvements, in work methods and systems. Management's efforts seemed to have been concentrated on revising the management organization and eliminating the former one-man rule of the company, and the raising of productivity.

"The major improvement in plant productivity was obtained from a straightforward, conventional, industrial engineering program established by a firm of consulting engineers. A rise in productivity of 30 percentage points was obtained, measured by operator productivity, from 85 percent of standard to 115 percent. Management reports the improvements were created as follows: ' . . . the earnings development program with individual operators was the most potent of the steps undertaken, contributing perhaps 11 percentage points of the total gain of 30 points. Next in influence were the weeding out of low earners . . . and the provision of training for supervisors and staff in interpersonal relations, each contributing about 5 percentage points to the total gain. The group consultation and problem resolution program with operators appears to have contributed about 3 percentage points. The balance of 6 percentage points can be viewed as arising from miscellaneous sources or from a combination of the several program elements.'

"The industrial engineers' section of the Weldon case history reports that the fundamental goal selected for concentration and agreed upon by all in management as the problem of first priority was raising employe earnings which were based on an incentive plan. The goal was reached in one year. This section reads just as would a typical case of resurrecting a disintegrated incentive plan. Some of the engineers' efforts were spent in ' . . . three- to four-hour production studies of the operator to estimate her performance potential.' The engineers encouraged the operator to change to more effective methods and to raise her skill. 'An operator was helped in this manner until an outcome was apparent, until her earnings increased or she was deemed unlikely to change.' During this period, ' . . . an effort was made to get rid of the remaining employes with chronically low production records and histories of frequent absence.' The success achieved in raising productivity at Weldon seems to have been obtained by using conventional practices on the plant floor. The approach followed was what any competent plant manager would have employed.

"Harwood-Weldon management may have designed its management organization on participative principles. But the managing style with respect to the production employes seemed to be quite firm; behaviorists might even label it authoritarian." I would add constrained by due process because it is unionized, albeit conventionally.

Distortions in PM Applications

Of even more interest is Fein's analysis of the much publicized General Food-Pet Food case in Topeka, Kansas, which is a non-union operation. Basically, what is claimed is that it was an innovative experiment in rescuing and revamping a low-morale workforce. But it really was a matter of running away from the original problems, in an Illinois plant, and building an ideal work environment through a careful selection of new personnel and the advantages of new physical facilities in Kansas.

"In discussing the General Food-Pet case, the HEW task force shows its myopia and bias toward the problems in plants which affect management and workers," Fein says. "Typical is their description of why General Foods management decided to build a new plant at Topeka: 'Management built this plant because the employes in an existing plant manifested many severe symptoms of alienation. Because of their indifference and inattention, the continuous process type of technology used in the plant was susceptible to frequent shutdowns, to product waste and to costly recycling. There were serious acts of sabotage and violence. Employes worked effectively for only a few hours a day and strongly resisted changes that would have resulted in a further utilization of manpower.'

"This statement sounds as if it were written by the PR department of a company which was preparing a public case for abandoning its old plant. Actually it was obtained from a paper prepared by Richard E. Walton of Harvard, one of the consultants to the HEW task force, specifically for the HEW project. Nowhere in the HEW report or Walton's paper is there any indication of the union's official attitude and position with regard to what occurred at the plant.

"In reporting the case of the GF-Topeka plant in *Harvard Business Review* and in his HEW paper, Walton omitted a most critical piece of information which greatly affects the interpretation of what occurred and why. Walton states that the key features of the new plant organization were: 'autonomous work groups . . . integrated support functions . . . challenging job assignments . . . job mobility and rewards for learning . . . facilitative leadership . . . managerial decision making for operators . . . self government for the plant community . . . congruent physical and social context . . . learning and evolution.' The full report of what occurred over a two-year period is too long to be repeated here, but it is available for reference.

"What was not reported by Walton in either of his two papers was the strategy for hiring employes for the new plant." This is described by L.D. Ketchum, Manager of Organization Development Operations at G-F. An ad was run in the local press:

"General Foods—Topeka plant needs production people: Work in a new, modern Gaines Pet Food Plant with an exciting new organization concept which will allow you to participate in all phases of plant operations.

"Qualifications: mechanical aptitude; willing to accept greater responsibility; willing to work rotating shifts; desire to learn multiple jobs and new skills.

"If you would like to work with an organization that emphasizes individual potential, learning and responsibility, with excellent earnings and benefits, job interviews will be conducted. . . ."

The hiring process proceeded as follows, according to Fein's description: 625 people applied. (Other reports say over 700 applied.) Screening by the State Employment Service and the team leaders eliminated 312. Many of these eliminated themselves. Testing eliminated 76, so 237 remained. The physical examination eliminated 18, and the balance went through an in-depth interview, an hour each, with three different team leaders and this eliminated 121. The team leaders then designed a selection weekend and began with 98, eliminated 35, leaving 63 who were offered jobs. King, a consultant to the program, adds that when the applicants were down to 98, they were invited to spend a Saturday at the plant for the final selections. After a one and a half hour tour of the plant, the applicants worked for two hours on a NASA problem exercise, to determine how they would react under different circumstances at work. The supervisors then selected 63 for jobs in the plant.

"Walton did not reveal that the new Topeka employes were screened for special skills and profiles to match the organization criteria that had been established for the new plant," Fein continues. "In a normal employe market, screening one out of four applicants is considered fairly tight. Here only one out of 10 was selected. The new Topeka employes were a special breed; they were 'non-union achievers' who preferred working in autonomous situations. They were obviously not typical of a cross-section of the Kankakee employes.

"Nowhere does Walton mention that the problem-ridden plant is located at Kankakee, Ill., and employs 1,200. At a 10-1 ratio, in hiring for a 1,200 employe plant, they would have to screen over 12,000. Where would all the people come from?

"Walton says: 'Using standard principles industrial engineers originally estimated 110 employes should man the plant. Yet the team concept, coupled with the integration of support activities into team responsibilities, has resulted in a manpower level of slightly less than 70 people.'

"Attributing the superior performance of the Topeka employes to the organization development principles completely ignores that the Topeka employes were carefully selected for the plant and may have had very different skills and attitudes from the Kankakee employes. Walton cannot use industrial engineers to sanctify his comparison because the comparison is not valid. Work measurement principles in industrial engineering require that the measurement criteria must be developed separately for each plant, unless it is demonstrated that the plants are identical. Common sense reveals that these two plants are not comparable, especially in the workforce. It is like putting together a basketball team of 8-footers to play a normal height team.

"The results obtained at Topeka are valid only for Topeka. This was a stacked experiment in a small plant with conditions set up and controlled to achieve a desired result. These employes were not a cross-section of the population, or even of Topeka. The plant and its operations are not typical of those in industry today. What are the other managers to do? Screen one in 10 employes and only hire these? And what about the other nine?

"The GF-Topeka case proves nothing of value for operation managers. Had the behaviorists gone to work on the Kankakee plant and shown how they converted a rundown plant, bursting with labor problems, into a plant where management and employes told glowingly of their accomplishments, the behaviorists would have earned the gratitude of everyone. Instead, they turned their backs on a plant which typifies the problems of the big city plants. Worse, they tantalize management with the prospect that, in building a new plant, with new equipment, with carefully selected employes and no union, productivity will be higher. Many managers have dreamed of relocating their plants into the wheat fields or the hills to escape from the big city syndrome. Is this Walton's message to managers in his article, 'How to Counter Alienation in the Plants'? And is this case the HEW task force's contribution to the solution of the problems of the big city plants?"

The Direction for Future Solutions

My object in citing these cases written up in the HEW report but analyzed by Fein is not to make the point that behaviorists are anti-union as a class. They are not. What is worse is that by and large, so many of them are indifferent. They are without conviction in the matter. Now such an attitude is understandable in value free engineers, but how are we to regard evangelistic behavorial scientists converted to participative managerial democracy who have failed to understand democracy's most fundamental tenet? Democracy cannot exist where management is free to give and to take without any countervailing force. Such "democracy" makes as much sense as a U.S. government without any institutionalized checks and balances. The labor movement will expect more than is offered if it is to tie in with the behaviorists. The opportunity is theirs.

One possibility for a new era lies in legislation introduced in February by Sen. Edward M. Kennedy (D-Mass.) with the joint sponsorship of 13 senators, called the Worker Alienation Research and Technical Assistance Act of 1973.

The bill provides $10 million for research into the problem of worker alienation in all occupations and technical assistance to those unions, workers, companies, state and local governments seeking to find ways to relieve this problem.

This bill, if passed, could mean the beginning of a new era in which more and more workers actually participate in the decision-making of the enterprise. It can usher in a new era for cooperation between behavorial scientists with a real democratic commitment, enlightened management and trade unionists. I am sure that is what the senators have in mind. Let us hope that Scott Myers' adventure in Orwellian Doublewrite becomes the exception rather than the rule when describing the behaviorist's future behavior.

The behaviorists have pointed up a problem. Their lack of knowledge of labor history may have led to an exaggeration of what they have come up with. Nevertheless, the problem is real. Its solution calls not only for technical competence, but moral commitment.

William W. Winpisinger is vice-president of the Machinists' Union of the AFL-CIO.

This article, based on a presentation to the Industrial Research Association in Toronto, Canada, is reprinted from the February 1973 issue of **AFL-CIO American Federationist.**

7

Job Satisfaction: A Union Response

William W. Winpisinger

After some years of seeking legislative alternatives to collective bargaining, plus even more years of academic discussion and debate on the pros and cons of union responsibilities in relation to public rights, it now appears that labor's good friends in government, intellectual and academic circles have discovered an interesting new malady. They've already provided it with a name, a diagnosis and even a cure.

The name is the "blue-collar blues." The diagnosis is that because younger workers are brighter and better educated than their fathers they refuse to accept working conditions that past generations took for granted. The cure consists of a shot of psychic penicillin known as job enrichment.

Rising Level of Alienation

There can be little doubt as to the existence of a rising tide of dissatisfaction, or alienation, among those who are increasingly and even sneeringly referred to as the Archie Bunkers of America.

Employers feel it in more absenteeism, more turnover and more strikes over working conditions. Politicians feel it in the perceptible shift of blue-collar workers from the principles of the New Deal to the philosophy of George Wallace. Unions feel it in the rising level of contract rejections and the growing number of defeats suffered by long established business representatives and officers in union elections.

Just a couple of months ago *Time* magazine, in an essay on the work ethic, noted that according to a Gallup poll taken in 1971, 19 percent of all workers expressed dissatisfaction with their jobs. This was viewed with some pessimism by the learned editors of the magazine. If they had chosen to be optimistic they could just as validly have noted that 81 percent of all workers seem to be satisfied with their jobs.

There is, of course, no way to prove it but I feel reasonably certain that at no time in the entire history of man would Gallup have found 100 percent happiness and job satisfaction in the labor force. I doubt if 100 percent of the ancient Egyptians who built the pyramids, or 100 percent of the medieval craftsmen who constructed the great cathedrals, or 100 percent of the 19th century Irishmen who laid the tracks for American railroads were so filled with job satisfaction that they consistently whistled while they worked.

The right to bitch about the job, or the boss, or the system, or even the union, is one of the inalienable rights of a free workforce. Whether workers today are generally happier than those in the so-called good old days is not provable one way or the other. Some claim the increasing atomization of work processes and the mind-deadening monotony of the modern assembly line cannot help but lead to anything except increasing alienation in the workforce. And yet the assembly line has been with us for a long time. The concept of the robotized worker, endlessly repeating one function, tightening the same bolt over and over, was already well established long before Charlie Chaplin satirized it in the movie *Modern Times* more than 40 years ago.

Strangely enough, Gallup's polls on worker dissatisfaction, which were started in 1949, consistently registered slow but steady increases in the level of worker satisfaction right up to 1969. Though workers throughout the 1950s and 1960s were never really affluent in the Galbraithian sense, they were making progress. On the whole, jobs were plentiful and the gap between what the average production worker earned and what the Bureau of Labor Statistics said he needed for a "modest but adequate" standard of living was narrowing. But then between 1969 and 1971 the overall rate of job satisfaction, according to Gallup, fell 6 percent. If this decrease were due to some substantial change in the nature of the jobs that people did I would have to agree with those who prescribe job enrichment as the answer to worker dissatisfaction.

Don't get me wrong. I am not opposed to efforts by management or industrial psychologists to make assembly line jobs less monotonous and more fulfilling. But the point is—and it may not be too palatable to some in management or government or academic circles—that just as job dissatisfaction in the workplace yielded to trade union solutions in the past, such dissatisfaction can be decreased to the extent that trade union solutions are applied today.

One of the reasons that worker satisfaction declined in the late 1960s and early 1970s is that worker income, in relation to inflation and taxation and the purchasing power of the dollar that was earned by labor, also declined.

Because of government policies leading to rising unemployment, establishing one-sided controls on wages and permitting multinational corporations to export thousands of American jobs to Hong Kong, Taiwan and other low-wage areas, the gap between what the average worker earns and what Hong Kong, Taiwan and other low-wage areas, the gap between what the average worker earns and what his family needs for a decent standard of living has been growing. So it should come as no suprise to anyone that worker dissatisfaction is also growing.

Dissatisfaction of Young Workers

The recent rash of strikes and other labor problems at the General Motors plant in Lordstown, Ohio, has been seized upon by those who write articles for learned journals as proof that even if the nature of the assembly line hasn't changed, the workforce has. As every student of industrial relations knows, the overwhelming majority of the workforce at Lordstown is young. On the basis of management's unhappy experiences with these kids, the experts have solemnly proclaimed the discovery of a new kind of workforce. They inform us that here is a generation that has never known a depression and thus has no interest in security; that grew up in a time of crass materialism and thus rejects the work ethic; that has been infected by the rebellion of youth and thus has no respect for authority. I have seen one scholarly analysis, in fact, that compares the "rebellion" at Lordstown in the early 1970s with the free speech movement at Berkeley in the early 1960s. And the conclusion was drawn that the nation's factories, like her colleges, would never be the same again.

Quite frankly, I submit that that kind of analysis overlooks one salient fact. The young workers at Lordstown were reacting against the same kind of grievances, in the same kind of way, as did generations of workers before them. They were rebelling against an obvious speedup; protesting safety violations; and reacting against working conditions that have been unilaterally imposed by a management that was determined to get tough in the name of efficiency. Anyone who thinks wildcats or slowdowns or even sabotage started at Lordstown doesn't know very much about the history of the American labor movement.

An almost identical series of incidents took place over much the same issues at Norwood, Ohio, at almost the same time but very few inferences were drawn about the changing nature of the work-force because, in this case, it was older workers who were involved.

Many people, including President Nixon, are viewing the decline of the work ethic in the United States with alarm. On the basis of my experience, which includes many day-to-day contacts with rank-and-file members of the Machinists, I can assure you that the work ethic is alive and well and living in a lot of good workplaces.

But what the aerospace workers and auto mechanics and machinists and airline mechanics and production workers we represent want, in the way of job satisfaction, is a wage that is commensurate with their skill.

If you want to enrich the job, enrich the pay check. The better the wage, the greater the job satisfaction. There is no better cure for the "blue-collar blues."

If you want to enrich the job, begin to decrease the number of hours a worker has to labor in order to earn a decent standard of living. Just as the increased productivity of mechanized assembly lines made it possible to decrease the workweek from 60 to 40 hours a couple of generations ago, the time has come to translate the increased productivity of automated processes into the kind of enrichment that comes from shorter workweeks, longer vacations and earlier retirements.

Environmental Safety

If you want to enrich the job, do something about the nerve-shattering noise, the heat and the fumes that are deafening, poisoning and destroying the health of American workers. Thousands of chemicals whose effect on humans has never been tested are being used in workplaces. Companies are willing to spend millions advertising quieter refrigerators or washing machines but are reluctant to spend one penny to provide a reasonably safe level of noise in their plants. And though we are now supposed to have a law that protects working people against some of the more obvious occupational hazards, industry is already fighting to undermine enforcement and the Nixon Administration has gone along with them by cutting the funds that are needed to make it effective.

If you want to enrich the jobs of the men and women who manufacture the goods that are needed for the functioning of our industrialized society, the time has come to re-evaluate the snobbery that makes it noble to possess a college degree and shameful to learn skills that involve a little bit of grease under the finger-nails. The best way to undermine a worker's morale and decrease his satisfaction with himself and his job is to make him feel that society looks down on him because he wears blue coveralls instead of a white collar. I think it is ironic that because of prevailing attitudes many kinds of skilled craftsmen are in short supply while thousands of college graduates are tripping over one another in search of jobs.

Some of the most dissatisfied people I know are those who got a college degree and then couldn't find a position that lived up to their expectations. And that has been especially true the last few years. A lot of college-trained people are driving cabs today; they would have had a lot more job satisfaction and made a lot more money if they had apprenticed as auto mechanics.

Participation in Management

If you want to enrich the job, give working people a greater sense of control over their working conditions. That's what they and their unions were seeking in the early 1960s when manage-ment was automating and retooling on a large scale. That's why we asked for advance consultation when employers intended to make major job changes. That's why we negotiated for clauses providing retraining and transfer rights and a fair share of the increased productivity that resulted from automation.

What workers resent—and what really causes alienation—are management decisions that rearrange job assignments or upset existing work schedules without reference to the rights of the workforce.

If you want to enrich the job, you must realize that no matter how dull or boring or dirty it may be, an individual worker must feel that he has not reached the end of the line. If a worker is to be reasonably satisfied with the job he has today he must have hope for something better tomorrow.

You know this is true in universities, in government and in management. Even an assembly line must have some chance of movement, even if it's only from a job that requires stooping down to one that involves standing erect. But here again, we are talking about a job problem for which unionism provides an an-swer. And the name of that answer is the negotiated seniority clause. Perhaps when workers first negotiated the right to bid on better shifts, overtime or promotions on the basis of length of service, they weren't thinking in terms of "job enrichment," but were only trying to restrict management's right to allocate jobs and shifts and overtime on the basis of favoritism. But even if they weren't thinking in terms of "job enrichment," in actual practice that's what they got.

It's true that many young workers in their twenties resent the fact that while they have to tighten the same old bolt in the same old spot a thousand times a day the guys in their forties are walking up and down the line with inspection sheets or running around the factory on forklifts.

They may resent and bitch about it now—but they also know that they are accumulating seniority which they can trade for a better job of their own some day.

These many ways in which jobs can be enriched may not be what management has in mind when it talks about job enrichment. On the basis of fairly extensive experience as a union representative, I find it hard to picture management enriching jobs at the expense of profits. In fact, I have a sneaking suspicion that "job enrichment" may be just another name for "time and motion" study. As labor historian Thomas Brooks said in a recent *Federationist* article, "Substituting the sociologist's questionnaire for the stopwatch is likely to be no gain for the workers. While workers have a stake in productivity it is not always identical with that of management. Job enrichment programs have cut jobs just as effectively as automation and stopwatches. And the rewards of productivity are not always equitably shared."

What some companies call job enrichment is really little more than the introduction of gimmicks such as doing away with time clocks or developing "work teams" or designing jobs to "maximize personal involvement"—whatever that means.

Outlook for the Future

In conclusion let me say that I know there are those who worry about what the younger generation is coming to and wonder whether the rebellious young workers of today will be willing to fill their father's shoes in the factory jobs of tomorrow. We can't generalize from isolated examples but I was very interested in an NBC television documentary recently that studied the dissatisfaction of young workers. The part that interested me the most was the transformation in an assembly line "hippie" who followed his electrician father's footsteps by becoming an apprentice and cutting his hair.

All the studies tend to prove that worker dissatisfaction diminishes with age. That's because older workers have accrued more of the kinds of job enrichment that unions have fought for—better wages, shorter hours, vested pensions, a right to have a say in their working conditions, the right to be promoted on the basis of seniority and all the rest. That's the kind of job enrichment that unions believe in.

Ted Mills is Director of the Quality of Life Institute, Washington, D.C. He was formerly Special Assistant to the Chairman of the Price Commission.

This article is adapted from an address to the Council of Public Affairs, Washington, D.C.

8

The Thirteenth Dilemma

Ted Mills

In Norway, England, Austria, France, Italy, and Japan, as well as here in the United States, a new concern for human values in the workplace is emerging. Printed media all over the West are beginning to feature stories of job dissatisfaction, worker ennui and apathy, and growing alienation and dissatisfaction. The subjects of job enrichment, dissatisfaction, job redesign, and humanization of work or quality of work are receiving more and more attention.

At the heart of this rapidly emerging phenomenon is the notion that a man or a woman inside the workplace is exactly the same man or woman he or she is outside, with the same passions, inconstancies, yearnings, values, and pride manifested at home or in the community. This is in sharp contrast with the opposing view that, once inside the workplace, people are economic commodities whose output we can quantify and whose worth at work is measurable with the stop watch, calculator, and cash register.

Perhaps the root source of this phenomenon is our stunning success in the last generation at the universal education of our young. Four out of every five men and women entering the U.S. work force are at least high school graduates, and one out of three of those has had a year or more of college, with all the expectations and insights that education often brings. Perhaps the root source is the growing mechanistic giantism, in which individuals virtually cease to exist, or be noticeable, something which most people don't like very much. Perhaps the root source is an intuitive sense that mechanism and its rationalist cousin have failed to be the god to end human misery and want and that what is needed is a search for a more rewarding god.

Whatever the root source, or combination of sources, there seems unquestionably to be a new focus on people and their needs and wants at work. What seems to be emerging is the somewhat astonishing assumption—to economists in particular—that men and women at work are not interchangeable cogs in a giant, artificial machine we call an enterprise or corporation. A growing body of experimentation and study is beginning to prove that turned-on *people* are a great deal more productive than turned-off people, even by mechanistic yardsticks. Undramatic little devices such as rotation of jobs, work enlargement, formation of work teams to replace hierarchies, and, above all, worker involvement in their own work design have, in instance after instance everywhere in the industrialized world, radically improved what the mechanistics call output and the economists call profit.

Now all of this doesn't sound very threatening to anyone. It's a kind of win-win situation, which benefits everybody at no one's expense. It doesn't seek to take from one and give to the other; it has impressive payoffs to all, when properly applied.

Yet much of organized labor in the world, and particularly in our own country, is suspicious that it's all a kind of trick devised to destroy or weaken union power. And much of organized management in every Western country, and particularly our own, is suspicious that it's a kind of trick to destroy or weaken the old working systems of autocratic control of organizations.

If the new concerns for the quality of life at work are symptomatic of a worldwide swing away from faith in mechanism to an as-yet-unidentified renaissance of older, nonmechanistic concerns with true human purpose, then the hesitance of our redoubtable old mechanistic institutions, like companies and unions, to greet that swing with open arms is understandable.

Yet, at the same time, if we as an industrial society are going to be able to cope with that swing, which seems to be taking place with ever-increasing social speed, we face a serious problem in trying to distinguish some of the realities of what is—and might be—happening from the rhetoric and claims on both sides of the question, a debate which is heating up daily. I have isolated 13 major areas of dilemma—13 obstacles that lie in the path of any of us who are contemplating this new phenomenon, and wondering what to do about it, if anything at all.

A normal inclination would be to try to convince the unconvinced that enthusiasm for a change in the way we regard work is *highly* justified, and that what we've seen so far in the quality of work phenomenon is only the beginning of a major new social trend which Senator Percy of Illinois has characterized as a major breakthrough.

But a more effective contribution would be the reverse tack, a warning *against* unjustified optimism.

What we are dealing with here is a big, complex, subtle, infinitely varied and changing field; which only the patient, the wise, and the farseeing can unravel; and turn into a positive social force. It's not a field of faddists, or the timid; or those afraid of change. It is a field filled with many obstacles or dilemmas.

The quality of work, the nature of the work experience, is profoundly related to and responsible for much of the changing quality of life in America. As special assistant to Jackson Grayson, head of the Price Commission, I helped to initiate an investigation of this correlation.

The more we investigated, at every level of our society from management to union hall, the more convinced we became that a new phenomenon was already in the process of erupting across the country. We developed a government project to expand on my solitary examination, which we called the Quality of Work Program.

What we proposed was not study. We proposed action: getting companies and unions together, to actively explore what might be done to improve the quality of life at work—where we spend most of our waking lives. Secretary Schultz felt such a project should be housed in the National Commission on Productivity (NCOP). The purpose of this article, however, is not to discuss that project specifically.

Senator Kennedy and others suggested that a government goal in the area of this program should be *reducing dissatisfaction*. Our program suggested the reverse. It proposed that government's goal should be to find ways to improve the *quality of work* in America, performed by and in the private sector. Ours was not a program designed to *study what's wrong*. It was a demonstration program designed to explore what's right.

1. This leads directly to the first dilemma on the list: *the dilemma of exactly what government's role in this exploding field should be.* Government can and should do a lot to encourage and seed *positive* private sector activity in the quality of work field. Government can help acquire, develop, and even create expertise, knowledge, statistics, and relevant economic and sociological research about what's happening. Government can improve and is improving the quality of work inside its own house. Government can and should attach to this field the growing importance it deserves.

Encouragement, help, research, and occasional seeding of private sector experiments is one thing. But for the private sector ever to rely on government to *provide initiative* is quite another. And there's the dilemma—for, unfortunately, the precedent for such reliance abounds, particularly in Europe, with its government-mandated industrial democracy and co-determination programs. But, here at home, in some of our Manpower programs, all too often private enterprise has sat on its hands waiting for a government grant before tackling its own problems of hiring or retraining the disadvantaged. The private sector becomes involved in social responsibility, most of the time, only when Uncle Sam pays it to do so.

If such an attitude were to arise in the quality of work field, it would prove disastrous. For quality of work effort can work and last only when it is conceived, gestated, born, and raised by the people who will live with it. Any real quality of work effort is a *very* private affair.

This of course demands that what's involved must be profoundly understood by all of its participants. And very, very often it isn't.

2. In that critical fact lies the second major dilemma of the field: *its semantic anarchy.* Terms are important in any area of endeavor. We all remember how, when we suddenly came to understand what "ecology" meant, we could in a word understand an entire process devoted to preservation of environmental resources. But what I call the quality of work field does not yet have a commonly accepted terminology, as some of you may have realized. Instead it has a dozen vocabularies.

Differing terms such as "job enrichment," "job redesign," "humanization of work," "job satisfaction," "worker motivation," "worker participation," "behavioral research," "organizational development," and a dozen other rubrics abound in the field. This variety confuses amateur and professional alike with such imprecision, and frequently leads to contradictory policies.

One has to be a scholar just to understand the terminology. There is the Tavistock socio-technical school, the Herzberg job-enrichment school, the sensitivity T-group school, the McGregor X/Y school, the worker participation school, the job design school, the industrial democracy school, to name only a handful, each with its own terms and concepts for workplace improvement.

Again and again old professionals in the area talk about "this field," for lack of a precise or common term. Again and again, particularly in Washington, "this field" is called the "behavioral field," as if its sole concern was with changing worker attitude and behavior, which is not the case at all. The dazzling array of semantic choice tends to bewilder managers and workers alike.

I like the term, "quality of work." It has in it the key word "quality," to differentiate its area of concern from the purely quantitative concerns of the mechanists and economists. And, it has in it the word "work" which implies a different focus than the smaller concepts of "job." "Job enrichment" is a *descriptive* term describing a single process. "Quality of work" is an *inclusive* term, identifying a set of concerns. It includes under its canopy *all* the theories and activities whose collective goal is better utilization of human resources in an industrial and post-industrial society.

A quality of work effort might include both job enrichment *and* organizational change, which job enrichment alone does not encompass. It might involve work-team formation *and* job re-design, as a single effort. Or it might be solely a new incentive or profit-sharing system. But all are concerned with improving the *quality*—not the quantity—of working life.

The term quality of work can be imagined as suggesting a file drawer filled with *all* extant notions, plans, and programs for workplace improvement. But as the term is defined here, the contents of the file drawer are not limited merely to schemes and action plans for better and more productive human attitudes and motivation. They include schemes and diagrams and plans for more scientific meshing of human and machine systems, the area some call industrial engineering or management science. And it includes models of more contemporary and effective organizational structures and ways to achieve them. The term quality of work suggests all three areas of concern: it is a synthesis of scientific management, behavioral psychology, and/or organizational development into one interdisciplinary function. The term implies a three-in-one effort.

A sub-dilemma, under the terminology dilemma, and to some a serious one, is the much misunderstood term "productivity." I won't go into that tragically misunderstood semantic can of worms, except to say that I like to differentiate carefully between the terms "labor productivity," and "capital productivity." Although the semantic distinction is quite different from the classic economic view of productivity normally used, I think it more accurately reflects industrial reality, and the fact that the people and techniques used by each area are vastly different, with different expertise and concerns. Many economists will argue that the impact of labor productivity is negligible on total productivity figures. The truth is that it is impossible to measure by purely economic, or quantitative means. As one economist has put it, it is the "measure of ignorance" in economic measurement. The ignorance is large. It is worth noting that the president of one of our largest enterprises told us that his highly automated company, a pioneer in productivity measurement, estimated that about 50% of their 6% productivity gain last year came from labor productivity increases, and the other 50% from capital productivity, at a much greater cost.

3. The troublesome semantics of the quality of work field

lead to a third common dilemma: *the frequent resistance of middle and senior management to quality of work activity.* Numerous senior managers find it hard to believe that notions to increase labor productivity are really of much pragmatic use to the enterprise, which is what many economists tell them. More often than not, such resistance to quality of work efforts stems simply from lack of understanding of the pragmatic three-in-one nature of such approaches. Occasionally there are managers who do understand, but consider such efforts as a distinct threat to management control. A few even see them as a threat to free-enterprise capitalism itself, which is, of course, sheer idiocy. Management resistance is diminishing—in about direct proportion to the startling news coming in from successful quality of work efforts.

4. The fourth dilemma is a companion dilemma: *the frequent resistance of unions, and union leadership to quality of work programs for their membership.* Some unions are deeply committed to such effort as a major union thrust, and cooperate wherever and however they can. Leonard Woodcock, President of the United Auto Workers (UAW), whose union is cooperating in the program made the following comments: "We've had a lot of discussion with regards to this [notice he, too, needed a term] within our union. It's not the sort of thing, really, that should be a problem of confrontation and collective bargaining. If any of the companies suddenly said to the UAW, 'O.K., we agree. We want to humanize the workplace. You do it. We wouldn't even know where to begin. We really don't understand the extent of the problem, or the basis of the problem.' Is this the general malaise in our society finding its way into the workplace? I suspect it is, to some degree. So what we would say, I think, is, 'We want experimentation, involving both the management and the union and the workers to try to find the answers.' "

As open and wise an attitude as Mr. Woodcock's is not typical of all unions. Some union leaders still see quality of work effort as a camouflaged trick to go after labor speedup, or job displacement, or as a union-weakening device, or all three. They miss its win-win character, in which the union *and* the worker benefit equally, if not more than the management.

Some union leaders don't agree with Leonard Woodcock that quality of work effort shouldn't be confrontation, or be related to collective bargaining; a couple of leaders even suggest that it's a management trick to get *around* collective bargaining.

Some union leaders are simply realistically cautious. One Union International President said, without saying no to his union's involvement, that getting his union into a position advocating improved quality of work would involve a major historic step for the union and for labor generally. To him, it suggests something almost radical in classic labor-management relations:

the notion of working together, as partners, in those aspects of working life which are social and not economic, which are qualitative and not solely quantitative. "Besides," he added, "we here in Washington don't do the deciding. It's the brothers who do the deciding. The whole democratic process, including my re-election, is involved."

5. This takes us to the fifth, and one of the most curious, dilemmas of the entire quality of work phenomenon. *It is that the members—the men and women, the younger and the older workers who comprise the union's strength—are not sending positive signals up to their leadership that work improvement is an important issue to them.* Or, rather, in one way they aren't. Job dissatisfaction, the fact that there are far more dumb jobs than dumb people to fill them, doesn't tend to be a ringing issue in union meetings, according to union observers.

This fact might at first seem to belie the observation that the social pendulum is swinging toward a new concern for the quality of life at work. Yet, as one labor leader pointed out, there *are* very clear signals and they are increasing in frequency.

But instead of being positive signals of anger and grievance, the visible signals are negative and passive, measurable in such growing counter-productive behavior as increased absenteeism, rising turnover, higher error rates, drug abuse and alcoholism, quality deterioration, and so on. There is little evidence anywhere that active, articulate job dissatisfaction has risen. There is some good evidence that it is declining. Union members in the over-publicized Lordstown, Ohio, plant of General Motors, however, emitted another signal which may be more to the point. It wasn't apathy, alienation, negativism, or anger. The word was *frustration.* They possessed an almost touching eagerness for a chance to participate in work decisions. Not in how to run a General Motors plant, but in how to make the Vega a better car.

6. That group of very young men, however, was vastly different from a similar group, of mixed age, in a steel mill. And there we come to dilemma number six in quality of work effort: *the almost infinite variety of workplaces in which such effort might take place.*

Even in the same company, two plants manufacturing the same product mix can differ as do the night and day. The ethnic makeup of the labor force can make a tremendous difference in the productive output of a work force, as can management strength, boldness, and pride, communicated downward. The technology, present or absent, and its age and intensity is a critical criterion. The personality of a plant or office manager often can revolutionize a workplace—for better or for worse—as can the quality and strength and consistency of local and national union leadership.

To attempt to make any generalizations about the American

workplace and American productivity is as error-prone as to generalize about American women. Thus the emphasis on how private, or almost personal, a quality of work effort must be.

7. The vast diversity of the nature and character of American workplaces leads to dilemma number seven: *the equally infinite diversity of alternatives for work change and workplace improvement.* What is important and successful here may prove a disaster there. A job enrichment program which works splendidly in one area of a manufacturing plant may fail in another simply because the nature of the tasks is such that enrichment is simply not possible. Many times it is said that the more automated an assembly line, the less possible is job enrichment. Yet it is also true that *organizational* change, such as the elimination of a layer or two or three of supervision, can work wonders in terms of productivity increases in which job enrichment is well-nigh impossible. It all depends.

8. Dilemma number eight in quality of work activity is an extremely serious one: *the length of time it takes for a sound, effective work-change effort to demonstrate its effectiveness to all concerned.* For one thing, if the activity is not painstakingly planned, and if careful diagnosis of problems and solutions is not made, the program can be a dead failure before it starts. Planning alone takes months. But implementation of the planning-learning of new ways to work, new ways to supervise or not supervise, new work processes, new technology, and new work rules can take years before the full impact of the changes can be felt and measured.

Often, before a year is finished, many of the desired human and economic outcomes are already discernible. But what makes work change so difficult for Americans, in particular, is understanding that a learning process requires a lot of time. It's slow. It's learning to do things differently, and see things differently, and work differently, and that, too, requires time.

One of the world's foremost authorities in quality of work, a Norwegian named Einar Thorsrud, stated that to gain full bottom-line impact from work and organizational change takes as much as five years of the process. To a nation as fond as we are of instant success, the quiet patience required to let a quality of work effort mature slowly and properly is a dilemma indeed.

9. And this fact leads to dilemma number nine: *the frequent failure to secure and/or keep the sanction, and approval of senior management in a quality of work process.* Obviously, if the plant manager or union leader is not himself deeply committed to the learning process that change requires of him, or if his understanding of its dimensions and objectives is not large, he can quite literally kill the project's chances of ever succeeding. But what applies to him applies to his superiors, all the way up to the top of

both the management and union involved. The case books are filled with stories of enthusiastic plant managers who were transferred out at a key moment of the process by a headquarters management which was literally totally unaware of what was happening in that plant. One of the most brilliant achievements in quality of work history, that of the Shell Refineries in England, fell into oblivion after four years of extraordinary improvement, simply because the managing director of the company was transferred out and a new uninformed managing director let the effort die because he didn't understand it. The absence of management and union sanction all the way up to chairman of the board and international president often turns out to be one of the most serious obstacles to a well-planned quality of work effort.

10. *Dilemma number ten is the complex problem of how to diffuse a successful quality of work effort.* By diffusion, the professionals mean the effective spread of the process throughout a plant, or company, or an industry. All too often, something very successful may occur in one plant, or more often in one part of one plant, and never be communicated or transferred to other parts of that plant, or other plants in the company. The result is little better than no effort at all.

The obstacles to diffusion are many. One common problem is that frequently the most successful quality of work innovations are undertaken in brand new plants, where no traditions or old habits prevail. What worked for General Foods in Topeka, Kansas, and for Proctor and Gamble in Lima, Ohio, in new plant situations, is difficult to diffuse to older plants where old capital and old hierarchial structures resist innovative modern techniques of work and organizational structure. Yet without diffusion, the effort is an exercise in futility.

11. *The diffusion dilemma leads directly to dilemma number eleven, which I call the Watergate dilemma: the frequency with which many involved in quality of work activities have expressed serious concern to me about full disclosure of what they are doing in the field, even to the union involved.* Much more activity in quality of work innovation is going on in this country than is publicly known. The reasons for secrecy include fear of union participation, a desire to prevent the competition from knowing what's been achieved, and fear that publicity could destroy a beginning effort.

Except for secrecy from unions, it's difficult to blame companies anxious to keep quality of work innovations at a low profile, to avoid over-expectation or jealousy by the rest of the company. Yet if secrecy pervades, if we are permitted to see only the top of the quality of work iceberg, how are we as a society to know what is really working and what failed, a necessity if we are to properly evaluate the effort? It's a major dilemma.

12. The twelfth dilemma is perhaps the most subtle obstacle in the way of the emerging quality of work phenomenon. *It is the fact that with ample justification, most American managers are simply gun-shy of any new notions which lay claim to being a new solution for management's many problems.*

In just a decade, they've been bombarded with the Operations Research movement, the Information Sciences movement, the Sensitivity Training movement, the Management Sciences movement, the Human Relations movement, the Organizational Development movement, to name only a few of the more important topical fads. Each was valid. Each provided important new insights into the difficult art of management. But more often than not, each was oversold and overreacted to. Each became a bandwagon. And none ever quite lived up to the shining objectivies announced by their enthusiastic proponents.

Those of us who seriously believe that the emerging quality of work activity is more than another new bandwagon fad, like the automation scare of the 1960's which almost everybody jumped on, should do our best to tell it like it really is. We should never represent it other than as a slow, infinitely complex, undramatic learning process, with no master plan or formula for certain success, no universally sure or predictable outcomes, no promised panaceas. It is an instrument for desirable change. It is neither slick, nor easy. It often takes place in noisy plants and dreary offices. If we permit it to be represented as anything other than what it is, we shall merely add to the existing dilemmas and invite already gun-shy managers and union leaders to adopt an inevitable and justifiable thumbs-down stance.

13. This article is entitled "The Thirteenth Dilemma" because the thirteenth not only involves all the others, but, in a sense, makes them trivial by comparison.

Because the thirteenth is a social dilemma.

It is an either-or question. Can unions and managements, separately or together, afford *not* to get actively involved in quality of work planning now?

The chairman of one billion-dollar company, which is perhaps the most advanced in quality of work innovations and planning in America, stated that he has demanded such commitment to change his workplace simply because he'd like his company to be in business ten years from now. The president of Volvo, in Sweden, perhaps the leading work quality innovator in Europe, put it somewhat differently. He said he's building a new nonassembly line auto plant simply because he'd like to have a work force ten years from now. The biggest companies in the world, AT&T and General Motors, *in just the past two years,* have both split the old industrial relations vice presidency in two, and named new vice presidents in charge of human resources. The signs of concern are everywhere and growing.

These men could be wrong. What seems to be an emerging social phenomenon may be no more than a passing, overpublicized, Western fad. The whole thing may be, as reputable labor leaders have said, merely the invention of a few liberal academics who like to see their names in print. It may be, as others allege, the degeneration of an already overpermissive society spreading its permissiveness to the workplace. It may be another phony, even dangerous, bandwagon.

But from what the polls tell us of increasing public disenchantment with big business and big labor, from what the published and unpublished statistics tell us of rising absenteeism and turnover, dropping productivity, rising error and reject rates, deteriorating quality and mounting prices of American goods and services in a world market where our economic leadership seems to be slipping, one might suspect that something very real and perhaps historic is happening. There seems to be substantial and growing factual evidence to lead one to believe that we are indeed witnessing the beginning of the beginning of a new value shift in Western society, away from Newtonian mechanism toward humanism, away from purely quantitative concerns toward qualitative concerns for the quality of life.

So the thirteenth dilemma poses essentially two options to businessmen and labor men, right about now, as history tells time.

Option One is believing that something *is* happening. It is the hard, easy way of trying to cope with the dilemmas of the phenomenon now, against a lot of skepticism and resistance, moving boldly, carefully, intelligently, but relatively painlessly, and trying to improve work quality as wisely as possible so that everybody benefits, at no one's expense. It's the preventive therapy, or counterattack option.

Option Two is refusing to believe that something is happening. It's the easy, hard way—easy now but perhaps hard later on if what now is only a small groundswell proves to be an early warning signal of serious social and economic dysfunction later in the decade. It's the wait-and-see option.

The thirteenth dilemma is the choice between these options.

Not surprisingly, I advocate choosing Option One. I subscribe to the old managerial axiom that problems are a lot harder to identify but easier to solve early, and a lot easier to identify but harder or impossible to solve later. Besides, in Option One's favor is fact: we're beginning to know for sure that preventive therapy, quality of work activity, does work, when carefully applied. We know that it is feasible to redesign work and organizations, without disrupting output, in ways which make human work increasingly rewarding, and eventually more productive for everyone's benefit. We know, from the growing literature of successful innovation here and abroad that it is possible to surmount every single one of the dilemmas I've cited, and unlock new dimensions of working life, some of them startlingly effective. The state of the emerging art of quality of work is good, and rapidly maturing. Option One is not just theory. It's a fact. If management *and* labor, separately and together, choose the first option, somewhere in the not-too-distant future lies a new, late-twentieth century declaration of interdependence in the area of quality of work and working life, a new work ethic of qualitative cooperation between employee and employer, and vice versa.

Walter A. Haas, Jr. is Chairman of the Board and Chief Executive Officer of the Levi Strauss Company, San Francisco, California.

This article is reprinted from the May-June 1974 issue of **Atlanta Economic Review,** *pp. 12-14.*

9
Humanizing the Work Scene

Walter A. Haas, Jr.

What is this work ethic which is supposedly changing so much that it has suddenly become a matter of national concern? As a point of reference, the book, *Work in America,* which is discussed elsewhere in this issue, says,". . .Thrift, hard work, and a capacity for deferring gratification historically were traits widely distributed among Americans. Moreover, as part of the legitimacy of the economic system, individual members of our society were to be credited or blamed for their own circumstances, according to the degree of their prosperity."

In the very old days, this work ethic stood its ground against change very well. Oversimplified, the ethic stated that a person's worth in the eyes of God varied with the degree to which he put his nose to the grindstone.

This ethic for self-deprivation, strength, and self-reliance condemned what it felt to be such crimes against nature as the 10-hour day, the 5-day week, and later the 8-hour day, social security, welfare, and similar programs. Each change had to be introduced despite conservative prophesies that "the world is going to hell in a handbasket."

Thrift, hard work, and a capacity for being able to defer gratification are certainly traits to be admired, but the winds of change are such that a rapidly increasing number of people—and it's not just the young—want to have their own voice in the mix and not just blindly follow the voice of the Puritan ethic.

What the youngsters and others are demanding is a reversal of what they consider a phony value system. They want to get things done without some compulsive person complaining about the length of their hair or the manner of their dress. They want to talk in definitely unpompous terms. They want to accomplish goals through unconventional means. They want to do something meaningful, to have fun at their work.

It's no wonder so many people—again not just the young—are abandoning the old work ethic in favor of what the current jargon calls the "self-actualization" ethic which, by definition, encourages people to seek out new and different ways of finding self-fulfillment. One can be an inventor, a social worker, a street corner musician, a craftsman, a poet, or you name it. One may spend time "bumming around" to find out who he or she really is, or, hopefully, enough people can find self-fulfillment in business and industry to enable us to maintain and strengthen the desirable elements of our modern society.

The new ethic inevitably leads to a challenge for management, not only in business, but equally in government, in labor, and in education. The challenge to management is to structure a work environment that is conducive to fulfilling the self-actualization ethic.

Whether or not the expectations held by new workers are valid, management today must provide fuller opportunities for people who view work as an end in itself. But the way to achieve this is fairly straightforward and basic: good supervision, a willingness to explain "why," clearly established and fair goals, frequent and candid feedback (oral and financial)—in short, recognition of the value and the contributions of each individual. Such techniques as job restructuring may be helpful in gaining a sense of participation and commitment, but in some situations this is impossible, and in any case should not be an "out" for poor supervision.

Many people have false notions of what work is all about. In point of fact, much work is dull, petty, and empty of meaning, even for top managers. Paper pushing is no fun, whether one is a GS-3 file clerk or the Secretary of Health, Education, and Welfare. Factory work can be repetitive whether a person is sewing a pair of pants or developing moon rockets. And even such "creative" tasks as assembling stained glass windows or cultivating an organic garden have their tedious moments.

If anything, modern conveniences have made housework more pleasant, but in today's liberated world it is not "cool" to be a devoted mother and housekeeper. Similarly, certain jobs which used to be valued, such as police and factory work, have lost prestige while others, teaching and TV announcing, for example, have become more glamorous. This should be recognized in assessing certain jobs.

The key factor in job satisfaction seems to be personal motivation. Despite equal pay and good working environments, there are happy and dissatisfied businessmen, doctors, plumbers, and sewing machine operators. Commitment can be facilitated by proper recognition, but nothing works without personal motivation.

One of the first things management must do is get in the proper position for meeting its challenges. It is simple to state what must be done, even if it is not simple to accomplish: keep your eyes and ears open, be tolerant, and don't be too quick to apply older standards to newer values. A tendency to be too quick to judge will negate a host of exuberant ideas, boundless amounts of energy, and wells of creativity. An increasing number of people have goals they want to accomplish through unconventional means, and most of them want to talk in definitely unpompous terms.

Now back to those challenges to management. Many companies seem to be rushing to job enrichment as *the* answer, but such is not necessarily the case. Many people do not necessarily want "rich" jobs. A woman in one of the Levi Strauss plants was an excellent employee and was promoted to a "richer" job—trimming and inspecting. The personnel manager, visiting the plant, asked her how she liked her work, only to be told that she didn't like it. The worker had been a top operator on a sewing job, had trained herself to perform well without demands on her attention, and was able to earn a good wage at the same time that she was free to daydream about her family, social life, or whatever. On her new job, she had to pay attention and could not daydream. She was a good and conscientious employee and enjoyed the unchallenging routine of the sewing operation which she did not consider to be dull and boring. It should be added that sewing in a garment plant is a highly structured job, one that pays far below the national manufacturing average wage.

It is hard not to consider a job as a sewing machine operator, performing the same repetitive function day after day and year after year, terribly boring and highly frustrating. Strangely enough, and most heartening for the apparel industry, a report released in 1973 by Emanuel Weintraub Associates indicates that most sewing operators like their jobs. The report is based on a survey taken in 1972 in 17 factories across the country in the categories of men's wear, women's wear, and home furnishings. Over 2,500 women participated in the survey, 70% of whom were union members. In answer to a survey designed to measure the extent of dissatisfaction among garment industry workers, only about one out of ten operators said that she did not like her job.

They are not all satisfied, but they are not dissatisfied because of boredom. Rather, their dissatisfaction is related to much more mundane areas: more job security; pay equal to that in nearby plants; more or different fringe benefits; and a four-day week or other changes in work shifts that would permit them more leisure time. A great many of the workers surveyed expressed a desire to have a greater voice in decision making, asking for occasional discussion meetings. In their answers, these women were not expressing a desire to have any controls over the business; they were simply expressing a desire for better communication with management.

Job enrichment is only one of many tools directed at humanizing the work scene and making it more rewarding. It would be disastrous to place an improper amount of emphasis on it. Jim Windle of the Department of Industrial Supervision at Purdue University has been quoted as believing job enrichment "is being oversold as the cure for alcoholism, absenteeism, and the whole gamut of society's ills, including the growing incidence of hangnails and warts." Management can easily provide an environment that satisfies the traditional work ethic because the nose-to-the-grindstone ground rules of that ethic are simple, clear, and few. But how does management provide the myriad of behavior opportunities needed by the *self-actualization* ethic?

Improving the Quality of Working Life

Creatively, Levi Strauss recently made a commitment to establish a job enrichment program, but for a long time it has been engaged in efforts to humanize the work environment and/or make work challenging and engrossing. These efforts included the following elements:
O Opening opportunities to women and minorities.
O Divisionalizing and diffusing decision-making authority to the lowest possible levels.
O Improving internal communications both upward and downward.
O Developing management-by-objectives programs.
O Establishing community affairs teams at our facilities, giving employees power and capabilities to deal with the needs of their communities.
O Sponsoring an involvement corps team.
O Eliminating the artificial distinction of exempt and nonexempt employees.
O Performing an employee opinion survey to improve upward communications
O Holding communications meetings for the same purpose.
O Insisting that the products marketed are of a wuality that employees can be proud to make and sell, and many more.

Levi's has, therefore, had many successes in humanizing the work scene, but it also has had some failures. Over a year ago one of the employees suggested that a program be structured so that employees could, within limits, arrive at work at various times and quit working at various times, just so long as 40 hours were put in each week. The idea has since become known as "flexi-time" or "flex time" and is becoming increasingly in vogue. The suggestion was sent to all department heads for reaction and was subsequently turned down because it was "impractical"—a euphemism meaning that managers would have to devote some energies to making the idea work and would have to put aside some work ethic values that consider flex time to be lax, unbusinesslike, molly-coddling, and/or a dirty Communist plot.

Probably the greatest single deterrent to humanizing work is the presence of the work ethic in management's value system. It assumes people must be kept in line for output to ensue and results in a great resistance to change. New ideas and behavior departures are smothered as quickly as possible so that "proper managerial control" can be kept intact.

The Challenge of Change

Late in 1972 an international convention of 150 of Levi's top management people was called. Its theme was "The Challenge of Change" which stressed that only those past techniques that will be valid in the future should be kept. Levi's has declared its intention to experiment with flex time and job enrichment. It will look at the inherently tedious job of sewing a pair of pants to see what alternative job designs can be made. The main emphasis will be on ways to increase employees' participation and their partnership in profits and pride.

There are a host of partial solutions, all of which are already in effect someplace, which warrant attention and/or trial by companies which really want to humanize the work scene. There are sabbaticals, paid time off for community work, provisions to do work at home, in-house educational opportunities, reduced work-weeks for individuals such as mothers who want to work but also want to be home when their children are, relaxed dress requirements, more participative organizational structures, company sponsorship of employee small business and handicraft activities, and an endless variety of other possibilities. A creative management should be able to experiment with and then implement the right combination from such possibilities to provide a more meaningful work environment.

These are all tools. Probably no company can, or should, have them all. But the managements which focus on experimentation and implementation should overcome the smug tendency to rely on individually biased approaches and can, instead, build a functional tool kit.

Experimenting and implementing are two different things. The decision by management to strike out in a new area is but half the battle. Penetrating the ranks of middle management and supervision that are imbued with the traditional work ethic is a chore that exasperates all but the most persevering. Consequently, when a company has espoused a particular program—be it job enrichment, sensitivity training, zero defects, or whatever—a disparity between the "party line" and the reality of implementation is uncovered. To put it bluntly, humanizing the work scene is a difficult task.

All of this experimentation will not be at the expense of providing society with a product and shareholders with a return on their investment. Levi's efforts in minority employment opportunities and a wide range of corporate social responsibility programs have been good business as well as good citizenship. A business's most important asset is its people, and a progressive management philosophy attracts and motivates the best people. Humanization of work and making a buck are not mutually exclusive, but it is only the creative manager who can find ways to achieve both goals.

William E. Reif is Associate Professor of Management at Arizona State University, Tempe, Arizona.

This article is reprinted from the May-June 1974 issue of **Atlanta Economic Review,** *pp. 38-42.*

10
"Work in America": A Review Article

William E. Reif

The quality of life at work has become the subject of much discussion, debate, and controversy by academicians, managers, union leaders, government officials, and the press. A significant input to this discussion was the report *Work in America*, which presented the findings of a special task force to the Secretary of Health, Education and Welfare. The report has generated a great deal of interest, not only because of what it says, but also because it was commissioned by a federal government agency for the purpose of establishing the basis for public policy and federal work strategies.

The report's potential influence on public policy should be of concern to all of us. For this reason there is a need to critically evaluate its content, especially the assumptions it makes about the nature and importance of work, and to see if the foundation it has built is solid, conceptually and practically, or whether it will develop cracks under cross-examination.

The first thing which attracts the critical eye is that the primary intent of the task force was not to approach the quality of working life controversy objectively and in a scientific manner. Instead, it assumed that the culprit was in hand. Its purpose then became one of supporting the argument that: (1) the quality of life at work is generally poor, (2) there are ready means of improving the situation, and (3) improving work life (work being the independent variable) will have a very positive effect on the quality of life in general. To this end the report does a respectable job of presenting its case by reviewing the findings of "much of the literature" and conducting a "large number" of interviews with blue-collar and white-collar workers. Unfortunately, the approach taken by the researchers allowed them to conveniently ignore most of the contradictory research that is available. As a result the final report is deficient, and to the unsuspecting reader who has little knowledge of the quality of work controversy, it is misleading in intention, reporting, and interpretation of findings.

The position taken by the task force is based on a series of assumptions about work, each of which should be questioned for its validity and general application to the "typical" worker and work situation. The assumptions, taken directly from the report, are as follows:

O   "We must always remember that the most important part of the quality of life is the quality of work."[1]

O   "The first chapter of the report discusses the functions of work: its centrality in the lives of most adults, its contribution to identity and self-esteem, and its utility in bringing order and meaning to life . . . if the opportunity to work is absent or if the nature of work is dissatisfying (or worse), severe repercussions are likely to be experienced in other parts of the social system."[2]

O   "Alienation exists when workers are unable to control their immediate work processes, to develop a sense of purpose and function which connects their jobs to the over-all organization of production, to belong to integrated industrial communities, and when they fail to become involved in the activity of work as a mode of personal self-expression."[3]

O   "The redesign of jobs is the keystone of this report."[4]

O   "Job redesign is the major tool with which we might make work more satisfying."[5]

The report contends that job redesign will serve to "decrease mental and physical health costs, increase productivity, and improve the quality of life for millions of Americans at all occupational levels."[6] Job redesign will accomplish these very desirable ends by making work more meaningful; that is, it will "contribute to self-esteem, to the sense of fulfillment through the mastering of one's self and one's environment, and to the sense that one is valued by society."[7]

The report closes its case with the statement, "People tend to become what they do."[8] Aside from being catchy, this kind of statement has no constructive purpose and is akin to another currently popular notion that "you are what you eat." Incidently, there may be greater support for the latter.

The way in which the task force presents its case at times interferes with the reader's ability to separate the grain from the chaff. The report tends to take on a missionary zeal that only serves to further remove the discussion of work in America from the realm of objectivity. One example of this is the quote from Sidney Harman's "Responsibilities of Businessmen," as follows:

"Work satisfaction—which is to say the attainment of a sense of purposefulness in his or her work, the achievement of a sense of personal worth and dignity—should be seen as a fundamental right of employees, and therefore a fundamental obligation of employers . . . the consistent implementation of this view throughout the business community is the most reliable assurance of the preservation and constructive development of the free enterprise system."[9]

If one is successful in wading through the rhetoric, he has to conclude, as was the intent, that job satisfaction is up there with flag, mom, and apple pie.

Some Contradictory Research

The purpose here is to present some of the contradictory research that was not included in the report. Although this section will be fairly critical of the task force's lack of concern for objectivity, the intent is to be constructive and to balance the extreme position taken in the report with information that is not consistent with the assumptions, findings, and recommendations contained therein.

The task force relied heavily on Abraham Maslow's hierarchy of needs theory, Frederick Herzberg's two-factor theory of motivation, and the University of Michigan Survey Research Center's widely quoted study, *Survey of Working Conditions*, to document its assumptions. These were: work is central to the lives of most people; the vast majority of workers are oriented to the satisfaction of higher order needs; and, since these needs are not satisfied, workers as a lot are dissatisfied. Higher order needs include the desire for comradeship (affiliation), esteem, autonomy, and self-actualization. The accompanying proposition is that they are satisfied at work primarily by intrinsic motivators, including interesting and challenging work, achievement, responsibility, recognition, advancement (based on merit), feedback about work performance, and the opportunity for personal growth and development on the job. Furthermore, the report contends that due to changes in attitudes toward work, and the changing needs, aspirations, and values of workers, more and more individuals are demanding satisfaction of these needs. According to the report, workers who do not feel this way represent "a small minority."

In building its case, the task force ignores research that would in any way discount the notion that most workers are high achievers. Considerable evidence *does* exist which suggests that many people do not actively seek greater responsibility, autonomy, and opportunity for creativity at work; workers can be satisfied with what others might consider to be dull, meaningless tasks; and, instead of intrinsic rewards (satisfaction from the work itself), some, perhaps many, people prefer security, decent working conditions, higher pay and fringe benefits, and other forms of extrinsic rewards.

The basic theories which the task team relied on so heavily for support are themselves under close scrutiny today as evidence continues to accumulate that is not consistent with their propositions. Herzberg's two-factor theory has been widely criticized, especially the prediction that hygiene variables—such as pay, working conditions, and relationships with one's superior and peers—can at best produce a condition of no dissatisfaction.[10] Also, there is evidence that the order of needs represented by Maslow's hierarchy may not apply to most individuals. There is reason to believe that an individual's desire for satisfying higher order needs is not necessarily contingent on the satisfaction of lower order needs; but, rather, he may be striving to achieve both simultaneously.[11] What this means, of course, is that management cannot ignore lower order needs because they are still sources of dissatisfaction for many workers. Or, looking at it in another way, the satisfaction of lower order (hygiene) needs may serve to motivate workers as well as the more talked about higher order needs.

The task force is very dependent on the *Survey of Working Conditions*, which it refers to as a "unique and monumental" study. The general conclusions drawn in the study are that American workers want "more autonomy in tackling their tasks, greater opportunity for increasing their skills, rewards that are directly connected to the intrinsic aspects of work, and greater participation in the design of work and the formulation of their tasks."[12] Although the task force readily accepted these generalizations, others have not, and for good reason.

The most outspoken critic of the Survey Research Center's study has been Mitchell Fein. By breaking out the data into 12 occupational groups Fein discovered there were wide differences in opinion about what is important at work and the extent to which the 23 working conditions factors used in the original study are present in workers' jobs.[13] He found that, when the blue-collar data are separated from all other occupational groups, the workers' needs are *reversed* from those reported in the study as representing the "composite worker." Essentially what happened is that in developing the profile of the "composite worker," the study failed to consider the old axiom that applying the arithmetic mean to heterogeneous data in effect renders the data and any interpretation thereof meaningless (no pun intended). The HEW report failed to take this into consideration and used the survey data as primary support for its statements about life at work.

Another example of the strong bias that pervades the report is found in Chapter 3, "Work and Health," which takes the approach that the improvement in work through job redesign "holds out opportunities for *avoiding* physical and mental illness and thereby avoiding medical care bills."[4] The chapter documents this proposition by referencing studies that relate instances of mental and physical deterioration of individuals who experience dissatisfaction from dull, repetitive, routine jobs and from having to operate in a general work environment characterized by poor relations with co-workers, lack of recognition, incongruity between job status and other life roles, and poor working conditions. The report goes on to draw a relationship between job dissatisfaction and problems of alcoholism, drug abuse, and suicide, which it contends are the individual's way of coping with the conditions of life at work. Conspicuously absent from the discussion are any contradictory research findings, and in their absence the reader is led to the conclusion that symptoms of mental and physical illnesses will disappear with the redesign of jobs.

The fact of the matter is that there are strong doubts about the true nature of the relationship between personal characteristics, working conditions, and the worker's health. For example, in a recent article the eminent psychologist, Robert N. McMurry, raised the question that if the authoritarian leadership style is so unpopular with employees, why is it so universally practiced? His answer, which would not be popular with the task force, is that authoritarian leadership is widely used because "it best suits the needs of most people for structure and guidance and freedom from the need to accept responsibility and to make decisions."[5] McMurry goes on to argue convincingly that for some people enriched jobs would *cause* mental and physical health problems, not cure them.

Chapter 4, "The Redesign of Jobs," is the most often quoted section in the report, since it contains the task force's primary recommendations for improving worker satisfaction. As in other chapters, the deficiency is not in what is included but in what is omitted. The report's solutions to unsatisfying work are supported for the most part by the same few case studies of workplace reform and innovation that are mentioned by nearly all other writers who are interested in job redesign and job enrichment. Included in this select group are the General Foods plant, Corning Glass, Texas Instruments, The Traveler's Insurance Companies, Proctor & Gamble, and AT&T. It is implied that these firms are representative of industry at large and that the positive results from job redesign experienced by them could be readily duplicated by others.

A close look at the conditions in which job redesign was implemented in these firms would lead one to conclude that they are more atypical than typical and their successful experiences more unique than representative. A prominent industrial engineer who studied the situation at the General Foods plant reported, "Comparing the performance of the Topeka workers to those of Kankakee (another, more representative, General Foods plant) is like comparing the Knicks basketball team to that of a local high school."[16] He continued:

"General Foods—Topeka is a controlled experiment in a small plant with conditions set up to achieve desired results. These employees are not a cross section of the population, or even of Topeka. The plant and its operation are not typical of those in industry today. The results obtained are valid only for this plant."[17]

This reviewer suggests that the same argument could be used in the case of Lincoln Electric Company, Proctor & Gamble, Texas Instruments, and most, if not all, of the others cited in the report.

Another theme that runs throughout Chapter 4 is the central role played by participative management in job redesign. The report develops its argument for participation to the point that increasing participation in workplace decisions will result in large gains in the physical and mental well-being of workers. Even though its position in favor of participation is not well documented, the task force, having by now become comfortable in doing so, encourages the reader to generalize that participative management is a universal cure for many company and worker ills.

While the report is not alone in its belief in participation, it has been the experience of many others that participative management is a very fragile concept and that positive results are contingent on a number of situational variables that are not widely distributed among individuals and organizations. Strauss and Rosenstein, in their critical examination of participation, refer to the concept as "one of the most overworked words of the decade," and caution against its indiscriminate use. They conclude that "A major reason for the failure of many participation schemes is their tendency to place emphasis on psychological rewards exclusively. Those plans which have elicited the most worker interest are those which gave the promise of improving the workers material rewards."[18]

In addition to an unwillingness to recognize contradictory research findings, the quality of the report is downgraded some what by internal inconsistencies. The contradictions presumably are due in part to the fact that the report was prepared by a team of researchers and, as acknowledged in the letter of transmittal, consensus was not always forthcoming. Nevertheless, the lack of consistency on key issues does raise questions about the capability of the task force to integrate its accumulation of information into a well-conceived and executed study of work in America.

Several inconsistencies are especially troublesome to the reviewer. To begin with, the report repeatedly speaks of the "anachronism of Taylorism" and refers to Tayloristic philosophies as outdated and ineffective. At the same time it strongly supports "participation in profits" as highly effective in increasing job satisfaction. Was not Frederick Taylor one of the men primarily responsible for the introduction of wage incentive plans that tied economic rewards to productivity and, along with his friend Henry Gantt, for their widespread use in industry today?

Another point that needs reconciling is the one concerning the importance of work. The task team takes a decidedly historical approach to understanding the function and importance of work—an argument that is central to its purpose. The approach is essentially extrapolative, with the assumption being that, given an understanding of the meaning of work to workers over the last half century, conclusions can be drawn about the importance of work today. In the next breath, however, the report emphasizes the recent changes in attitudes toward work, implying that the relationship between man and work is a whole new ballgame. If this is true, is it also not possible that one of the recent changes in attitudes toward work is the *lack of importance* work holds for some people and that meaning in life can be found outside the job? There is increasing evidence that this is the case, contrary to the generalizations in the report.[19]

Another source of confusion is the seemingly ambivalent feelings of the members of the task team toward the rather distinct roles of intrinsic and extrinsic rewards in increasing job satisfaction. While they admit that there are factors other than job content responsible for satisfaction and dissatisfaction at work, they make job redesign the keystone of the report, and state that intrinsic motivators are the independent variables in the quality of working life equation. In similar fashion, they argue that work is the independent variable in the quality of life equation and then go on to make repeated references to the cultural, social, political, educational, and economic considerations that also have a hand in determining what constitutes "quality." All of this tends to confuse the reader, at least this reader, so that he is not really sure what the task force is saying, or not saying.

Finally, the task force appears to be uncertain about what it thinks is the relationship between job satisfaction and productivity. It is generally assumed throughout the report that productivity is dependent on job satisfaction, hence the great concern for increasing job satisfaction through job redesign, education, and job mobility (Chapters 4 and 5). On the other hand, the report treats productivity as the real payoff from job redesign. Does this possibly denote a shift in assumptions from satisfaction causes performance to performance causes satisfaction? If it does, such a shift would be more in line with recent evidence that satisfaction *is the result* of an individual's being rewarded for good job performance, but would be inconsistent with the tone of the report.[20] Obviously, treating performance as the causal variable would require about a 180° shift in assumptions and approach, and in the end it is not clear where the report stands on this all important issue.

The object of this rather critical examination of *Work in America* was not to manufacture an argument counter to that of the report, for, after all, that would be practicing what this reviewer has taken the task team to task for doing. Hopefully what has been accomplished is a balancing of the views expressed in the report with contradictory research that supplies some of the missing pieces to a true picture of the complex nature of work.

In studying the report it is most important that one keep in mind the assumptions that are made about workers and work, and understand how these assumptions can affect conclusions and recommendations. Assumptions, unless clearly defined, can be used to blind the eyes of the researcher so that he only considers sources of information that support some preconceived notion of what is or what ought to be. This reviewer has attempted to piece together the implied assumptions, and for the most part has found them to be self-serving. It appears that too often the task team's efforts were guided down predetermined paths to conclusions that preceded the investigation.

Contributions of the HEW Report

In spite of its shortcomings the report does provide valuable input to the quality of working life controversy. It does a commendable job of bringing attention to a number of work-related problems that should be of concern to everyone. There is no doubt that some workers are locked into meaningless jobs, and that their dissatisfaction is being expressed in terms of alienation, high absenteeism and turnover, poor workmanship, restricted output, and the pressing social problems of poor mental and physical health, alcoholism, and drug abuse. (Please keep in mind that what constitutes a "meaningless" job can only be defined by the job holder.) The magnitude of these problems, however, has not as yet been determined and until it is, it is just as wrong to assume that job dissatisfaction is running rampant in industry as it is to assume that it does not exist.

Answers will come as improvements are made in diagnostic skills that enable the attitudes, values, and beliefs of workers to be measured accurately, the sources and nature of dissatisfaction to be known, and proper corrective action to be taken. Cures must be applied contingently in order for the prognosis to be favorable. There are no simple remedies for the "common" ailments associated with work because ailments are not common, in the sense of being universal, but are usually found to be unique to a particular set of variables that comprise a work situation. For most organizations, to buy a cure-all is to buy a dream, or perhaps a nightmare.[21]

Another contribution of the report is the emphasis it places on job redesign as a means of improving the quality of life at work. Those of us who have been conducting research and writing in the area of job enrichment/job enlargement welcome the publicity that this part has received. The one problem is that the report leaves the false impression that job redesign is a panacea. Little consideration is given to the fact that techniques of job redesign, such as job enrichment, were never intended to be solutions to all problems of motivation and productivity, but were designed to deal with problems where *job content* was diagnosed as the root cause. To expect the design of jobs to do more than that is contrary to all evidence currently available.

It must also be recognized that job redesign does not automatically result in increases in job satisfaction and performance, nor can it be applied to all job situations that are in need of enrichment. There are organizational considerations, among them economic, technological, and managerial constraints, that can restrict its use.[22] The report takes a very casual approach to the problems that are involved in job redesign and ignores completely some of the real gut issues of implementation.[23]

The report would have been more effective in promoting job redesign if it had used the examples of "successes" in a more restrictive, but objective, way. The case studies are billed as being representative of most firms, and the strong inference is that everyone should be able to experience like results. More realistically, the companies presented are not typical and their results should not be generalized. What their results do show is that job redesign can be extremely effective under certain conditions that are supportive of management's efforts to provide for the satisfaction of individual and organizational needs. If the task team had concentrated on identifying the conditions that must exist for the concept to be effective, it would have measurably contributed to present knowledge.

The report makes a contribution by stressing the work-related problems of education and mobility. There is no quarrel with its contention that workers who have restricted mobility, for whatever reasons, and either are overeducated or lack the knowledge and skills for meeting job requirements are prime candidates for dissatisfaction. When one realizes that the half-life of engineers and other highly technically qualified professionals is five to seven years, the problems associated with knowledge obsolescence take on urgency. The report is being overly conservative when it speaks of "mid-career changes." In the future there will be a need for many workers to become retrained or trained for entirely new careers five or six times in their working life.

The report's proposed solution to this problem is really not new, since sabbaticals have existed in education for years and have more recently been adopted by industry, albeit on a limited basis. Moreover, the widely practiced concept of management by objectives encourages the setting of personal development objectives and considers the manager's growth and development to be part of his job and something for which he will be held accountable. What is worth mentioning are the two alternative models of worker retraining suggested by the task team: basic worker self-renewal program and universal worker self-renewal program. In discussing these concepts, the report questions the value of present education, as far as preparing individuals for careers, and deplores the low correlation between education and job requirements. The observation that the design of work is lagging behind changes that have occurred among workers, including their educational achievements, is strongly supported by this reviewer.

Conclusion

Although the full impact of *Work in America* is yet to be determined, several observations are in order. The report is obviously a call for government action. This is clearly spelled out in the first paragraph of The Summary: "Truly effective responses (to the frustrations of life in a mass society) are far more likely to be made if the obscure and complex sources of discontent are sorted out, and the lever of public policy is appropriately placed."[24]

The greatest deficiency in the report is that the obscure and complex sources of discontent were not sorted out. Furthermore, the recommendations that were made throughout the report and the federal work strategies proposed at the end were not based on hard evidence, but were formulated from largely undocumented assumptions, oversimplifications, and generalizations that do not meet the standards of scientific investigation. How many times has the lever of public policy been "appropriately" placed under similar circumstances and what has been the result? Although the question is rhetorical, it is this reviewer's opinion that the extent to which policy makers depend on the report as a source of information is the extent to which policies made will prescribe solutions to problems that may not exist, ignore problems that do exist, and apply whatever action is deemed necessary, indiscriminately to all.

Once the report is put in proper perspective it begins to have some value. One must realize that the task force does not approach the quality of working life controversy objectively. Rather, it enters with a decidedly humanitarian bias and with a predisposition that, with the exception of a very small minority, individuals desire to self-actualize in their jobs, find they cannot, and thus are dissatisfied; second, that the reasons they cannot self-actualize are primarily associated with the meaningless tasks they are required to perform; and, third, that the solution can most readily be found in job redesign. To this end the report does an admirable job.

In the process of arguing its case, the task force pulls together selected information that does contribute to an understanding of some of the issues involved in turning job dissatisfaction into satisfaction. The concern for work-related problems of not just blue-collar workers but also white-collar, managerial, and professional, and the regard for the special problems of young, older, minority, and women workers give proper dimension to the study. Also, establishing the relationship between work and health underlines the need to give more weight to such considerations in managerial decisions.

The report's suggested reforms and innovations in the workplace, which primarily involve job redesign, are warranted and, if applied contingently, can have very positive effects on workers' attitudes and behavior. Finally, the recognition of worker retraining as a partial solution to problems of job mobility is welcomed. Management would be well advised to acknowledge the relationship between education and work and begin to take more seriously the need to provide for continual growth and development on the job, not just for the sake of the worker but as a means of increasing the organization's ability to achieve its objectives.

---

1. *Work in America*, Report of a Special Task Force to the Secretary of Health, Education and Welfare (Cambridge, The M.I.T. Press, 1973), pp. vii-viii.

2. Ibid., p. xv.

3. Ibid., p. 22.

4. Ibid., p. xvii.

5. Ibid., p. 121.

6. Ibid., p. xviii.

7. Ibid., p. 5.

8. Ibid., p. 6.

9. Ibid., p. 25.

10. See Valerie M. Backman, "The Herzberg Controversy," *Personnel Psychology*, vol. 24, no. 2, 1971, p. 155; and William E. Reif and Fred Luthans, "Does Job Enrichment Really Pay Off?" *California Management Review*, vol. XV, no. 1, 1972, p. 30.

11. Robert M. Monczka, William E. Reif, and John W. Newstrom, "Perceived Satisfaction With and Importance of Direct Economic, Indirect Economic, and Psychosocial Rewards: Support For a Contingency Approach to Organizational Reward Systems" (unpublished paper, 1974).

12. *Work in America*, p. 13.

13. Mitchell Fein, "The Real Needs and Goals of Blue Collar Workers," *The Conference Board Record*, February 1973, p. 26.

14. *Work in America*, p. 76.

15. Robert N. McMurry, "Management's Achilles Heel: Over-Dependence," *Michigan Business Review*, November 1973, p. 14.

16. Mitchell Fein, "Job Enrichment Does Not Work" (unpublished paper, 1973), pp. 11-12.

17. Ibid., p. 12.

18. George Strauss and Eliezer Rosenstein, "Workers Participation: A Critical View," *Industrial Relations*, vol. 9, no. 2, 1970, p. 213.

19. See Charles L. Hulin and Milton R. Blood, "Job Enlargement, Individual Differences, and Worker Responses," *Psychological Bulletin*, vol. 69, no. 1, 1968, p. 41; and Milton R. Blood and Charles L. Hulin, "Alienation, Environmental Characteristics, and Worker Responses," *Journal of Applied Psychology*, June 1967, p. 284.

20. Charles N. Greene, "The Satisfaction-Performance Controversy," *Business Horizons*, vol. 15, no. 5, 1972, p. 31.

21. For those interested in taking a diagnostic approach to job redesign see: William E. Reif and Ronald C. Tinnell, "A Diagnostic Approach to Job Enrichment," *MSU Business Topics*, Autumn 1973, p. 29; and Robert M. Monczka and William E. Reif, "A Contingency Approach to Job Enrichment Design," *Human Resource Management*, Winter 1974.

22. Reif and Tinnell, "A Diagnostic Approach . . .," pp. 30-34.

23. *Work in America*, pp. 111-115.

24. Ibid., p. xv.

PART TWO
Practice and Applications

Roy W. Walters is President of Roy W. Walters & Associates, Inc., Glen Rock, New Jersey.

11
Job Enrichment: Challenge of the Seventies

Roy W. Walters

Work itself, and only work, can motivate workers.

This simple but vital idea lies at the heart of job enrichment. It has launched a revolution in management's approach to its basic task, the mobilizing of human resources.

A long and continuing bout of inflation has made it more difficult for management to reach its "traditional" goals of keeping costs down and increasing sales and profits. At the same time, government regulations and public opinion have increased the pressure on business to meet new social goals: improve quality and safety, clean up the environment, and cure social ills.

Business cannot hope to meet such challenges unless it can increase productivity. But productivity increases have hit a monumental snag. Instead of more output per man-hour, company after company is experiencing low output, poor quality production, increased employee turnover, absenteeism, lateness, threats of unionization, excessive overtime, and, more recently, alcoholism and drug addiction. Managers claim that they are unable to meet the objectives established by higher management and that the problems listed here are the chief reasons.

Managers further state that the personnel specialists are hiring the wrong kinds of workers, or that they don't understand what is wrong with the young people today. "They certainly aren't like we were when we were their age." They go on to say that they can't understand why they aren't motivated when "we treat them so well."

Interviews with thousands of workers, at all levels, indicate that they are not really concerned with how well they are treated. The intolerable working conditions of the twenties and thirties have disappeared from the scene. Most workers are treated well. Now what they are saying is that they want to be *used well*. Being trapped eight hours a day on a dull job is a helpless, hopeless feeling. Many members of the older generation have placidly accepted this as their lot in life. But the younger generation-- which represents better than 50% of the membership of most organizations--will not accept this. They rebel against it by controlling production, permitting errors by careless attitude, quitting and moving on, being late, being absent, beating the drum for unionization (which can only bargain for more goodies), drinking, and using dope.

The apathy and sometimes open hostility which characterize the behavior of today's worker have been studied at length by Frederick Herzberg. According to Professor Herzberg's hygiene-motivation theory, such personnel factors as spiraling wages, liberal fringe benefits, reduction of time spent at work, human relations training programs, and communication through house organs are simply "hygiene." They may avoid job dissatisfaction, but they do not motivate.

Union leaders, corporation presidents, and behavioral scientists have recognized the fact that the widely accepted incentives of the last 40 years are no longer effective in combating boredom and discontent on the post-industrial scene, from the assembly line to the executive suite.

Professor Herzberg proposes growth or motivator factors conducive to job satisfaction -- achievement, recognition, work itself, responsibility, advancement, growth.

He distinguishes between horizontal job loading (increasing the number of bolts the worker is expected to tighten a day or adding another meaningless task such as a routine clerical activity) and vertical job enrichment, which increases the employee's freedom and accountability while gradually introducing him to more difficult tasks.

This adherence to Herzberg's theory of vertical expansion must be accompanied by an equally important aspect of job enrichment. A feedback, or a constant and immediate opportunity for the employee to know how he is performing, must be incorporated into the work. Most jobs don't have feedback built into them or, if they do, it comes from the boss in an embarrassing and degrading manner which results in tension. When the worker receives feedback directly from the recipient of his efforts in the normal process of work, his perspective of the end results of his labors is increased.

Organizations that wish to survive, to say nothing of growing, must begin by improving the management of their human resources. They must begin to change existing dull jobs, and they must prevent the creation of additional dull jobs. Successive layers of management must not be allowed to hold the routine and insignificant decisions to their bosoms. They must not be used as checkers of subordinates' work. They must prevent creation of additional rigid rules, practices, and regulations. Too many executives and managers behave in such a way that they deny their subordinates the thrill and excitement of analyzing a problem, arriving at a solution, and being held responsible for implementing a new process or procedure.

Job enrichment seems to hold the solution to problems of this kind. Rearranging work processes and work flows so that workers have a constant feeling of growth and development has been tried successfully in a number of organizations. Analyzing work content and folding in functions that precede a stripped job, pulling back functions that follow the stripped job, pulling down from the boss items of decision making, or levels of authorization, and bringing in functions from another department, all represent possibilities for job enrichment.

We have enriched jobs at all levels in a number of organizations. Job enrichment is not confined to the lowest clerical or production worker. Foremen, supervisors, salesmen, and middle managers all tend to react positively to the process.

A large insurance company wanted to test the impact of job enrichment on company-wide problems, such as negative employee attitudes, absenteeism, turnover, and performance that was low in both quantity and quality. For experimental purposes management picked essentially identical groups of keypunch operators. Their jobs were repetitive and boring, and their working behavior presented virtually all the problems the company wanted to overcome.

In one group -- the control group -- no change was made in existing job structures. In the other -- the experimental group -- jobs were modified along job enrichment lines. For example:

Each operator took all responsibility for her own unit of work -- setting and meeting schedules, accuracy, and time records.

Operators were authorized to send coding errors back to the originating department.

If questions arose about the work, operators were instructed to discuss them with client departments rather than with their own supervisors.

Some operators were given the additional option of not

verifying their work.

The job enrichment trial lasted a year. Employee attitude surveys and statistical performance measures taken before and after the trial were compared for the control and experimental groups. The results:

O Positive employee attitudes, as revealed by the questionnaires, increased 16.5% in the experimental group, and by an insignificant amount -- 0.5% -- in the control group.

O Absenteeism dropped 24.1% in the experimental group, while it actually rose 29% in the control group.

O The error rate for experienced operators in the experimental group was reduced 35.3%.

O Hourly volume rose 29.6% for the experimental group, and only 8.1% for the control group.

O As a result of these changes, the company saved an estimated $64,000 during the trial. Additional potential savings of about $92,000 were estimated

A bank used job enrichment to improve product productivity in its corporate-trust stock transfer and billing operations. To simplify work flow and reduce manpower needs, the bank emphasized two principles of job enrichment: (1) increasing the accountability of employees at all levels, and (2) combining several repetitive and formerly separate tasks into larger work units.

Stock transfers are now handled by 25% fewer people, and overtime has been cut from 50 hours a week to zero. The trick was to cut the number of separate, fragmented steps in the transfer process from nine to six. The jobs of a transfer clerk and a stop board clerk were combined. And the separate functions of checking, balancing, and matching up after issuance of certificates were combined.

In the registration process, the jobs of 3 tellers and 9 sorters and writers were merged into a single function handled by 8 employees. Each dealt with all aspects of the job, instead of just one. Each employee received more responsibility. The bank got better control and backup, as well as speedier transfers. Within two weeks the pilot group was issuing 30% more certificates per man-hour. Manpower requirements were cut from 20 workers to 16. Similar changes in billing saved 240 supervisory hours of overtime.

Within three months after the job enrichment trial started, actual savings reached an annual rate of $6,200 and another $24,000 of savings was proposed. The savings came from reduced manpower requirements. Of a work group of 125 people, 7 were saved immediately and 5 more were possible -- a 9.6% improvement.

A sales district significantly increased the order input and dollar volume of its sales force with a job enrichment program for both salesmen and support people. As a start, the program focused on those aspects of the district manager's job that could be delegated down the line. The objective was to give the members of the sales force more of a sense of growth and responsibility.

The district manager loaded the jobs of the salesmen vertically by letting them make the credit arrangements for their customers. He picked a different salesman each time to chair the weekly sales meeting. He involved salesmen in setting their own quotas. He assigned one salesman the responsibility for presenting a public seminar. Its success led to a promotion for that individual.

Vertical loading was also applied to support jobs. Technical support people were made responsible for entire product areas, rather than products scattered in many areas. They were asked to prepare bimonthly presentations on new developments in their areas. One man with a flair for words was chosen to prepare a regular newsletter for customers. Wherever possible, in line with the positive approach of job enrichment, the enlarged responsibilities were treated as recognition for a job well done.

In this program the simplest ideas were implemented first, and the success to date assures that more enrichment will follow. Besides increased sales productivity, the program has paid off in greater professionalism in salesmen's attitudes toward their jobs and in more creative use of the time of the sales manager.

A large brokerage house used job enrichment to restructure its operating cashiers department for annual savings pegged at almost $25,000 after only six months, and an eventual projected payoff of at least $104,000 per year.

Two sections were affected—Receive and Deliver. The guiding principle in both cases was the same: to upgrade clerical jobs by vertically loading into them some of the tasks previously performed by higher grade clerical workers and supervisors. This in turn, resulted in some supervisory jobs being upgraded or eliminated.

In the Receive Section, the jobs of 12 blotter clerks and 5 trouble clerks were combined into 17 more challenging positions. Eventually the jobs of 5 buy-in clerks will also be merged, leading to 22 varied clerks jobs. At that point, the buy-in supervisor's job will gradually be eliminated.

In another phase of the Receive operation, clerks formerly doing only routine work were made responsible for researching and correcting any troubles associated with their work (previously the responsibility of trouble clerks). The trouble clerks, then, began performing tasks previously performed by lead clerks and supervisors.

In the Deliver Section, blotter and street clerks have taken over reclaiming work from trouble clerks, whose jobs have been eliminated. These productivity improvements have resulted in moving a blotter operation from the night shift to the day shift thus eliminating the job of the night blotter supervisor.

The savings in both sections in the first six months came from elimination of three clerical salaries -- in addition to the 2/3 reduction in items to be reclaimed in the Deliver Section. Job redesigns projected but not yet implemented are expected to save another $35,000 in Receive and $44,000 in Deliver. It may also be possible to combine the Receive and Deliver Sections, and thus save another $15,000 in supervisory salary.

A large chemical company had a problem with the job of laboratory technician. It seems that the technicians felt that their abilities and experience were being wasted.

The technicians set up the appropriate apparatus, recorded data, and supervised laboratory assistants who carried out simpler operations. The technicians were professionally qualified people, but lacked the university degrees possessed by the scientists. After several meetings, management decided to change the job of the laboratory technicians by adding the following items:

1. Technicians were given responsibility for project planning, work scheduling, and target setting.
2. Certain technicians were allowed to requisition materials and equipment.
3. Each technician was given his own work group to supervise.
4. Certain technicians were made responsible for devising and implementing a training program for their junior staff.
5. Certain technicians were given the responsibility of interviewing candidates for laboratory assistant jobs.
6. Technicians were given responsibility for appraising the performance of their laboratory assistants.

The results have been substantial. Quality of reports improved dramatically along with ideas and suggestions. Morale and productivity also increased.

The technicians now feel more responsible about their jobs and handle their projects as managers. The scientists have more time to do pure research and are giving up more and more of their routine duties to the technicians.

A manufacturing plant decided to enrich the jobs of 60 film operators. The work consisted of three departments that processed film in two separate lines. The first line had 3 stations of 10 men each, and the second line had 3 stations of 5 men each. A control department of 10 men set up the work, created job specifications, dealt with customers, set priorities, and controlled all schedules. The quality of the output was inspected by a team of 5 men at the end of the process.

The following items were built into the job:

1. Two stations were combined into teams handling the work of high-volume customers.

2. The inspection station was eliminated and quality control responsibility was delegated to the station on the second line.

3. Provision was made for feedback of customer rejects to the station operator involved.

4. Certain operations were provided with customer specifications and permitted to do the process planning.

5. Certain operators were delegated the authority to set priorities.

6. Certain operators were assigned work with customers on specified types of problems and the number of operators in the control department was reduced.

7. Certain operators were trained in quality control procedures and reported their findings periodically at station meetings.

8. Operators set their own goals.

Quality went up 8% and production rose 7% with a slight reduction in the number of employees. Morale is high and union grievances have dropped 25%.

These capsule case histories focus on the results of job enrichment. Now let's briefly summarize the techniques, keeping in mind that the basic idea is to redesign and enrich jobs to increase their content of the "motivators" -- responsibility, achievement, recognition, task interest, advancement, and personal growth. The techniques are:

1. *Natural units of work.* Fragmented tasks are combined into a larger logical grouping. Instead of 10 workers each performing one of 10 steps in an assembly process, for example, each worker might perform all 10, working on a smaller number of products.

2. *Job module design.* Tasks and natural units of tasks are assembled into larger job modules. To add challenge and significance, a natural grouping may be enlarged still more by bringing in other tasks that precede, follow, or are otherwise related. Particularly important is "vertical loading" -- adding to the job meaningful responsibilities from a higher job level. In some cases these tasks and responsibilities may even be brought in from other departments.

3. *Client relationships.* The worker's direct involvement with the "customers" of his effort gives him a greater sense of his accountability from day to day.

4. *Feedback on performance.* The worker should get this from client relationships, supervision, and benchmarks built into the job process itself. It lets him know how he is performing, how others view his work, and how to correct errors.

This is not to say that job enrichment is a cure-all. We believe there is no such thing as an all-purpose technique, and that successful management has to draw on many disciplines. The strength of job enrichment is that it takes a broad and flexible viewpoint, and it views the organization as a total behavioral system.

The traditional structuring of work -- making the workers conform to the technology or the organization -- has now become counterproductive. Workers -- especially younger ones -- consider it a right to work at a job that holds their interest and lets them use their skills to the fullest.

The case histories presented here show how some companies have benefited both themselves and their workers by recognizing the power of work as a motivator. Job enrichment also has a wider significance. There is increasing evidence that such social problems as drug abuse are linked to the widespread boredom, frustration, and alienation of workers in their jobs. Business may look first at the immediate economic benefits of job enrichment. But in the longer run it may be equally important as a way of protecting our stake in a stable and productive society.

Robert Schrank is Project Specialist, Division of National Affairs, The Ford Foundation.

12
On Ending Worker Alienation

Robert Schrank

General Foods Corporation is probably best known to the average citizen for Post breakfast cereal and Jello. They also make pet food. The Gaines Pet Food plant in Topeka, Kansas, is a tiny segment, 120 employees, in a multinational corporation whose annual sales exceed two billion dollars.

In the recent discussions about the quality of working life, the Topeka plant has repeatedly been cited as a prototype workplace. Writing in the *Harvard Business Review* Richard E. Walton, for example, cited the Topeka operation as an example of "How to Counter Alienation in the Plant." This paper is about a recent visit I made to the Topeka plant. It is also a review of some of the issues involved in the discussions of rising worker dissatisfaction.

The Topeka plant has been in operation for 2½ years. The original Gaines Pet Food operation is in Kankakee, Illinois. Lyman Ketchum, who became manager at Kankakee in 1966, is largely credited with the planning and development of the Topeka plan. Ketchum describes the Kankakee operation as it was when he took over:

At that time, rapidly expanding volumes caused overtime operations. Kankakee had a young work force with 53 percent of the males under 28, and 35 percent of the females under 28. It was a capable work force. Rapid turnover in the management ranks, mostly for positive reasons of promotion to other parts of the General Foods system, was evident.

The *management organization* had made extensive use of National Training Laboratories and University of Illinois training programs, the latter at the foreman level and at the middle-management level. But the productivity problems at Kankakee were serious enough to cause General Foods to consider a new pet food plant.

In a sense, this was the beginning of a journey that Ketchum describes as begun in a traditional management concept of a pyramidal organization and culminating in what he now conceives as a highly participative, almost circular, open system organization at the Topeka plant. Walton, in the *Harvard Business Review*, speaking about worker alienation makes two points:

1. The current alienation is not merely a phase that will pass in due time.
2. The innovations needed to correct the problem can simultaneously *enhance the quality of work life* (thereby lessening alienation) and improve productivity. (emphasis added)

Because the Walton article is representative of the views of many behavioral scientists who are concerned with workplace problems, I will use it to discuss some of the issues involved.

An underlying assumption of many people concerned with improving life at the workplace is that any change or improvement must also be reflected in an increase in production. Such an assumption tends to make workers and union people suspicious that it may be just another scheme to get more production out of them; all workplace changes tend to be sponsored by management, with little union or worker participation, thus reinforcing their suspicion that it is a scheme to increase productivity.

Walton was involved in the planning of the Topeka plant. Ketchum describes the work of Walton and other behavioral scientists:

> Our enthusiasm for the practicality of behavioral science grew. We invited Dick Walton (Harvard), Don King (Purdue), and Earl Wolf (University of Illinois). The significant difference between this approach and all of our previous uses of behavioral science knowledge and talent was application of the principles at the *level of the first-line supervisor*, rather than at the top of the organization.

What Ketchum describes as his convergence to a behavioral science approach is further elucidated by Walton's source of worker alienation, the six "Roots of Conflict:"

1. Employees want challenge and personal growth, but work tends to be simplified and specialties tend to be

used repeatedly in work assignments. This pattern exploits the narrow skills of a worker, while limiting his or her opportunities to broaden or develop.

2. Employees want to be included in patterns of mutual influence; they want egalitarian treatment. But organizations are characterized by tall hierarchies, status differentials, and chains of command.

3. Employee commitment to an organization is increasingly influenced by the intrinsic interest of the work itself, the human dignity afforded by management, and the social responsibility reflected in the organization's products. Yet organization practices still emphasize material rewards and employment security and neglect other employee concerns.

4. What employees want from careers, they are apt to want right now. But when organizations design job hierarchies and career paths, they continue to assume that today's workers are as willing to postpone gratifications as were yesterday's workers.

5. Employees want more attention to the emotional aspects of organizational life, such as individual self-esteem, openness between people, and expressions of warmth. Yet organizations emphasize rationality and seldom legitimize the emotional part of the organizational experience.

6. Employees are becoming less driven by competitive urges, less likely to identify competition as the "American Way." Nevertheless, managers continue to plan career patterns, organize work, and design reward systems as if employees valued competition as highly as they used to.

Ketchum, with consultants like Walton, planned the new facility to meet the objectives quoted earlier. The main features of the design as summarized in the Walton article were:
- autonomous work groups
- integrated support functions
- challenging job assignments
- job mobility and rewards for learning
- facilitative leadership
- "managerial" decision information for operators
- self-government for the plant community

— congruent physical and social context
— learning and evolution (assessment and evaluation)

During my visit to the Topeka plant I had an opportunity to observe the operation and speak with a number of people in management and production. The plant is located on the outskirts of Topeka off a main highway, in what not long ago must have been a wheatfield. The building looks like a windowless 15 or 20 story office tower. The square structure encloses a series of huge grain elevator-type storage bins. It is painted white and is lit up at night. At the base of the tower to one side is a more typical one-story commercial factory type structure that covers about a square city block. This is a new canned dog food plant as well as the receiving, packing and shipping area.

The entire Topeka operation is run around the clock by 120 employees. The plant offers an interesting contrast between a continuous process operation and a more traditional manufacturing operation in packaging and warehousing. The work is divided into three groups:

— processing — 8 per shift
— packaging, warehousing — 18 per shift
— management, engineering, or office - 24

How employees were hired. The first employees were recruited more than two years ago through the Kansas Employment Service. About 1200 people applied for jobs; the Employment Service interviews eliminated 600. Team leaders (once called foremen) carried on the interviewing, finally hiring 63 people. The starting rate was $3.40 per hour. (It is now $3.60) The average age of those hired is 30. All employees are high school graduates. One has two years of college. One is female. Fifteen are minority group members.

Criteria for employment were based on work history, with emphasis on a high level of initiative, decision-making ability, and most important, the ability to work as part of a team. (A personal "interaction test" was utilized in the beginning, but then dropped as it was found to be unreliable.)

As work groups were being assembled, prospective employees were interviewed by the team leader (part of management) to see if they would "fit in." Presently all applicants are interviewed by the work groups. If a prospective employee is not approved by the group, he is not hired. All new employees come through the packaging/warehousing group, suggesting this as the lower-status group in the plant. The team leader's job is salaried, the other employees are paid hourly. Of the six team leaders, three came from the Kankakee plant of General Foods, and three are new to the corporation.

Pay scale. The problems of an equitable pay scale have not been completely resolved at Topeka. The original concept was to match salary scale to the individual's knowledge of the plant operations. A new employee starts at the base rate. When the group feels he is ready, he moves from $3.60 to $3.80. The objective is to keep moving up the scale until $4.28 is reached — usually within a year. A committee of employees and management is presently trying to develop a "more equitable wage structure," but its success is uncertain. I did get a sense from some employees of an uneasiness about wages relative to responsibility. This may prove to be a greater problem over time than it has been during the first years of plant operation. While the hiring of new employees seems highly participative, it also harbors shades of potential nepotism through keeping out individuals or groups who do not "fit in." As one employee put it, "one of the fellas just did not fit in — he lacked initiative and could not make decisions when confronted with real problems." Unlike a situation involving a union dispute, there is no procedure for redress outside the existing institutional structure. What prevents a group from "ganging up" on an individual?

Benefits. The plant has a forty-hour, five-day work week. There are no time clocks. Benefits include nine holidays, two weeks vacation a year, five days sick leave approved by the group team leader, and hospitalization through a major insurance concern. Employees are covered by an insurance company hospitalization policy similar to Blue Cross. Average overtime has been four to eight hours a week.

Absenteeism at Topeka runs about one percent. No record is kept of lateness, since people tend to make up time if they come in late. The work group deals with problems of habitual lateness with a warning system as well as the authority to terminate if necessary.

Starting a New Topeka

The management people at Topeka (who are identifiable from the rest of the workforce) emphasized repeatedly that it is much easier to start up a new plant than it is to introduce the Topeka concepts into an existing plant under union contract. "When you have a union situation, you have very different problems," one management person said. "You are limited by the collective bargaining process." He also commented on problems related to the wage scales in Topeka. Because the employees did not participate in establishing the wage scale they tend to be suspicious of it, he said, adding that, if they had it to do over again, the planners would have taken a different approach.

The number of people in the Topeka plant is small, and employees do express the feeling that they have freedom to communicate with anyone they want. They do not have to make appointments, nor do they have to get approval from one level of supervision to see the next.

I queried management about how large an organization could maintain the kind of openness and informality that exists at Topeka. Though I strongly disagree, they felt that the size of the plant was not the critical factor in determining the level of openness. They felt the critical variable was the size of the work group. (The number 17 seemed to be maximum workable group size.) They felt that with a group that size it was possible to have optimum communication within the team, one of two critical elements for a successful work group. The second element is that the relationship between the employees and management be one of basic trust: "If you can win trust, then employees will accept what you are doing." The management people emphasized that in order to win trust there must be full participation, good communication and an open atmosphere in the plant.

There is some evidence to suggest that the question of participation and openness is very much related to plant magnitudes. It is one thing to have an open McGregor (type "Y") management in a plant where 30 or 40 people are present at any given time. It is another thing in a plant of 2,000 or 10,000. It is like comparing a Mom and Pop grocery with A&P. The number of people working in a plant is a critical variable determining the level of openness. In a large organization there is an inevitable control factor. Some one must initiate the direction of the plant. Small units of operation are required to achieve a participative atmosphere in order to function smoothly.

I tried to get some background from Topeka management people who had worked at Kankakee on how they saw the work relationship in that plant. They said that because the Kankakee plant is organized in the American Federation of Grain Millers, it has little or no flexibility. They expressed the view that the union in Kankakee was an obstacle to change — that the union sees its influence being undermined by management's efforts to improve work relationships. One person said: "If people can go and get understanding from the employer, they don't need the union to represent them." A quick glimpse at the history of industry management exposes this notion as fallacious. In the overwhelming majority of cases management tends to be fraught with favoritism and employees unrepresented by a union have been subject to the capricious behavior of immediate supervisors. It is unfortunate that many behavioral scientists and industrial engineers concerned with workplace problems (Walton excepted here) fail to understand the role of the union as a form of worker participation as well as an important change factor at the workplace.

As is the case with most behavioral scientists who write on this subject, Walton, who is most supportive of union participation in other things he has written, fails to mention the role of the union at the workplace in his six needs factors.[1] Union people argue that such factors as Walton's "patterns of mutual influence," "self-esteem," "openness," etc., can be achieved only if employees feel they are not subject to the whims and fancies of management, including low-level supervisors. Trade unionists point out that people at the production level are often the victims of new production schemes that ignore their interests. Ketchum indicated consultation to the first supervisor's level in the planning for Topeka. When then was the participation of the workers in planning the new plant? Could the union have been involved in the planning for Topeka? No one I spoke to in Topeka seemed to be able to lucidly consider the question. Could the reason for this be that unions are still looked upon as outside organizations?

The Topeka Plant Operations

Processing. Gaines dog food consists of corn, soya, pre-mixed vitamins and meat meal. The processing section is automated. Percentages of the mix are predetermined. The process group or team consists of eight people per shift. They run the entire processing operation, beginning with the receipt of raw material via freight-cars which dump them into floor bins where they are then conveyed to storage. The batch man weighs the incoming material, recording the weights in order to insure maximum productivity from the raw material. The expander adds moisture to the product. The dryer takes out moisture for storage. Coating reels apply a tallow which gives the dog food a fatty, meat-like taste even though it is a vegetable. Dust is mixed in to color the Gravy Train red. It is then moved to bins for final packaging.

The whole process is monitored in the fifth-floor control room. This is a large room with a control board about 8 x 30 feet divided into five or six different sections. Two or three people might be in the control room at any one time monitoring the process on a computer. The objective of the processing group is to produce a minimum of 100 tons of dog food per shift, and to keep the packaging room continually supplied with enough processed dog food so that they never run out of material for packaging.

The process team has few, if any, routine functions. They do a small amount of maintenance such as periodic lubrication and monitor the equipment trying to avoid breakdowns. They may attempt to speed up the equipment and try to surpass the 100 ton a shift objective. A red light may go on, signaling a malfunction. The men in the control room will decide what to do. They say that sometimes dog food clogs a chute, or is hung up in one of the feeder bins, and it has to be cleaned. The team is a typical operations maintenance crew where initiative, decision-making, and teamwork are essential to the smooth functioning of the process. Not at all unusual for this type of operation. We also need to keep in mind that only one out of twelve persons interviewed was hired at Topeka precisely because of demonstrated ability in these areas. Judging from my brief visit, this group of workers has a high level of freedom at the workplace, resulting in a high level of satisfaction. A correlation that may be more universal than is presently acknowledged. This was borne out by one of the processors who had been a machinist on the Santa Fe railroad for five years. He likes the Gaines plant "300 percent better," he said, "because I am not stuck on a lathe, turning railroad wheels." Now a trouble shooter, he is free to roam the plant almost at will. He enjoys a number of other freedoms that I will discuss later.

The process team experience at Topeka supports the research of Eva Mueller at the Institute of Social Research, University of Michigan, indicating that workers in automated-type operations tend to be more satisfied with their work than those in traditional production line operations. Some of the processing men had worked on the packaging line. I asked them about that. They said they enjoyed the line experience, since they were getting the bugs out of packaging and they also had a better understanding of the line problems. They saw working on the packaging line as a part of learning the whole process, but were glad to be off it, though they were aware that they would be back on the line periodically.

I was informed that the goal of 300 tons of dog food a day was reached quite often. Prior to the week that I was there, a 400 ton day had been achieved. The employees described the drive for tonnage as "friendly, fierce competition which made the job more interesting." Employees also expressed the feeling that, "management trust us, and that makes this the best place I ever worked." Yet, one cannot help but wonder what the employees at the Kankakee plant of General Foods are feeling about what is happening at Topeka. With but sparse information at hand, I attempted some comparisons between the Kankakee and Topeka production. Topeka is reaching its average of 300 tons a day with 72 people. Kankakee turns out 900 tons a day with 1200 people. We should at least parenthetically acknowledge here the tremendous investment that General Foods has made in building a modern, automated plant. A ratio of tons to people comes out as follows: 4.2 tons per employee in Topeka as against 0.7 tons per employee at Kankakee. Based on comparable wage scales a powerful argument could be made that the Topeka workers have not shared with General Foods the fruits of the increased production. How then are the benefits of increased production divided?

Mitchell Fein, a noted industrial engineer, has argued that, allowing for the $10-million cost of the new plant, which gets amortized over an extended period, the employee effort at Topeka deserves a bonus rate that would give the Topeka workers a share of the increased profit. The issue of sharing the benefits of increased productivity needs to be dealt with by people concerned with workplace problems if workers and unions are to overcome their strong reservations that workplace improvement is simply a scheme to increase production.

Warehousing, Packaging, Shipping. While the processing part of the Topeka plant is a modern, automated operation, the warehousing and packaging is in many ways quite traditional. Workers stand all day long at filling stations, holding or feeding boxes or bags. At one station the worker takes a bag, opens it and puts it under the machine, which automatically drops down a pre-weighed amount of dog food. It then goes onto a conveyer through a sewing machine, which closes the bag, and then to a pallet for warehousing. I would characterize this work as highly repetitive, boring and monotonous, with little autonomy, no growth and no place to go but processing. There remains that lack of freedom to walk around, and socialize: that I have suggested is a critical element in job satisfaction. Yet because workers, like the rest of us, are not of one mold, one worker I spoke to said he liked the packaging line because he did "not want to think about the work anyway." The packaging line, in contrast to processing and because of the nature of the technology, hardly meets any of Walton's conditions for ending alienation. It is high Chaplin-Modern Times material. One of the team leaders said he did not mind the line because he did not have to stay there; he could rotate to processing. There may be a lesson in this example of two very different types of jobs in the same plant. Given the premise that some jobs like packaging and warehousing are lousy, that some lousy jobs are with us to stay, and that some jobs are better than others, then maybe we need to rotate the "dirty work" as they have done in the Topeka plant.

I wonder what will happen over time in Topeka as the jobs in processing become the status position and workers from packaging want to move up. I was told there would be a natural circulation in the plant, and that processing workers would go back to putting in time in the warehousing section. I would predict that over time, the processing group will become the elite and there will be less and less willingness to go back to packaging and warehousing.

Some Theoretical Considerations

In the *Harvard Business Review* Walton cites the Topeka plant as a model for decreasing worker alienation. Topeka is an interesting micro-case study of contrasts between two technologies: one a continuous process type operation and the other a traditional repetitive manufacturing operation, both going on in the same plant. What can be learned from the General Foods

Topeka plant experience? What does the Topeka experience say about Walton's six "Roots of Conflict" as sources of alienation? How does Topeka compare to other manufacturing plants?Much of the literature dealing with workplace problems uses Maslow's concept of a needs hierarchy as the theoretical base. Maslow suggested, as did Marx and Engels, that when man has satisfied his basic needs: food, shelter and clothing, he becomes concerned with a higher order of needs. Engels suggested that culture begins with the production of surplus — meaning that surplus permits time for things other than acquiring food, shelter, and clothing. Maslow, in a similar vein, suggested that when basic needs are satisfied man becomes concerned with a higher order of needs having to do with autonomy, creativity and self-actualization.

Walton's definition of workplace problems in the "Roots of Conflict" is similar to the views of other behavioral scientists and differs to the extent that he does not include Maslow's factors of "creativity" and "self-actualization." Walton, I am quite sure, would argue that his non-acceptance of these two factors makes his position considerably different from other behavioral scientists. Well, maybe it does, but I would argue that a more basic issue at stake is the relationship of the individual to the institution. Can an individual worker as Walton suggests achieve autonomy or self control in an institution which has as its primary, and in many cases only, objective increased profit?

I am fearful that at least some of the definitions of workplace problems have grown out of the behavioral science gardens of people's needs, satisfactions, wishes, and wants. Some of the difficulty may be semantic, including concepts such as needs, autonomy, and control are highly relative. (Compared to what?) For instance, how one's value system looks at manual work. Intellectuals tend to view manual work as some kind of horror. They would be surprised that many manual workers are horrified at the prospect of having to sit and write all day. One's frame of reference may have more to do with how work is perceived rather than some claimed objectivity of a test or questionnaire. Terms like needs, satisfaction, autonomy, growth and most important, alienation have become so all-encompassing that I am not sure they have any distinct meaning any longer.

Let us examine Marx and Maslow as two extremes, leaving aside Walton for the moment. A basic difference between Marx and Maslow is that Marx's assumptions about alienation are based on the conflict between the private ownership of the means and products of production and the social nature of the factory. Marx uses the term alienation to describe the factory workers' relation to the raw material, the process or means, and the finished product, over none of which does he have control. The concept is based on an economic and social relationship. Maslow's concept of alienation, on the other hand, is based primarily on the psychological needs of some individuals.

Once again, Walton excerpts himself from Maslovian influence and has stated he would not apply the terms "creativity" or "self-actualization" to factory workers because it is unrealistic. Maslow himself, in *Eupsychian Management*, acknowledges that he did not think of such concepts as self-actualization or peak experiences applying to factory workers. He further pointed out that he had never tested his self-actualization material on subjects other than college students. It seems odd that many writers other than Walton dealing with workers and workplace problems seized on the Maslow schema as an explanation of worker dissatisfaction without at least questioning the basis of concepts such as autonomy, participation, creativity or self-actualization as they apply to mass production workplaces. I have an uneasy feeling that many people who suggest such concepts could be applied to mass production technology were either ignorant of what goes on in manufacturing plants or vulgarized the meaning of these concepts. The latter could be interpreted as creating straw men to avoid dealing with real ones, i.e., excusing inadequate pay and poor working conditions by concentrating on individual psyches.

The Nature of Mass Production

Any discussion of workplace problems requires some understanding of mass production technology, which is based on some locked-in granite assumptions. All process and manufacture are pre-designed, pre-engineered, and pre-planned down to the smallest detail. "Time is money." In order to guarantee cost replication and interchangeability, every step of the production process is planned, engineered and timed. Schedules must be strictly adhered to. No deviation from a specification is permitted. The successful completion of the final product, including costs, depends upon everyone adhering to a master plan. Given this as the basic nature of mass production, where can there possibly be opportunities for such highly individualistic activity as autonomy, creatively and self-actualization? I am afraid they are few—if any at all. Then why do social scientists concered with workplace problems keep suggesting this paradigm, and insist management can overcome boredom, monotony and alienation among factory workers by giving them an opportunity to be creative, autonomous and self-actualizing? It is either ignorance about how mass production systems operate or a vulgar definition of what enhances the quality of work life. At any rate it will not help to bring about badly needed changes.

In many years of working in and around factories, I did not observe many factory workers who had much concern about autonomy, creativity or self-actualization. There was much concern over pay, security, working conditions, and, most importantly, dignified treatment. The latter was usually achieved by unionization, since people were no longer subject to capricious behavior of supervisors. The level of freedom to circulate in the plant was a critical element in how workers felt about the place. Many people writing on workplace problems are not familiar with the culture of the people who inhabit factories. Social scientists tend to seek out pathologies, and in the process lose the quality of the whole gestalt.

Workers' lives, like most peoples', are divided between work, leisure, family, chores, etc. Yet, there do seem to be some universals everyone, including school teachers want — shorter work hours, probably to be more autonomous, travel, go fishing, be creative, build something (do-it-yourself), self-actualize, or start a new career. And, like most other people, workers understand the limitations on satisfying their needs and desires in the factory. They are very much aware of both the magic and the curse of mass production technology. It is magical to see a batch of raw material start in at one end of a plant and come out as a working thingamajig on the other. It may also be a curse to keep doing the same little task over and over again, but they know that this is the secret of the magic. Workers understand this as a group; it is "our secret." They make the best of the life in the plant with humor, camaraderie and what sometimes becomes a rich social life. When they do participate in decision making, it is mostly through collective bargaining by controls over safety and agreements on productivity levels, etc.

Marx suggested a collective sense of alienation as a source of worker discontent which would create continuous problems for capitalist societies. "Countering alienation," then, could be considered from the viewpoint of worker unrest as a threat to corporate stability. Or, it might be considered from the viewpoint of the individual worker being unhappy and dissatisfied with his job.

Most people concerned with workplace problems today, however, both in Europe and in the U.S., start with a psychological or individual pathological approach rather than the socio-economic mirror to reflect on these issues. There is also a socio-technical school that suggests human and technological needs can be made congruent. The process department at Topeka may be a prototype for this approach.

Contemporary difficulty with Marx's concept of alienation grows out of grave doubts over whether socialist or worker ownership and control of the means of production has given the workers on the plant floor any greater autonomy or control over the means of production, or the finished product, than workers in capitalist countries. In socialist countries, factory workers find themselves in a relationship with the means of production that seems to be endemic to factories; highly repetitive work, pre-planned and pre-engineered. There seems to be some exception in how plants are run in Yugoslavia to the extent that workers have some say in who manages and how. But the organization of the work process itself and the tasks remain similar to all factory production techniques.[2] Marx's concept of alienation failed to note that it was, inherent in the nature of mass production technology, *regardless of who owned it*. The socialist countries, far from finding a new way to produce things, have, if anything, emulated the efficiency of the capitalistic model to its smallest detail.

The American labor movement has traditionally dealt with "alienation" by seeking the most for its workers in pay and benefits, while reducing the amount of time they spend at the job. Until we find an alternative to the factory system, history may yet reveal that this is the best and most universal response to a negative situation.

Craftsmanship vs. Mass Production

Some of the suggestions for improving the quality of work life reflect a nostalgia for the return to craftsmanship. In his 1844 manuscripts, Marx expresses a sadness over the decline of the Renaissance craftsman. Concepts such as autonomy, creativity, decision-making, and control of one's tools are qualities that are associated with hand work. While I am extremely empathetic with that nostalgia, I am also convinced that notions of bringing back craftsmanship are based on either fantasy or ignorance about mass production. There is so little of traditional craftsmanship surviving, I do not think we even know what the term means anymore.

I spent about 15 years of my early working life as a skilled machinist and a toolmaker. Many people consider that craftsmanship. It was not craftsmanship in the traditional sense. I made no decisions about the raw material, the process, or the product. My skill, as distinguished from craftsmanship, was the ability to follow extremely detailed instruction to very fine tolerances. That requires a certain kind of skill, not craftsmanship, and above all, no creativity. I remember my old boss, to whom I was apprenticed, repeating over and over, follow the prints. He was referring, of course to the blueprints.

I tried to discover the decline of craftsmanship. I found some clues in *Art and the Industrial Revolution* by Klingender. He talks about the end of craftsmanship, relating how in 1830 the owners of the Wedgewood Pottery hired a salesman to find out what people were interested in buying. The Queen on a horse seemed to be of popular interest. Wedgewood hired a designer to create a series of ceramics with the Queen on a horseback motif. That act of engaging a salesman and a designer, both of whom were responding to a market, was the beginning of the end of craftsmanship. Klingender says as a result of the designer, the Wedgewood potter became, at best, an "inventor" who could now decide how to do it, but no longer what to do.

As engineers moved into factory production, the "how to do it" became the next victim. Now companies decided what was the best way to do it. The best known of these work engineers was Frederick Taylor. He was obsessed with the idea that a man should be like a part of the machine. Thus, even the "inventor," trying to decide "how to do it" soon disappeared when equipment and machinery were designed for specific functions, and workers lost control over the method as well as the product.

The final blow came with the notion of interchangeability of parts. The result was Taylor's phenomenally successful effort to fragment all tasks to their smallest element so as to eliminate any possible judgment on the part of the worker — thus assuring no variation in the final product. And it worked. The factory proved to be productive beyond the engineer's wildest dreams. This success is called the industrial revolution; that it was.

One Further General Observation

The term "Hawthorne effect" grew out of the psychological impact of considerable attention paid to workers in experiments at the Hawthorne works of Western Electric in 1929. The workers in that experiment felt they were quite special, and so behaved by feeling better about themselves and their work. Their behavior was influenced by the effort of just being in the experiment. What is the effect on workers today of an unusual amount of attention from television, news and magazine stories, and an endless stream of visitors? Topeka provides us with our first clues. Workers become celebrities. They read about themselves, see one another on television, and are continuously interviewed. This is beyond Hawthorne. This is the "Topeka euphoria."

Topeka and the "Roots of Conflict"

I would like to look at Walton's six "Roots of Conflict" or alienation, and apply them to Topeka, using processing and packaging as differential settings. The plant should be accepted as is, given that the product, the formula and process at Topeka are all established and fixed by the technology.

What happens when an employee has mastered all the functions within the plant? How does he achieve what Walton calls broadening his opportunities to assure his development? Within the universe of the Topeka plant, an employee, carefully screened as a high achiever, is able to master nearly everything there is to know in a few months. One can argue that after that there is no place to broaden yourself but *out* of the plant. That concept should support a high turnover rate since the plant, because of its small size, has limited opportunities. (Or does one go somewhere else in General Foods? Are there opportunities for the bottom of the pyramid to move up?)

Applying the first "Root of Conflict" (challenge and growth vs. simplification and repetition) to the packaging plant, it is difficult to see the development of a growth pattern. A few simple line operations (I counted nine at most) are endlessly repeated. The line operator must keep up with the machine, filling a box or bag every few seconds. There is little opportunity for growth or challenge occuring when one does nine movements by rote. One fellow on the line said he liked it because he "didn't have to think about dog food anymore." The machine designer to me kept saying, "automate these jobs out." Applying my own criteria of level of freedom, the line operator has little or no freedom to move around and socialize that the processing group has. To leave his station, he must obtain relief, which is a good indicator that work is rigidly designed.

Applying "challenge and personal growth" to the processing group, one gets a different picture. Here the key factor is the computer, which actually controls the process. The process workers make corrections suggested by the computer and trouble shoots when the computer indicates malfunction. *The process worker has no direct line function.* His work is not repetitive. There is an element of surprise which creates interest. Most important, he has total freedom to move around, socialize, hide, talk, use the telephone and visit other parts of the workplace. Given decent wages, benefits and working conditions, I believe the most neglected element of worker satisfaction is the freedom to socialize at the workplace. This means full use of the telephones to make and receive calls, to have available all the general amenities which satisfy the need for personal interaction. The freedom to interact is *real.* The notions of "growth," "challenge," and "autonomy" in a fixed, repetitive operation tend to be an illusion.

The process workers at Topeka have the freedoms indicated. We sat around in the computer control room for a couple of hours and had a most enjoyable kaffeeklatsch. I repeat, for emphasis, these non-work, or what I have called the freedom aspects of the job, may be more important as job satisfiers than trying to build autonomy, creativity, and self-actualization into repetitive tasks which have been precisely designed to eliminate all those elements.

To suggest "personal growth" as a result of the rotation of some repetitive task is fallacious. The greatest benefit of rotation may be to increase one's socializing orbit. Rotation may reduce monotony or boredom for some workers, but the reduction of a negative element does not necessarily create its opposite: a positive element. Design and tooling technology require that every step in the production process be performed according to specification. The sequence of steps may be rearranged, but I would hope that is not what is meant by "challenge" or "autonomy."

Walton's second "Root of Conflict" is the employees desire to be included in "patterns of mutual influence." In the planning group for the Topeka plant, no workers were included. Management people did the planning. Yet much of the writing about Topeka is how good it is for the workers. The "mutual influence" of the Topeka employees is limited to what the computer or packaging line permits — no more, no less. If one looks for a pattern beyond Topeka into General Foods, it becomes quite vague. Lyman Ketchum acknowledges his own lack of influence in General Foods in a paper he presented to the Arden House Conference on the Quality of Working Life.

Walton says that organizations are "characterized by tall hierarchies." Within the Topeka plant there is not much of a hierarchy because of the small size of the operation. What about the tall hierarchy of General Foods? It is difficult to find any evidence that it has changed as a result of Topeka. Topeka is a small island in the sea of General Foods. Because the island is small, the hierarchy is small. But it is there. There is a hierarchical delineation of decision-making responsiblity. That is the way factories are run. As suggested earlier, we do not know any other way. There is an effort in Topeka to hide the hierarchy because I suspect some of the local people might like to get rid of it; but do they have an alternative? What has happened in Topeka is that the processing jobs have been homogenized. A workforce was recruited with a strong capacity to handle these jobs. The status hierarchies that exist in a traditional plant like Kankakee will emerge in time as differential capability gets reflected in the wage scale and as the plant size increases.

Hierarchies tend to develop and harden as organizations based on the pyramidal design become institutionalized. I predict that will happen in Topeka. We simply have not yet developed an operational model of a plant organization that is not hierarchical. What is sometimes done instead is to make the chain of command more subtle, hoping in that way to "hide" the hierarchy. In that sense Topeka's operation becomes game playing, and the foreman becomes a "team leader." He is responsible for the team's activity. He is a "human relations" supervisor which should make him a better team leader, as long as the team wins the productivity goal.

If conflict develops in Topeka, I think the team leader will become once again the foreman. Let the home office of General Foods become disenchanted with production at Topeka, and the current foggy hierarchy of responsibility will disappear. The pyramid will light up like Las Vegas at midnight. The Topeka plant, like all continuous process plants of this nature, requires a high level of judgment from its process operators in order to keep it moving. It is unfortunate that this simple fact of technology tends to get confused with eliminating alienation through autonomy, control and decision-making.

The third Walton conflict states that: "Employee commitment to an organization is increasingly influenced by the intrinsic interest of the work itself," the human dignity afforded by management, and the social responsibility reflected in the organization's "products." This notion is set forth by Frederick Herzberg in his work enrichment paper, suggesting that job satisfaction must be part of the work itself. He calls benefits "hygiene factors" and suggests that they will not overcome dissatisfaction that stems from the work itself. This concept of job enrichment represents another longing to get back to craftsmanship — a return to the good old days. In a way it was Marx's longing too. A noble idea, but most often suggested by people more knowledgeable in philosophy or the behavioral sciences than in technology. Start with the salesman and the designer at Wedgewood, now add design, tool, production and industrial engineers and it should be obvious that craftsmanship in the plant or factory is over. Yet, the dream and desire to return to the village smithy remains. It appears in literature quite regularly — usually under the guise of "job enlargement," "autonomy," and "skill development," all of which are contradictory to mass production techniques. Enriching a job in manufacture means adding repetitive tasks. That does not make it creative or autonomous, nor does it stimulate growth. Some workers prefer multiple tasks, others prefer a single task, but neither should be called "a higher order of need."

Process work at Topeka is not craftsmanship. It has an important element of challenge because it is trouble shooting. It can be compared to a servicing function rather than a manufacturing operation. That can be challenging because one may make decisions about what is wrong and why. On the other hand, the packaging line at Topeka is limited to a few simple, repetitive, boring operations in front of a filling machine. Behavioral scientists underestimate workers when they suggest that by adding together repetitive tasks they have enriched a job and made it challenging. I strongly believe that the intrinsic reward given the process workers at Topeka is the freedom they enjoy in the plant. The freedom involves not only being able to roam and socialize at will; it also has the status of feeling more like managers than workers — of not being line operators. The satisfaction that comes from this freedom is the key factor in creating the commitment to pet food and General Foods.

The "human dignity" that Walton speaks of is a management style at Topeka. Having met Lyman Ketchum on a number of occasions, I would give him a large share of the credit for that. It would be my hunch that in managing any plant, Ketchum would create a McGreggor (type "Y") humanistic open management operation. But the "Ketchums" may be unusual in management. I often wonder why, after all the years of human relations talk in management, so little of it seems to have taken hold.

As for social responsibility reflected in the organization's products, I must confess, I was overwhelmed by the amount of pet food produced in this country. Topeka makes 300-400 tons a shift. The entire industry manufactures approximately two million tons of dog food a year! That tells us something about productivity.

I am not a dog hater! When I was a kid we had a dog. He used to get the scraps off the table. That was a good way to recycle garbage and feed your dog. I would find it difficult to get any sense of social responsibility from making dog food or a large portion of the huge variety of other mass produced items factory workers make. But that judgment very much depends on one's value system. From a social responsibility point of view, it would seem to me to be an alienating experience to make 300 tons of dog food a day out of nature's beautiful raw materials that could feed hungry children.

Topeka and the Unions

The grain handlers union has made some efforts to organize Topeka but without success. They believe Topeka was set up to eliminate the union and, over time, the workers will pay for it as a result of diminished security. Mitchell Fein argues quite vehemently that General Foods has not made an equitable distribution of the increased profits which result from increased productivity at Topeka. Union people argue that this factor gets lost in the issues of job satisfaction. Productivity is four times higher at Topeka than in Kankakee.

Walton says that organizational practice still emphasizes material rewards — employment security — and neglects other employee concerns. In Maslow's hierarchy of needs schema, when the intrinsic rewards of security, safety, food, shelter and clothing are taken care of, a higher order of need develops. The difficulty with these concepts is deciding when the basic need for security and safety has been achieved. This is a highly relative matter, depending on education, place, *expectation*, and most importantly, the relationship of the rewards to the individual employee and the company profits. Sharing some of the increased profit with the 72 plant employees would demonstrate the egalitarianism Walton speaks about. One of the reasons that unions are suspect of workplace behaviorists is their failure to consider how the benefits of increased productivity are shared.

Walton's fourth "Root of Conflict" ("What employees want from careers, they are apt to want *right now*"), somehow suggests that today's worker is less able or willing to postpone gratification.

While money is still the most important gratifier of all, it is no longer the only one. There are many others, including the amenities and freedoms at the workplace. If "instant gratifiers" such as participation, job enrichment, autonomous work groups, etc., are seen as substitutes for income, however, workplace problems will be exacerbated. In a consumer society, it is the things that money can buy that enable workers to become status gratified. It is what they can own that is important. Are they different from the rest of society? I think not. It is mythical to suggest that job hierarchies and career paths can be designed to give workers instant gratification. Upward mobility is always limited by less room at the top of the pyramid. To suggest otherwise creates false expectations.

The processing division of the Topeka plant satisfies what I consider the kind of gratification possible at the workplace — freedom to socialize, and the opportunity not to be stuck in one spot with one task. Similar situations exist in many process type operations, such as chemical and food processing plants, which are often dependent on the kind of team work done at Topeka.

Because process workers are on standby or monitoring a good part of the time, they can sit around, drink coffee or coke, talk, smoke, scratch themselves — all of which I define as the schmooze factor, which is a social group interaction about a subject matter not particularly related to the goals or objectives of the organization. I sat with three men in the control room in Topeka having coffee, our feet up on the table. While they kept an eye on that big board, we schmoozed about whether it is better to live in the city or the country, whether girls in Topeka wear brassieres, and what unions can do for you, anyhow. Once somebody suggested, "Why don't we speed the mill grinder or the conveyer a bit?" That precipitated the pushing of a button. Then we went back to schmoozing. Schmoozing is common in offices, universities, processing plants, and many service industries. It occurs much less in manufacturing plants and, at times, almost surreptitiously. It would have been impossible for me to sit with three workers on a manufacturing line without permission of the management if it were not a coffee break, a lunch hour, or after work. Similarly, in the packaging room at Topeka, you could not schmooze with someone on the line unless he was given relief.

How are the differences between process and packaging handled in Topeka? There is a rotation. I call it sharing the lousy jobs. I have a strong hunch that this may well be the only way society can begin to deal with necessary, but undesirable work.

Walton's fifth "Root of Conflict" is the employees' need for attention to their "emotional aspects," such as individual self-esteem, openness, expressions of warmth, etc. That exists in Topeka because of the smallness of the plant, the degree that one fits into the team, and the management style. The qualities of openness, warmth, and support are interesting because they are social qualities controlled by the institutional atmosphere. Does the institution permit employees to visit, have access to a variety of areas, support one another, use the telephone — in a word to schmooze? These qualities are not related to the work itself as suggested by Herzberg and others. They are influenced by the nature of the work and how it is organized. work can be organized in ways that permit a maximum amount of freedom on the job. The opposite seems to be the case in most manufacturing plants, unfortunately, they are designed with a maximum amount of employee time at a given spot. I consider this a most important dissatisfier because it deprives factory workers of freedoms enjoyed by most white collar and service workers.

A short time ago, before a Senate Subcommittee on workplace problems, I testified that the first thing I would do for blue collar workers to increase their work satisfaction is to grant them equal rights with the rest of us by permitting them free use of the telephone. Those of us who take it for granted underestimate the role of the telephone as a socializer and, as a reliever of monotony and boredom. How many times during the day might a white collar worker or a professional pick up the phone and dial a friend? The discussion might be inconsequential or silly, but it helps relieve tedium, and so makes the work easier. The telephone creates a vast network for intimate contact in an unrelated world.

Walton's sixth "Root of Conflict" has to do with lessened competition among workers. Topeka does not serve as an example. Quite the contrary — a large part of its success is the high motivation that comes from the fierce competitions. The first is to beat that 300 tons of dog food a shift. I would not have believed that workers could get that excited over producing dog food. The second is to beat the next shift and then beat packaging. The third is to know the most about the plant. That will eventually create a hierarchy based on the smartest is the firstest. Who is the chief beneficiary of this competitiveness? The company, of course. Unions would say this business of workers competing against each other creates speed-ups and will end by victimizing those who cannot compete. Elements of that appear in Topeka already. Workers say things like: "If he can't cut the mustard, he'll have to go." Although the autonomous work group may seem like a highly democratic structure, I am not sure that some form of protection for individuals is not needed to guard against repression and unjust behavior. The situation is not non-analogous to a university professor without tenure.

Unions have been a major factor in reducing competitiveness by trying to reach agreements as to what constitutes a fair day's work. I do not know that there is a fair day's work at Topeka. One management person said the men were so anxious to increase the output that on occasion they would endanger the equipment by overspeeding it in an attempt to break shift records.

It is unfortunate for those who are trying to improve workplaces that Topeka does not have a union. The Topeka process plant is a demonstration of what a particular technology and a humane management can do. With the Kankakee plant of General Foods under contract to a union, the Topeka experiment will be seen, rightly or wrongly, as a way to get rid of the union. I do not believe that was at all the motivation of the management group that designed the Topeka plant. Management tends to see unions in an adversary role, so if you can avoid having them, why not. Worker participation will always be highly questionable if there is no way for workers to be assured of certain basic securities — somewhat like tenure for professors. Another new plant is being considered in Lafayette. The union issue will come up there again. Can the management consider a role for the union?

The increased productivity of Topeka over Kankakee has cost a number of workers their jobs. The issue of "security" in the face of a new model workplace is not dealt with either at Topeka or by writers about Topeka. What happens in an existing plant when production is increased with the support and help of the workers and some of them then become superfluous? The behavioral scientists feeling of group support is expressed when workers behave as a team and support each other in face of possible layoffs. When a worker says, "I'm concerned about this man whom I've been working with. I don't want him to lose his job," this is a real sense of commitment and involves the most non-alienated behavior.

On the plant level the union may express the best humanitarian non-alienated qualities of the workforce. People concerned with quality of life at the workplace need to understand the role of unions. Unfortunately, many are employed by management, and so they tend to be less than fearless on this issue. It would be extremely helpful if business management schools, writers, and others concerned with the institutions of work would begin to think about the role of the union in humanizing the workplace. The unions too, will need to begin to understand more about the nature of work organization and how workplaces operate. If they insist on limiting their role to traditional collective bargaining issues, then the problems of workplace reorganization may just pass them by. The UAW has recognized this problem in its recent bargaining with the auto industry. Joint committees were established to examine issues of workplace organization and operation. A giant step forward for a major union. People concerned with workplaces should understand that unions have been dealing with workplace problems for a long time, and they are an important institution of participation. Without the reparticipation, suspicion will continue to grow amongst labor people that workplace changes are designed to counter union organization. To catch up the issue of workplace reorganization in an anti-union charge would be most unfortunate — but the movement toward improving the quality of life will be impaired without worker inputs and participation vis-a-vis the union.

The Topeka plant is an example of what can be achieved with a small, new, continuous process plant, a carefully selected group of employees, and a highly humane local management. The experience can be very helpful in learning more about humanizing workplaces. The people involved in planning and developing should be congratulated for their efforts in spite of the shortcomings I have cited.

---

1. Walton is quick to disassociate himself from behavioral scientists who would "avoid" or "get rid of" unions. In his working paper "QWL Indicators—Prospects and Problems" (Graduate School of Business Administration, Harvard University), he includes a variety of criteria for improving the quality of working life which have long been the subject of collective bargaining and the goals of labor legislation. The existence of unions, however, is not cited. Walton does mention productivity bargaining under "Revitalization and Reform" in the *HBR* article discussed here.

2. Ichak Adizes, "Industrial Democracy, Yogoslav Style."

Harold M.F. Rush is in management research for The Conference Board.

This article is reprinted from the April 1973 issue of **The Conference Board RECORD,** *pp. 34-39.*

13

A Nonpartisan View of Participative Management

Harold M. F. Rush

Introduction

The principles of participative management, behavioral scientists argue, may be applied at any level of the organization. Indeed, many of the firms participating in a recent Conference Board study report using participative methods for a large number of activities—even if they do not always use them for lower level employees.

In all the activities examined here, there are differences in the management styles of the OD companies and the non-OD companies. While rank-and-file employee participation is practiced in some non-OD companies in almost all of the activities, its use is found to be considerably less than in OD companies.

Profile of Worker Discontent

"Alienation" is a word that seems to appear today whenever there is a discussion of the characteristics of America's workforce. Social critics frequently attribute the alienated workers' discontent to the "dehumanization of work," and many a polemic has been directed against poor quality of the working life. Indeed, the problem of poor motivation—when it's argued to result in lowered productivity—is obvious cause for concern among the business community and to the nation as a whole. This year that concern became official with the report of a special inquiry by HEW into the problem of worker alienation.[1]

While it is generally agreed that a large part of the working population is apathetic—disenchanted by the work it does—a similar consensus on the remedy for the situation is wanting. Some see the solution as a matter of shortening the hours or lessening the number of days worked in order to provide more leisure or elective time for workers. Others prescribe revisions of work sequences in several kinds of job design, hoping to enlarge or enrich the jobs people hold. Still others recommend greater worker involvement in the decisions that affect them through the practice of "participative management."

Participation is a recurring theme in the management literature of the past two decades, for the concepts of employee participation are cardinal tenets of the behavioral science or "organization development" school of managing. Partisans of participative management often display missionary zeal as champions of a new order in which employees join with management in setting goals, solving problems, and managing tasks and jobs on an everyday basis.

Still, the question remains: is participative management an ideal or a reality? In pursuit of an answer, The Conference Board recently completed a study of methods designed to improve the effectiveness of business organizations.[2] The 147 U.S. and Canadian firms that participated in the study were designated, by a panel of nationally known behavioral science theorists and practitioners, as "OD companies" or "non-OD companies"—that is, as firms that actually practice the concepts of *organization development* or as those that do not. Each company was surveyed in detail about several kinds of corporate activities, and the responses of the OD and non-OD companies were compared.

Although the sample was small—45 OD and 102 non-OD companies—and the possiblity of "rater bias" must be taken into account, there is good reason to conclude from the results of the study that the OD companies do, in fact, try more often than non-OD companies to translate the concepts of participation into actual practice. And this would seem to confirm the differences in the relative value placed upon participative management philosophy by the two groups of companies.

Measuring Participation

Participation may occur in any number of circumstances and at any of all hierarchical levels of the organization. However, although there is widespread intellectual acceptance of the concept of participation as a means of humanizing work and of gaining greater employee motivation, in most instances, according to the survey, *participation occurs only at the upper levels of the organization.* Still, proponents of the participative style management insist that the concept be applied wherever appropriate, in all jobs and at all levels of the organization. And for them, the "acid test" of commitment to real participation is the involvement of employees at the rank-and-file level of the organization. Thus, measuring degrees of involvement becomes important.

The most commonly used methods of assessing employee attitudes is through some kind of systematic attitude measurement. This is usually accomplished by a detailed survey administered at periodic intervals, or at a time of change in policy or practice. Of the 102 non-OD companies participating in The Conference Board's study, only 38% report the use of such surveys, compared with 71% of the OD companies. Only 16% of the non-OD companies include employees at all levels in these surveys, while 29% of the OD companies cover the whole organization in their surveys.

Attitude Survey Practices		Table 1.
	Non-OD Companies (N = 102)	*OD Companies* (N = 45)
Company conducts systematic surveys	39 (38%)	32 (71%)
Surveys include all organizational levels	16 (16%)	13 (29%)
Surveys include nonmanagement, "white collar" employees	19 (19%)	14 (31%)
Surveys include "blue collar" employees	15 (15%)	12 (27%)
All those surveyed received feedback	34 (33%)	28 (62%)
Work groups use survey data for own improvement	9 (8%)	23 (51%)

Moreover, of those companies that do not include the entire organization, 31% of the OD companies report that white collar, nonmanagerial employees are surveyed, and 27% say they include blue collar employees. White collar employees are included in attitude surveys by only 19% of the non-OD companies, and blue collar employees by just 15% (Table 1).

What happens to the information after it is collected varies from company to company. Generally it is used to assess the fundamental climate of the organization—the problems employees encounter in the course of their work, their understanding of goals and objectives that determine the quantity, pace, and quality of their work, and the nature of the interpersonal relationships that are considered so vital to the work environment. Sometimes management may compare these attitudes with attitudes at another point of time, or may assess employee acceptance of changes effected or anticipated. Whatever the uses of the attitude surveys, most behavioral scientists agree that the persons participating in the surveys have a right to know the results, whether or not the findings put the company and management in a favorable light. Thus, it is interesting to note that only a third of the non-OD companies The Conference Board studied give such feedback to their employee participants, while more than 60% of the OD companies regularly furnish results to those surveyed (Table 1).

A psychologist employed by a large international chemical company complained about his company's use of attitude survey data. "Too often," he stated, "we ask for employee attitudes and opinions in great detail, but in most cases, once we have the data, nothing is done with it. And this is because the employees are telling management things that management doesn't want to hear, so management ignores the findings. Then they wonder why we continue to have discontent, grievances, and strikes. It would be better not to ask the employees what they believe and feel than to ask them and do nothing. For this reason, I wish we didn't go through the motions of collecting attitudinal data. At least we wouldn't be insulting the employees."

That such survey data can be extremely valuable is a feeling shared by many of the managers who responded to the Board's questions. They believe that sources of dissatisfaction uncovered by elaborate surveys in which employees speak candidly, and with anonymity, may be a most valuable source of information about working conditions and practices for management. Some even believe that the survey data can be used as a basis for modifications, corrections, or improvements by the employees themselves, since those closest to the problem have a better grasp of its entirety and are most capable of correcting it—an obvious example of the application of shared responsibility. More than half of the OD companies, compared with only 8% of the non-OD companies, report using attitude survey data as the basis for improving employee work situations (Table 1).

Group Problem Solving

It is common knowledge that the growth and effectiveness of

individuals and organizations are closely tied to their ability to identify and solve the problems they encounter. In business firms these problems may be related to the economic or material aspects of the organization, or they may take the form of interpersonal problems between peers, subordinates, and superiors as they relate to each other in the work environment. Often the problems are both economic and interpersonal.

Working on the premise that "all of us know more than any one of us knows," many organizations undertake problem identification and resolution in a group setting. Here, ideally, several perspectives and kinds of expertise can be brought to bear upon the problem. Further, this participative-group approach to problem solving is undertaken on the assumption that people will be more committed to overcoming a problem if they have helped to decide upon the strategy to be used.

How frequently is the approach taken? Nearly half of the non-OD companies in the Board's study responded that they use participative-group methods of problem solving, and virtually all the OD companies report similar methods (Table 2). But a more pronounced difference between the designated groups appears when we analyze the composition of the problem solving groups.

Problem Solving and Goal Setting	Table 2.	
	Non-OD Companies (N = 102)	*OD Companies* (N = 45)
Company uses participative-group methods of problem solving	48 (47%)	44 (98%)
All levels participate in problem solving	7 (6%)	18 (40%)
Lower management and rank and file participate in problem solving	4 (4%)	7 (16%)
Rank and file help to set short-range goals	0 (0%)	14 (31%)

Forty percent of the OD companies report that they use group methods for problem solving at all levels within the organization, wherever appropriate. This contrasts sharply with the 6% of the non-OD firms that report involvement of all levels and jobs in the group problem solving process.

Among those companies that do not use participative-group methods at all levels, seven firms (16%) in the OD group of companies do at least involve lower management and rank-and-file employees in the acitivity. Four firms (4%) in the non-OD group do the same.

Although a large number of non-OD companies report using some participative-group methods for problem solving, few carry the process into the lower levels of the organization. Thus, the participatory approach remains confined to the upper ranks of management and among scientific and professional employees. By comparison, a majority of the OD firms include employees at lower levels.

Goal Setting

In the matter of goal setting, a process closely allied to problem solving, appropriateness of participation is considered a key variable. For example, lower levels of the corporate hierarchy are thought to have neither the perspective nor the expertise to establish the long-range goals of the organization. The appropriate level for this kind of goal setting is clearly at the top of the organization, where responsibility and accountability for the larger goals and objectives lie.

In the setting of short-range goals, however, it is thought practicable to include those persons responsible for achieving them. For these goals not only have shorter time spans, but their achievement can be more easily controlled through the efforts of employees at the work group level. Behavioral scientists posit, moreover, that it is not only appropriate but most desirable in terms of motivation that the employees who have responsiblity for working towards short-range goals have a voice in establishing the goals.

Of course, work groups do not set goals at random. Short-range goals are established within the larger framework of long-range corporate goals, even in the most permissive or participative organizations. Further, the level of employees who help to set short-range goals is highly dependent upon the scope and nature of the goals under consideration. The Conference Board study reveals that while participation in the setting of short-goals may take place at all levels of supervision, it is noticeably lacking at the rank-and-file employee level. Even among the OD companies, only 14 firms—less than a third of the OD company sample—report the involvement of rank-and-file in short-range goal setting (Table 2). But, even that small number of companies stands in marked contrast to the non-OD companies, *none* of which report involvement at that level.

Communication

In a very real sense, communication is the lifeblood of an organization's operation. Communication is also, for behavioral scientists as well as practitioners, a major focus of organization development programs. They speak of communication in terms of the *process*, as distinguished from the media. Communication for them includes everything that transpires as people attempt to convey information, ideas, or feelings, and feedback is an integral component. The exercises used to improve communication among individuals and groups most often take place in face-to-face small group settings, and the emphasis is on experiential learning, rather than intellectual or "head level" learning.

The Conference Board study shows that such exercises take place almost exclusively at the managerial levels of the companies. Seventeen (17%) of the non-OD companies report experience-based communication activities, but only two of them include all employee levels in their programs. Two others conduct special exercises to improve communication exclusively among rank-and-file employees. While 38 (84%) of the OD companies conduct experience-based activities, only twelve include all levels. Eight of the OD companies (18%) hold communication improvement activities at the rank-and-file level. Exercises to improve communication between rank-and-file employees and their superiors, first line supervision, are reported by only 3% of the non-OD sample; the figure is 18% for the OD sample (Table 3).

Communication Improvement and Conflict Resolution		Table 3.
	Non-OD Companies (N = 102)	*OD Companies* (N = 45)
Companies using experiential exercises to improve communication process	17 (17%)	38 (84%)
Communication exercises include all organizational levels	2 (2%)	12 (27%)
Communication exercises *within* rank and file groups	2 (2%)	8 (18%)
Communication *between* rank and file and first-line supervision	3 (3%)	8 (18%)
Company has conflict resolution activities	22 (22%)	33 (73%)
Conflict resolution involves rank and file	0 (0%)	1 (2%)

Conflict Resolution

Companies particularly interested in organizational development often undertake special exercises to bring interpersonal conflict out in the open—to identify its sources and deal with the issues. Increasingly the emphasis in these exercises is less on resolution than on management of conflict, but, the primary aim is to bring conflicting parties together in a situation which allows them to deal with their problems in an atmosphere of objectivity. Here, it is hoped, that hitherto unexpressed and unexamined resentment or animosity, which so often impede communication and collaboration, can be aired and perhaps "evaporated."

The Conference Board's inquiry into conflict resolution activities yielded mixed results. Among the non-OD companies, less than one-fourth of them report having adopted this behavioral technique. Among the OD companies, however, almost three-fourths claim they make some kind of special effort to resolve or manage conflict (Table 3). As was true in the case of experience-based communication techniques, there is little evidence that companies are concerned with personal conflict among lower level employees. Only one of the OD companies reported conflict resolution exercises for rank-and-file employees, and none of the non-OD companies reported its use at that level (Table 3).

Team Building

Proponents of the behavioral science approach stress the importance of cooperative and collaborative team effort. To critics who decry this approach by citing the old saw about a camel being a horse designed by a committee, they point out that, in a modern company, people work in a social setting where groups are a fact of life. Therefore, they believe a managerial style that capitalizes upon the existence of groups is preferable to a style characterized by dealing on a one-to-one basis with subordinates.

Behavioralists insist, moreover, that cohesiveness, common purpose, open communication, and real collaboration are what must be striven for if a "group" is to design the horse rather than the camel—acknowledging that an aggregation of people does not automatically make a group, nor a committee a team. They say that, in the ideal organization development model, real teams can play a crucial role in achieving organizational effectiveness.

Team building can, and does, according to our study, take many forms. Most often it consists of special meetings between a supervisor and the "work family" that reports to him. Frequently these meetings are held away from the work site and employ the services of a professional "third party" who observes the interactions and helps guide the activities of the participants. The work teams identify and deal with, in specific terms, any problems that seem to impede their effectiveness—whether these be related to interpersonal communication, inadequate equipment or systems, poor work process design, attendance and turnover, productivity, or a host of other concerns. The ground rules include getting the problems and issues "out on the table" and working them through until a satisfactory solution is achieved.

While team building could be considered appropriate and effective at any level of the organization, since people must interact in one way or another in the course of their jobs, it nevertheless has not yet seen widespread use at lower levels. Only 20% of the OD companies include rank-and-file employees in team building, and only 4% of the non-OD companies do so (Table 4).

Teams and Task Forces		Table 4.
	Non-OD Companies (N = 102)	OD Companies (N = 45)
Team building for rank and file	4 (4%)	9 (20%)
Intergroup building for rank and file	4 (4%)	5 (11%)
Task forces include rank and file	10 (10%)	20 (44%)

Intergroup Relations

The aim of intergroup building is like that of team building—to help people to work together better—but this practice involves bringing together two interfacing work groups where collaboration is considered vital. These groups may be units from the same department or they may be from different functional segments of the organization—research and development with manufacturing, for example, or manufacturing with sales. But they are brought together to explore and attempt to resolve a problem related to their cooperation or lack thereof.

In their meetings the two groups identify and analyze specific barriers to collaboration and effectiveness. Usually teams with representatives from both groups are formed, and these propose solutions to the barriers or undertake action projects to improve the intergroup effort.

There is as little incidence of intergroup building as of team building among rank-and-file employees investigated by the Board's study. It takes place in only four of the non-OD companies, and among the OD companies it occurs in only five instances (Table 4).

Task Forces

Task forces, ad hoc groups, and other "temporary systems"

are used widely in business firms. They are called by many different names, but their common trait is their temporary nature, although "temporary" may refer to one week or several years. Their membership varies. They may be a "horizontal slice" of the organization—a peer group; they may be a "vertical slice" of the organization—persons within a department or function with direct reporting relationships, and usually representing several hierarchical levels; or they may be a "diagonal slice" of the organization—representatives of several reporting levels and kinds of jobs.

At any rate, they represent a company's attempt to bring to bear several kinds of expertise and differing perspectives on a problem, or to provide the various organizational levels and functions the opportunity to have some influence on the project.

Companies that practice organization development often see another value in the use of task forces—their tendency to "democratize." In other words, by creating relationships and shared responsibility among individuals who are not "officially" peers, a kind of leveling takes place which seems to foster cooperation and creativity. Especially in the vertical- or diagonal-slice task forces, there is a built-in mechanism for upward and downward communication, because members come from multiple organizational levels. It is not surprising, then, that the OD companies studied include rank and file in task forces with greater frequency than non-OD companies—44% of the OD companies, versus 10% of the non-OD companies (Table 4).

Autonomous Work Groups

Among the many remedies offered to counter worker alienation is one that carries the concepts of participation beyond the traditional means of involving employees in decisions that affect them—the autonomous work group. The term can be somewhat misleading, since autonomy is a relative thing in large business organizations, and since work groups are neither totally self-sufficient nor self-contained. However, a few companies have experimented with organizing such work groups, and these have been composed of persons and jobs with common linkages and dependencies brought together with the idea that they will develop into self-managing micro-organizations.

Clearly, these so-called autonomous work groups exist within the framework of the larger organization and their goals and objectives are determined within the objectives of the total organization. However, they do have a pronounced degree of independence that exceeds that of work groups in more traditional organization structures. Members frequently set their own schedules, handle the division of labor within the work group, and inspect and evaluate their own output. They also control their own personnel problems such as attendance and productivity. They may even select and train new members.

Each member of the group is accountable to the rest of the group for his own behavior and contribution, while the group *as a whole* is accountable to management, and its performance is evaluated on this basis. Since there is no boss within the group, they are sometimes referred to as "leaderless" work groups.

Sometimes the autonomous work groups are established only among scientific and professional employees, but they also are formed occasionally among production workers and other lower level employees. In fact, thirteen (29%) of the OD companies the Board surveyed report the existence of autonomous work groups at the rank-and-file level. Among the non-OD companies, seven firms (7%) report that they have such groups (Table 5).

Peer Evaluation

Members of autonomous work groups not only evaluate each other's performance, but they may also seek to regulate each other's behavior and performance. Another form of peer evaluation can occur in work settings that do not have autonomous work groups. Some companies have experimented with this, asking employees to evaluate other employees with whom they presumably have sufficient contact to permit judgment of their performance. Their evaluations may then be used in regular performance reviews, or when an employee is being considered for a raise in pay or a promotion to a higher level job. There is little evidence, however, that peer evaluations are used widely at *any* level, though a few firms studied—one of the non-OD companies and 4 of the OD companies—have used them even with rank-and-file employees (Table 5).

Autonomous Groups and Peer Evaluations	Non-OD Companies (N = 102)	OD Companies (N = 45)
Company has autonomous/ "leaderless" work groups	7 (7%)	13 (29%)
Rank and file perform peer evaluations	1 (1%)	4 (9%)

Table 5.

From the foregoing indications there is evidence that some companies at least are trying to employ the minds as well as the hands of lower-level employees. (Participation in matters such as collecting money in United Fund campaigns or deciding upon the cafeteria menu is, of course, quite a different matter from participation in making decisions that affect on-the-job performance.) It may simply be a matter of believing a maxim of the behavioral scientists: creativity, imagination, and ingenuity in solving organizational problems are not the special province of the better educated and higher level elite of the organization. Instead, they are qualities widely distributed among the population.

---

1.   *Work in America* (Cambridge, Mass., The MIT Press, 1973).

2.   Harold M.F. Rush, *Organization Development: A Reconnaissance,* to be published by The Conference Board, spring 1973.

Richard N. Arthur is President of Arthur Associates, Inc., Holland, Michigan. He was formerly Senior Vice President of Donnelly Mirrors, Inc.

14
Return On Involvement

Richard N. Arthur

As we discuss our experiences in this article, we would like you to keep in mind that we have been involved in this for some twenty years. Donnelly had a great deal of help doing this; however, there is so much more awareness of participative management today, that most of you could accomplish in from three to five years what it took them some twenty years to accomplish.

There are four dominant styles of management: Autocratic, Benevolent Autocratic, Consultative, and Participative. Most companies today use a combination of the first three. We doubt that there is such a thing as a purely autocratic, benevolent, or consultative style, but rather a blending of all three. However, there is a dominant style found in every organization. The fourth style of management available is participative. Note that I do not say permissive but participative. This has been our choice of styles. I might point out that when an organization decides to become participative, ironically enough it is often *decided* in an autocratic manner. This is not necessarily bad, as it is the responsibility of top management to choose the style of management. A word of caution, participative management *cannot* be implemented autocratically.

Donnelly's motivation for selecting participative management was to maximize profits. We could say that we chose this style because of its concern for the dignity of man, and this would indeed be true. However, from the purely business point of view, we use it to maximize profits.

We would like to give you a profile of Donnelly Mirrors, Inc. They were founded in 1905, are family owned, and employ about 600 people. They have four manufacturing plants in Holland, Michigan which are nonunion, and one plant in Europe located near Dublin, Ireland that is unionized. Products are automotive and high volume in nature.

Since 1952 they have had a compounded growth of about 14%, but then so have a lot of companies. Productivity per person has more than doubled; not everyone could say that. Most significantly, their main products sell for less today than they did in 1952, and profits are as good or better.

Wages and benefits are in the top ten of the area, and all employees enjoy frequent monthly bonuses as well. We point this out only to show that bonuses are not a substitute for inadequate wages. When bonuses are used in this manner, they lose their impact. We would like to emphasize that they have only one bonus plan. The traditional executive bonus and stock option plan was discontinued in 1973.

To use more current history, since 1967 quality in production has increased by about 8.5%. When this occurs, usually more goods are returned by customers; however, in this case returned goods have gone from .028 to .0011. There is one customer to whom they ship three and four semi-truck loads per week, and at the end of the year they can literally bring back all the returned goods in a station wagon. The returned goods figure from them is .0002.

The next three items can be directly related to the removing of time clocks and placing all personnel on salary. Absenteeism dropped from 5% to under 1%, tardiness has gone from 6% to under 1%, and employee turnover averages about one-half of 1% per month; including summer help, retirees, terminations, and so on.

The fundamental basis of participative management is the building of *trust*. Without trust we could have accomplished very few of the things we are now going to describe to you.

The people are very much involved in the setting of their standards. Please note, I *do not* say they set their standards, but they are involved in the setting of standards. This happens after they are made aware of customer needs.

Production personnel have also been involved in the purchase of machinery. Some time ago, an engineer, a purchasing agent, and a machine operator flew to California to check out a machine to be purchased. They did make some suggestions that would improve the equipment, and when the machine arrived you can be sure that the operator, along with the engineer, were committed to making it function properly.

They also have created a climate where people will eliminate their own jobs. The policy says, "If you eliminate your job which results in a cost reduction, [and of course it almost always would] we guarantee you indefinite employment. Furthermore, we will give you six months to find a job that pays as much or more than your present position." Because of this policy, one operation, involving thirty-six people, reduced their manpower to eighteen. This was done through suggestions made by the operators in cooperation with one another across three shifts. That meant eighteen people had to find work that paid them as much or more, elsewhere in the plant. They were in a growth period at the time and business was good, so all found new jobs within three or four months. There was trauma associated with this. Even though a person has job security, he is somewhat nervous until he finds out specifically where he is going to be working, and on what. It may sound like a dangerous practice to guarantee people employment. But when you consider that turnover is roughly ten percent, which means they could eliminate 60 jobs per year, and that their growth averages fourteen percent, which would mean at least another 80 jobs per year, they could in effect eliminate 140 jobs each year without laying one person off. Any company this size would be hard pressed to eliminate that many jobs each year.

The people are also involved in setting their yearly pay packages. This is how it works. Over a five-year period they have increased wages by $850,000.00 and have had cost reductions of $1,500,000.00 to cover the increases. Let me point out that 40% of all net cost reductions made go into their bonus pool.

The process for establishing a yearly increase is really rather simple. They have an Employees Committee structure made up from all levels of the company. After they have digested all the material available that would relate to a wage package, like the cost of living increases, area wage average, what the U.A.W. is doing or planning on doing, they pick what they feel is a fair figure. They then meet in what is called the Donnelly Committee where every level of the company is represented, from the Executive Workteam down through the organization. During this meeting each representative is asked what they think the annual package should be. They call out a number which is written on the blackboard. Incidentally, during this process other representatives can question them on their rationale for picking a specific figure, and they frequently do. When each person has voiced his or her opinion, invariably we find that seventy-five or eighty percent of the representatives have lined up behind one figure. When this happens, they try to close the issue as soon as possible by getting total commitment to that figure. Normally, these sessions take from forty-five minutes to an hour.

On a recent pay package, the figure established was 10%. At the time, they had a payroll of about $3 million, so the pay package would cost the company $300,000. Therefore, they needed cost reductions of $450,000 to cover the cost. Because we are working with annualized figures you must have from one and one-half to two times the amount of the package.

The committee representatives then returned to their areas to seek cost reduction commitments from all the teams that would total at least $450,000. When they met with them approximately one month later to tally the results, the total commitment to cost reductions was approximately $600,000. They then said, okay, the 10% package is yours. Let me point out that fringe benefits also come out of this package. If the people want an extra week's vacation added to their benefits, with a cost of 2%, they would take 8% in cash for a total of 10%.

Let me mention that cost reductions come from throughout the company, not just from production areas. The purchasing department, for example, for the past five years has saved at least $150,000 in the purchase of materials. The list in Figure 1 will give some idea of the type, source, and value of various cost reductions. Please note that none are gigantic; it pays to think small.

Let's take a look and see what participative management has done to Donnelly's business. They are the dominant source of the three main products that they supply. They are one of the few, if not the only, vendors that have three-year contracts from any of the Big Three automobile manufacturers.

They have had an excellent experience with the starting up of a brand new product that involved supplying one of the Big Three with 100% of their requirements. By the end of the third month they were breaking even in this product line, and in the fourth month started to make a profit. They also started up a new operation in Ireland and by the end of the second month this operation was breaking even, and made money in the third month. The plant in Ireland supplies Europe, Japan, and Australia and is dominant as a supplier in those areas.

They are also encouraged by their present customers to get involved in other products, usually ones that they are having trouble with internally, or products for which they cannot find good sources. Just recently, they were asked to take over a product, and it has resulted in about $3 million worth of additional sales.

We feel it is important to point out to you that Donnelly and one or two others are not the only ones that have had a measure of success with this program. Let's take a look at some data involving nine companies and eleven plants. One organization applied the plan separately in two plants, and another included two plants under the same measurement. The firms studied represented a wide variety of environments and circumstances. Eight companies

Figure 1: Cost Reductions

Cost Reduction	Source	Total Annual Savings
Increase Rate Assembly, Inspection Was: 759/Shift — 8 Is: 2,000/Shift — 14	Production	$ 5,234
Glass Price Reduction by Switching Volume to Customer Save 3.5cents/Sq. Ft. — 400,000 Sq. Ft.	Purchasing	9,240
Savings on Boats Save $.89/Lite on 13,200 Lites	Engineering	11,760
Eliminate Overseas Pallets 34/Month X $14.00 Savings	Shipping & Purchasing	5,712
Meter — Ottawa Avenue Sewer to Eliminate Paying on all Water Going Through Sewer	Lab	4,584
Eliminate Operation on Vanity $.025 X 1,455,200 pieces	Production	36,380
Vinyl Stud on Vanity Versus Purchased Labor: 485 Shifts X $30.00 = $14,500 Material: $4.50/1,000 = $13,096	Purchasing	27,646
1st Surface Mirror — Use 1 Per. Vs. 2 660,700 Pieces @ $.0078	Engineering & Production	5,100
Eliminate Mold Repair Due to Low Pressure Closing Device	Quality Control	10,000
Mold. 12″ Mirror from 3,080 to 3,200 pcs. $.0006 X 1,287,400 Pieces	Production	772
Elimination of Business Luncheons	Office	22,000
Elimination of Two Company Cars	Office	4,600
Dropped the Donnelly Mirrors and Replaced With Donnelly News	Office	2,250

have contracts with national unions and one had an independent union. The number of employees per firm ranged from 30 to 1,200, but the majority of plants were in the 100 to 400 range.

Productivity changes were measured by comparing the ratio of the sales value of production to total payroll costs in the first two years of operation.

Figure 2*

Company	First-Year Relative Efficiency	Second-Year Relative Efficiency	Two-Year Average Relative Efficiency (Unweighted)
A	14.9	10.9	12.9
B	21.9	12.7	17.3
C	16.7	13.2	15.0
D	36.7	29.3	33.0
E	28.9	49.4	39.2
F	32.9	42.9	37.9
G	38.7	25.1	31.9
H	14.1	16.5	15.3
I	12.9	23.2	18.1
J	6.8	13.7	10.3
Average (unweighted)	22.5	23.7	23.1

*From Lesieur (1958), p. 113.

This study would indicate, at least to me, that any company present would be capable of increasing their productivity at least 25% with a well-directed effort. Only you can determine if the effort would be worthwhile to your organization.

We are often asked if this plan can work where very detailed work standards cannot be set. We offer as an example a Tool and Die Shop where the word "standards" would be quite out of place:

1. Employment—approximately 60, all highly skilled or working toward that end.
2. Average bonus the first year—4.5% per month; second year—it reached 9% and at last report was in the neighborhood of 18% per month.
3. They are shipping about 30% more in finished products *without* adding additional personnel.
4. They started with two supervisors; when one left they requested that he not be replaced. Each person assumed

more responsibility and after six months experience, all went well.

5. A major problem of management in a tool and die shop is turnover. The law of supply and demand enables these skilled craftsmen to be very mobile. In this case over a two-year period only two men have left, and one of them was requested to leave.

6. About 90% of all suggestions made have been considered useful, and tool damage and machine down time have been reduced significantly.

What about the size of the facility? Does it present insurmountable obstacles? Size does make a difference. A plant with 50 people can be brought to a high level of understanding in two or three months from the day you begin. A plant of 1,000 could take twelve months or more, but time is really the only major restriction, and the leadership skill and commitment has a direct effect on the time element.

Let's take a look at a company with 1,000 employees:

Over a fourteen-year period they have earned bonuses 84% of the time; with bonuses ranging from 5.5% to 20%. They have two international unions involved, and have had an outstanding labor relations history over those fourteen years.

Their program has had such a positive effect on the productivity, that they have been able to integrate vertically, adding to profits. Before the plan began, they were purchasing 50% of their component parts outside; today that figure is less than 20%.

Another company is even larger with some 2,000 employees and three independent unions.

Again, over a fourteen-year period, they have earned bonuses 87% of the time, ranging up to 20%. They have had 25,000 suggestions submitted in that time, with the great majority being useful.

Will participative management produce results *without* a bonus system involved? There is no question about it, some amazing results have been obtained without the benefit of a bonus plan. It is true that we do not know how long this would continue without a pay-off of some kind. We do suspect though, that some results would continue just because people feel involved and are being treated with dignity.

We would like to give you one illustration of achievement where a bonus plan could not be installed. The plant employs 12,000 people, has a union contract, and manufactures a variety of products. The experiment was confined to one assembly line involving 30 people, and produced these results:

Allowable rejects for wire harnesses the first time through, 37.6%; established from years of history. Actual rejects, from 4% to 10% (identical lines around them were running from 37.6% up to 50%).

To accomplish this, the supervisor met with this line at the end of each day, and together they established the quality and quantity goals for the next day. He also encouraged suggestions to improve the process and rapidly implemented any he received. This whole process took about fifteen minutes per day and was held after working hours.

The day we talked with the supervisor he was arranging to have an automobile brought into the plant with their wire harness installed so they could all see how their efforts fit into the scheme of things. In brief, he showed an interest in his people, he involved them and gave them feedback.

In summary, we believe that a great deal of creativity existed in our people, and we took steps to tap it by involving them in decisions that directly affected them, where they had the training and competence to make those decisions. It is a fact that this potential exists everywhere, but it has to be unleashed, and *you* are the one that can bring it about!

Stephen H. Fuller is Vice President of the Personnel Administration and Development Staff at General Motors.

This article is adapted from the "1973 Report on Progress in Areas of Public Concern," General Motors Technical Center, Warren, Michigan.

15
Employe Development and the Modern Work Force

Stephen H. Fuller

Dramatic forces of change are at work in our society to-day. There are signs of crisis in almost every major institution. Many of these center around people — the desire of individuals for a higher quality of life in their everyday lives and on the job.

Industrial concerns are being subjected to intense pressures seeking improvements in the work place and in the work environment. We hear and read a lot about "blue collar blues," "dehumanization of workers," "monotony on the assembly line" and "worker alienation."

Obviously, we in General Motors are concerned about the increasing criticism being directed toward the assembly line and other aspects of our business. Some false and very damaging impressions are being created in the public mind about the attitude of industrial management toward the new values and expectations of their employes.

It would be easy to console ourselves with the fact that the magnitude of our personnel problems has been blown way out of proportion. It would be easy to explain away part of our problems by asserting that the expressions of frustration and unrest in America's industrial plants and offices are but a reflection of conditions being experienced in society as a whole.

For us to neglect these concerns would constitute a failure to make a constructive response to them, and we would lose an unparalleled opportunity for additional innovations in the personnel function. We recognize that we do have people problems. And our concern is not limited to "blue collar" workers — it includes the needs and desires of all our employes. We cannot ignore the increasing public concern about the quality of life in the work place — any more than we can ignore the higher public expectations in such fields as safety, pollution, service and customer relations.

Quite a bit has been printed about such things as job rotation, job enrichment and employe motivation. Most of these programs are nice to talk and write about. But they usually fail to achieve significant or enduring improvements when applied as individual projects. In our opinion, there is no one plan, one program, or one solution which can be applied effectively in all situations.

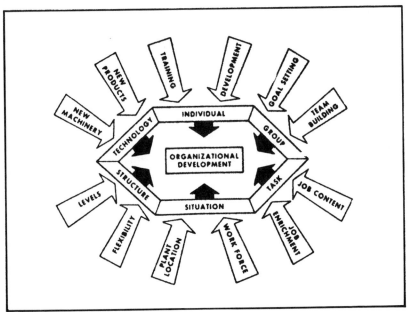

Elements of Organizational Development Build-Up

Organizational Development

Our approach at General Motors — which is called "Organizational Development" — is based on scientific analysis and follow-up improvement action involving a wide variety of activities which encompass all major elements of the organization. Let me illustrate what I mean.

If we were to seek changes through the individual employe,

two areas we might concentrate on would be training and other forms of personnel development. Improvement in the group process might involve goal setting or team building. If we want to effect a more efficient or more gratifying execution of the task itself, changes in job content or various types of job enrichment might be attempted.

The situation at any given location at any given time will have a major influence on the types of action programs which would be most desirable. Situation factors might include the location of the plant, the makeup of the work force, the kind of supervision received, the organizational climate or the current stage of development from the standpoint of the human organization. Structural improvements might involve changes in the

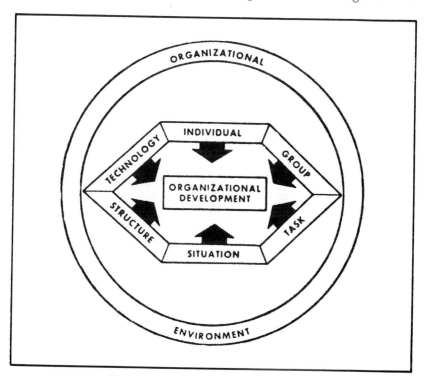

The Overall Organizational Environment

number of levels, relationships, flexibility and the communication process within the organization. We also must take into account the effects of technology — with new machinery, new products, new processes and the machine-man relationship being only a few examples. And finally, the overall organizational environment has a very important influence over all aspects of change.

Our approach is designed to evaluate the total organization and to map realistic corrective strategy which integrates all inter-related elements and takes into account their combined effects on organizational effectiveness. As a result, we are concerned not only with job enrichment and employe motivation, but also other activities such as increased employe involvement, better communications and training, team building and planned personnel development involving every employe.

Improvements also are sought through changes in such areas as job content, supervisory relationships, organizational structures and in the overall working environment. Highly important, we continue to learn as a corporation through a strong program of action-oriented research.

These are all basic elements of GM's philosophy of Organizational Development — a management concept which has gained wide acceptance throughout the Corporation and continues to grow. Its successful application depends on management's acceptance of change as a way of life, while putting people up front along with other basic elements of the organization.

The GM-ISR Project

One of the most significant projects in the field of Organizational Development involved a pilot study by General Motors utilizing the resources of the Institute for Social Research of the University of Michigan. Initiated in 1969, the GM-ISR Project marked the beginning of a long-range, scientifically-based program of Organizational Development within General Motors. Four General Motors plants were involved.

The GM-ISR Project had two major goals:

1) To seek long-term improvements in the human organization of General Motors.

2) To stimulate new concepts of managing people that are more consistent with the changing nature of the modern work force.

A survey was initially conducted among both hourly and salaried employes at the four GM plants to identify opportunities to improve plant performance. Using the information from the University of Michigan surveys which we conducted, organizational development activities were then developed and implemented by GM management. Major emphasis was placed on increased involvement of all employes — along with improved training and information sharing — in an attempt to develop a more participative type of organization.

The Project — as a result of surveys conducted over the past four years — has shown that there is a clear relationship between plant performance and how employes feel about the organizational climate, quality of management and employe-management relationships.

Our experience has demonstrated that concentrated and continuing efforts to bring about improvements in these areas also can result in significant advances in employe morale and motivation, job satisfaction, labor relations and overall performance.

The Project has not only produced improvements at the plant locations involved but, even more importantly, it has served as a valuable test bed for experimenting with new and innovative approaches. From these activities have come improved management concepts concerning people — concepts which provide some of the fundamentals for GM's Organizational Development program.

Organizational Development Activities

There is no Corporation-wide package program. Rather, ours is a broad and highly flexible management philosophy which is applied differently in each organization and is undergoing constant change as we gain new knowledge and experience. Our Personnel Administration and Development Staff provides a variety of resources and services to assist operational units and to coordinate Corporation-wide efforts.

Organizational Development (OD) activities in GM have undergone extensive expansion during the past three years. More than 100 organizational development specialists are working in 40 GM plants or staff activities in the United States, Canada and several overseas subsidiaries.

To give you a better understanding of the magnitude and variety of our activities in this field, let me briefly cover some specific examples of people-oriented projects now going on in various General Motors operations.

A number of projects are designed to strengthen the foreman's job. One concept involves the assignment of an hourly employe to assist each production foreman in nonsupervisory functions. The foreman has more time to manage his work group and provide more personalized leadership to his people. This redefinition and strengthening of the foreman's job has been highly successful in improving work performance and relations between the foreman and his people.

Special attention is being devoted to control of absenteeism. In two major efforts, Buick and Oldsmobile Divisions went to their foremen and hourly employes for help in improving attendance — and the results were significant.

The Oldsmobile Division's Press Plant has a quality improvement program that emphasizes people involvement by encouraging the "people on the floor" — working with their foremen — to actually develop a plan of action for building higher quality hood and fender panels. The results have been significant improvements in quality, reduced repair costs and better employe attitudes.

The Individual Quality Program at Delco Electronics Division encourages both hourly and salaried employes to participate in establishing departmental and individual goals in a variety of areas. Major results have been reduced product repairs, decreased maintenance and improved attendance.

The use of measurement tools has increased substantially during the past year. The most highly regarded measurement instrument is the questionnaire survey which is being used to measure organizational effectiveness, to measure employe attitudes about their organization and the management environment, and to solicit ideas and suggestions from employes about means of improvement.

People Oriented Activities

It would be misleading to imply that all of GM's efforts in Organizational Development have been successful. However, many projects have shown significant results.

New operations offer promising activities for people-oriented experiments and can serve as an example of what we are attempting to accomplish. Highly important to the success of these programs is the need to establish mutual trust, understanding and cooperation among all employes.

Changes in the supervisory structure of a plant can increase employe participation at all levels. At one new plant, the title of foreman has been replaced by that of area supervisor. More importantly, the area supervisor is a part of a flatter organizational structure. There are no general foremen or department superintendents. Management believes that this shortens and improves lines of communication. In addition, area supervisors become more self-sufficient because of greater responsibilities.

Other innovations being tried at new operations include the elimination of traditional barriers between salaried and hourly employes. These include removal of time clocks, and elimination of separate dining rooms and parking spaces for hourly, salaried and management personnel. One of the efforts to promote mutual trust has been the elimination of military-type uniforms for plant security people.

Special emphasis is also being given to orientation programs for new employes. A typical session might last for two days and all employes are required to attend. The program might include a lecture on motivation theory, a review of basic facts about the corporation and the plant and an exercise in team decision-making.

We also are experimenting with new types of assembly techniques. Preliminary work included studies of assembly technology at several outside companies — including Volvo and SAAB operations in Sweden. Using this information, General Motors Assembly Division designed its own team-built experiment.

In a two-month project at GM's Assembly Research Center in Flint, five employes worked together to build trucks in a stall located away from the assembly line.

First, the five-member team observed a disassembly of the Kutaway van they were to assemble. They made notes on the sequence of operations, separated operations into areas of responsibility and worked out their own assembly procedures and problems. It is estimated that each team member learned about 70 operations more than are needed by the average employe working on an assembly line.

The team bettered conventional assembly time, and the quality of the stall-built vehicles was very high. In addition, an attitude survey given before and after the experiment indicated a significant improvement in the employes' satisfaction with their work.

Because of that successful project, we plan to test the potential of the team-built concept in low-volume production situations.

In addition to local projects, there also are corporate-level Organizational Development activities.

For instance, GM and the United Auto Workers have established a joint Committee to Improve the Quality of Work Life. The committee has the responsibility for evaluating people-oriented programs, developing new projects, obtaining necessary outside counseling and effecting improvements in the work environment.

As part of the committee's efforts, a project to analyze the effects of Organizational Development activities on relationships among union officials, plant management and represented employes is being considered.

In a separate effort, GM is working with two Purdue University professors at the Central Foundry Plant in Defiance, Ohio. They already have interviewed members of management and union officials in an effort to determine if the two groups hold false perceptions of each other. Information from the interviews has been shared with participants as a means of promoting greater cooperation and communication between labor and management.

Employe Attitudes of Behavior

In a way, our people problems appear to pose a dilemma. Cost and competitive pressures have never been more intense. Yet, achievement of a higher quality of life in our plants and offices is being interpreted by some as involving higher costs — thereby decreasing our competitive capability.

We do not view this as an either/or situation. Our challenge is not people versus profit; it is people and profit. We have to operate a successful business to maintain employment levels and to provide satisfactory wages and benefits. Conversely, our success depends on people — not just the few in management — but all of the people of General Motors, working together toward common goals.

Our people-oriented activities are designed to improve employe attitudes and behavior — and to increase job satisfaction. They also seek to increase the contributions which all employes can make to our success — through greater involvement and participation, through better training, information and other resources and tools.

When we involve our employes in this type of cooperative, understanding relationship, we all benefit. The employes win and so does GM.

Conclusion

In conclusion, let me say that General Motors recognizes and is attempting to respond to reasonable expectations and aspirations of its employes at every level. Management and employes alike are accepting the challenge of change in a constructive, cooperative manner which is strengthening the effectiveness of our entire organization while also improving the quality of work life for everyone involved.

For without our people, we can accomplish nothing. With them, anything.

Norman Edmonds is in the Corporate Management Services and Planning Department, Travelers Insurance Companies.

16

Job Enrichment at The Travelers

Norman Edmonds

The Travelers has had an active program of Job Enrichment or motivation since early 1969. Today, I would like to give you an insight into why we became involved with Job Enrichment, present some of the concepts for implementing Job Enrichment, and show you what sort of results are made possible through the implementation of this concept.

The insurance industry is not unlike other businesses in the United States today. Most of our companies have fine programs of employee benefits. Our working conditions and pay have never been better. In Job Enrichment seminars one of the first things we do is to ask the participants to work with the seminar leader to compile a list of things that our company does for them. We have gotten as many as 60 separate and distinct employee benefits. We have never gotten fewer than 40. Suffice it to say that our company, and undoubtedly yours, is taking very good care of our employees. We want people to like their surroundings and their company, and by and large they do. We want them to stay with us and be motivated towards greater productivity. The question then becomes, has the employee benefit program been successful in terms of reducing turnover, reducing absenteeism, improving the quality and quantity of work, and improving the attitude of employees toward the company. I think that if we were to look at the statistics from any major corporation in the country today we would find that, in fact, it has not. Turnover is at an all-time high, absenteeism in many companies is soaring, particularly on Mondays and Fridays and the day immediately before and immediately after a holiday. The quality of work has declined to the extent that many companies have had to initiate complicated programs of quality control and checking. The Zero Defects program is a good example. The quantity of work has also suffered. There are repeated pleas for increased productivity as one of our major weapons against inflation.

Why hasn't this approach to the motivation of employees worked? We hear many answers. One is that there is a generation gap, that we in business just don't understand those young people. Another is that people are making too much money; they don't need to work as they did perhaps 20 years ago. Third, there is generally a "bad attitude" prevailing these days. Our younger workers are more revolutionary in their attitude and do not adhere to philosophies of some of their older counterparts. And lastly, the problem could be that we are much too permissive with our employees. We expected a good day's work for a good day's pay, but now we are making too many allowances. We tend to think that this logic is superficial and that really these conditions are actually symptoms of a larger problem.

What sort of environment are we now living in? If we were to look at the evolution of man's technology from 1900 to 1972 a very interesting picture would emerge. Included in this evolution of technology are such criteria as the number of computers in use and the number of telephones in use. Incidentally, the one hundred millionth telephone was installed just last year. In man's ability to produce horsepower, and any other technological indices that you can think of, we note that from 1900 to 1930 man's progress was quite evolutionary and orderly. From 1930 to 1972 it was quite *revolutionary*. We have shown here an exponential curve, a curve that will theoretically not reach the other side of the graph when compared to the base of 1900 to 1930. The purpose of this graph is to demonstrate that people who are coming to us now have been exposed to an incredible amount of knowledge. It has been said that people graduating from high school today are operating from a greater knowledge base than college graduates of only 10 years ago. It has further been stated that the half-life of engineering knowledge today is something less than eight years or stated another way, 50% of what an engineer learned in college eight years ago is of no use to him today.

Therefore, accepting the thesis that employees are generally better equipped and more knowledgeable than they were perhaps 10 to 20 years ago, we can plot their learning needs on a graph. This graph shows the learning level or learning ability of an employee plotted against time on a job. You can all probably recall your own experience as a young trainee. You were quite anxious to learn and make a good impression. Often during the training period we can observe the behavior of young employees straining to grasp any and all available knowledge concerning their new job. They take materials home for further study and often work through their lunch hour. These people are highly motivated, highly qualified and capable of absorbing large amounts of information. Compare that to the way jobs are typically structured in an organization. The trainee is fed only a small part of the job and as his time in the position increases, responsibilities are eventually added. As he approaches the later stages of his career, he reaches a maximum level of responsibility and a maximum opportunity for new learning and achievement.

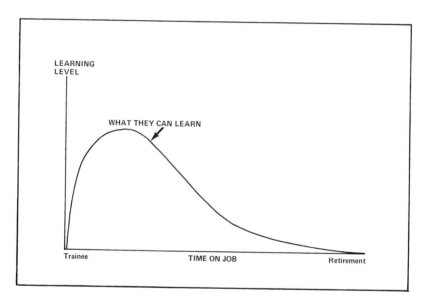

When we place these two graphs on a single chart we can see there is an incredible amount of waste in terms of matching employee abilities with the jobs assigned to them. As managers we have two alternatives. First, we can try to fit the ability of our employees to their jobs, as they are presently structured. Simply stated, this would indicate that if you have a Mickey Mouse job you should hire Mickey Mouse. The other alternative is to structure the jobs to meet abilities, learning levels and achievement needs of our employees. Both of these alternatives are workable. However, I submit that structuring the jobs to the abilities of the people is certainly the most profitable.

Now let's examine the concept of Job Enrichment and how it addresses itself to the previously-mentioned problems. We have established the fact that our companies, generally, have taken good care of such things as pay, job surroundings, supervision, benefits, security, etc. -- factors referred to as the job context or surroundings. The items you see here serve to keep our employees from being dissatisfied with their job situation. That is to say without any of the items shown on this slide, our people would be unhappy. But, I think that we have proved fairly conclusively that maximum application of all of these factors does not necessarily serve to make our employees happy with their jobs.

The major point is that these factors have nothing at all to do with the work itself. What makes people happy and satisfied is *what* they do. What makes them unhappy and dissatisfied is the environment in which they work. Taking this concept one step further then, what are those things that turn employees on?

Achievement, a chance to really feel that they are getting

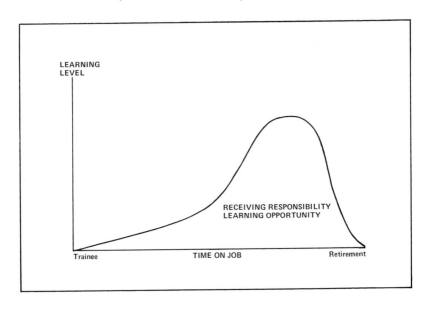

something worthwhile done on their own. Recognition, to be able to see and measure your own progress, to see the result of your work and have others recognize your accomplishments. Employees want responsibility, the opportunity to actively participate in the decisions affecting their work. The work itself must be interesting. People want a job that they find interesting. Something involved. Lastly, there should be opportunities for advancement and growth, to use new knowledge and skills for a tougher job -- a chance to achieve again. These are what we call the *motivators*. The factors of job environment previously shown to you are called "hygiene or maintenance factors." Given the fact that people are generally satisfied with their working conditions and their pay, how can we build the motivators into our jobs? How can we enrich these jobs to maximize the abilities and talents of employees?

Implementing Concepts

We have in job enrichment what are known as implementing concepts or techniques for enriching work.

Natural Units of Work -- This describes a particular way of distributing work items among employees. Traditionally, work items are distributed in a manner that only considers current workload or employee experience. An underwriter, for example, is assigned to process a particular group of applications, because he happens

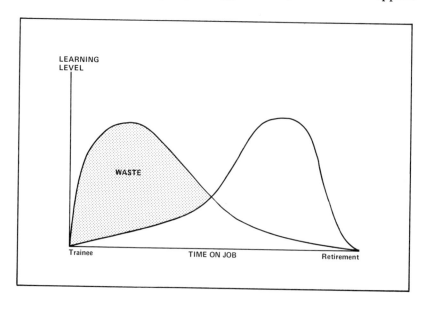

to have a light workload at the time. Another day, a second underwriter is assigned a similar group of applications because he has a light workload. The result is that these particular assignments have no real meaning or personal value for either underwriter. Each is simply processing paper. Natural work units permit a different situation. Each underwriter would be given *continuing* responsibility for his own group of work items. For example, an underwriter would be given the responsibility for handling applications from a particular and specific group of persons requesting insurance coverage. That underwriter would be accountable and responsible for handling requests of this group on a regular basis. There are at least five possible work divisions which can be made: geographic, organizational, alphabetical, customer-related, or type of business. Combinations of these groupings are also possible, such as geographic-numerical where a claims processor, for example, could be assigned to claims from the Pacific Northwest for claim amounts up to a specific amount. Natural work units identify areas of responsibility while heightening interest in the job and its tasks.

The next implementer is client relationships. For every business and business function, there are recipients, people or organizations on the receiving end of a product or a service from the workers. In the case of a claims adjuster, for instance, the recipient is the claimant or a person external to the organization. The recipient could be internal such as a data tapewriter who receives source

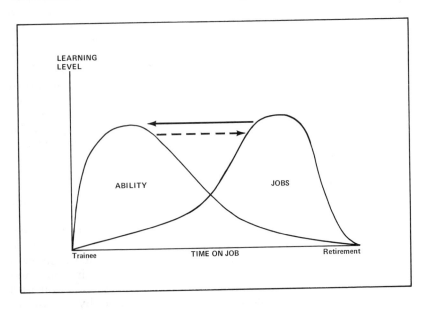

documents from the Marketing Division of her company. However, for many workers their product or service rarely goes to the same recipient on a regular basis and at the same time the input for their job rarely comes from the same source on a regular basis. The work is distributed in a random fashion. When the recipient of a person's work is always different, the worker usually lacks a sense of identity with or commitment to any particular recipient. Client relationships require that we reverse this pattern of constantly changing contacts. People react best when a continuing relationship with a readily identifiable client is established. A full and interesting client relationship has been developed when a worker contacts, and is contacted by his client; *personally* deals with that client; commits himself to good performance for his client; feels responsible in the case of error or poor service; identifies with his client; interest increases when he feels his client is his and his *alone*. When we discussed natural units of work, we focused on work items. In client relationships, we looked at who received our product or service. In our third implementing concept, we will examine job tasks. It has been said that it is the nature of jobs to get worse, not better. Many jobs have been broken into simpler jobs for the purpose of achieving maximum efficiency and error control. The automobile assembly line is a good example of this. While the assembly line produces greater number of cars, it has also produced a fragmented, unsatisfying and demoralizing segmentation of tasks. It has been demonstrated time and again that this type of work structure will cause dissatisfaction; decrease production, and increase error-rates, absenteeism and turnover. Combining tasks can counter this source of dissatisfaction. To do this we assemble *related* tasks to form a *full* job which we call "the job module." By combining some elements of the job before and after the enrichment process, we can provide interest, challenge and a feeling of responsibility. Within a well-designed job module, a worker becomes the *manager* of his particular job. Many operations in the insurance industry have been over-simplified in the name of efficiency, and should be re-examined for the possibility of recreating what was probably a strong Job Module in the first place.

The next concept is *vertical loading* ... a way of pushing responsibility down from higher levels and giving workers more control of their own jobs. People do not feel the need to meet production schedules and goals set for them by someone else. In most work situations the worker does the work, while the supervisor or manager retains responsibility for planning, directing, and controlling the work. People can and do gain satisfaction as a result of meeting schedules, goals and standards set by themselves which we have found are usually higher than those set by management. He begins to manage his own functions. Part of Job Enrichment is "greenlighting" or brainstorming ways to improve jobs to increase their motivational value. Examination of these greenlight items shows that many of them relate to loading back into workers' jobs functions that have drifted upward over the years. We find, for instance, that tasks which years ago were being performed on the general office floor have somehow found their way into private offices.

The next implementing concept is *task feedback*. A worker's performance generally has some measurable result. This could be in terms of customer satisfaction, the number of work items completed, or product quality, to name but a few. Feedback in most instances comes to the worker through the supervisor in the form of general comments related to work results. Although this may be helpful it has very little motivational effect. There are other examples of this kind of feedback. Performance may be discussed only when it is poor. Performance records may be kept at high levels. Errors are checked and corrected by supervisors. Errors are often sent to special units for correction. Quality inspection is done by someone other than the original worker.

Most workers want to see how well they are doing and what their progress has been. I can guarantee that bowling would not be nearly as popular as it is if there were a curtain across the alley and the bowler could not see or hear falling pins. Even poor bowlers want to see their results immediately and attempt to correct defects in their delivery to improve their game. Most people respond the same way to work situations, when they find out how good they are and see what is necessary to improve. Feedback is most effective when it comes directly from the work itself, immediately, as or quickly as possible, frequently and regularly. It simply requires that you identify the desired results of job performance and set up a means which allows the worker to receive the results on a *regular* basis. To recap, the five motivators we've discussed, (Achievement, Recognition, Task Interest, Responsibility and Advancement) are the general labels describing job experiences that *satisfy* people. The implementers offer a much more specific framework for identifying detailed changes in jobs that can increase motivation. Implementers take us out of theory and into the actual details of changing or re-designing jobs.

Using these concepts and other techniques, we have implemented Job Enrichment in jobs ranging from accounting clerks to computer schedulers. A logical question at this point would be, "How well does Job Enrichment work, if it works at all?" I would now like to share with you some results from one of our early implementations in a keypunch unit. We selected the keypunch job because it is probably one of the most difficult to enrich. The reason is that once a person has learned the keyboard skills, it is a very straightforward and routine kind of job experience. One is tied to a machine. And the opportunity for varying the interaction between machine and operator is distinctly limited. We felt that if we could enrich this job, we could enrich any job. Since this was one of our first attempts at Job Enrichment, we set up a controlled experiment. An experimental or achieving group was selected for the implementation of Job Enrichment. A control group of similar size and workload in a different location was also selected. Both groups were measured and the results were compared at the end of one year.

One of the indicators selected for use in measuring comparative performance was *thru-put rate*, or the number of cards each group produced per hour. As you can see, both groups were fairly similar in thru-put at the start of the experiment. After nine months, the achieving group increased thru-put by 39.6%, while the control group increase was only 8.1%. Stated another way, the achieving group had increased its capacity to process work by nearly 40%.

Attitude surveys were also administered before and after Job Enrichment. This survey essentially measures how people react to their job experience or the content of their job. Although nine categories of job attitude were measured, we have selected four as being representative of the operators' reactions before and after the enrichment experience. The categories are: the job provides opportunities, the job provides feedback, the job is not too closely supervised and the job is worth putting effort into. As you can see, in every case the operators experienced an improved reaction to their job. These results are particularly significant because of the kind of job we were trying to enrich. Taped interviews, held with the operators before and after Job Enrichment, tended to verify the test results. While these interviews do not give a quantitative picture of changing responses to the jobs, they do reflect some positive attitudinal changes. Before Job Enrichment the operators were saying such things as "I would like a job with more responsibilities." "I do the same job all day long. If I thought I would have to do this for even six more months, I wouldn't." "It's not the money; you couldn't really be happy if that is all you are working for." In the interviews after Job Enrichment comments such as these were recorded. "I feel good because the responsibility rests with me." "Everyone knows their job; you work as a team." "Now I have a complete job." "We are allowed to make decisions." The next category of measurement relates to the quality of work performed by the achieving group. Before Job Enrichment, approximately 40% of the operators in the achieving group were punching work of outstanding quality. An error rate of ½ of 1% or less was considered outstanding. At the end of the Job Enrichment experience, 55% of the operators had achieved an outstanding rating. Poor work is rated as being anything over a 4% error ratio. This slide illustrates that operators in the poor-rated group decreased by 50%. Previous to Job Enrichment, the collective error-ratio of the achieving group was 1.53%. At the end of the enrichment period this rate had been reduced 99%.

Absence statistics were obtained for both the achieving and control group for two periods of time, 11 months prior to Job Enrichment and 11 months after the initiation of Job Enrichment. All operators employed at the end of a period were included. An absence was considered to be any sick time or unpaid personal time. As you can see, the absence ratio in the achieving group was poorer than the absence ratio in the control group prior to the study. At the end of the period of enrichment, that situation had reversed itself. The achieving group absences improved by 24%, while the control group absence was 29% poorer, or a 53% differential in absence ratio during the Job Enrichment period.

We at The Travelers do not consider Job Enrichment to be a cure-all for the critical manpower problems facing management. We have, however, been able to successfully demonstrate that Job Enrichment is an effective workable tool. Subsequent implementation of this technique has shown results significantly higher than those discussed today. We have found that the concept of Job Enrichment is not limited to clerical positions alone, but that it has much broader application to a wide range of positions within an organization, including those in management. Our future plans call for expanding implementation efforts as requests come to us from line managers. Job Enrichment is not something management imposes upon line departments. In fact, to be successful, Job Enrichment should be voluntarily initiated by the department manager. The insurance industry is well known for its investment in the careful recruiting, selection and training of the most qualified people available in the job market. We view Job Enrichment as a method for assisting management in realizing the maximum return from that investment through the maximum utilization of the skills and abilities of the people we hire by making basic and simple changes in the way their jobs are structured. All we have been talking about here today is a systematic application of common sense backed by theory and technology.

Sam Zagoria is Director of the Labor-Management Relations Service sponsored by the National League of Cities, U.S. Conference of Mayors, and National Association of Counties.

This article is adapted from a speech given at the U.S. Conference of Mayors, San Francisco, 1973.

17
Improving Job Satisfaction in Local Governments

Sam Zagoria

The public employer, faced with the need for more and better services, also is faced with rising costs of goods and materials and escalating personnel costs, and confronts a protesting constituency when more tax levies are suggested. Better ways are needed to utilize the full talents and capabilities of local government work forces.

The public employee, steadily younger, better educated, more traveled, more independent, wants more responsibility, more variety, more opportunity for growth and advancement from his job, and a greater feeling of accomplishment. Employees in the public as well as the private sector are infected by a spreading malaise which is modifying old assumptions about work and is beginning to force new definitions of jobs. These changes include a broadening of worker responsibilities, rotation of jobs, a steady spread of the four-day workweek, and increased proposals to allow workers to choose their own hours.

The symptoms of the worker malaise, in a period of substantial unemployment and tight job markets, are usually submerged lest the employee be struck by an even greater ailment—no job at all. But some employers recognize that just below the surface is the disenchantment of a growing number of employees who see themselves engaged in joyless, dehumanizing chores which will last throughout their work lives.

The warning signs are abundant. A broad industry study by Harold L. Sheppard of the Upjohn Institute for Employment Research found that "there is no question that job dissatisfaction is increasing." Fully a third of the workers interviewed were unhappy, convinced that they had reached a dead end in their work lives. The study also found "increasing signs . . . of job malaise" in public jobs.

A study of clerical workers which was reported in the *Harvard Business Review* showed "burgeoning discontent" among the nation's approximately 13 million clerical employees. It concluded: "Clerical employees are beginning to feel like mere cogs in a great impersonal bureaucracy, and there is a growing tendency to see management as a nameless, faceless mask of authority and indifference."

Some years ago, the *President's Manpower Report* contained a survey showing that only 50 to 68% of blue- and white-collar workers viewed their work as interesting; 35 to 64% saw good use made of their skills and talents; and 39 to 68% had a feeling of job satisfaction. A good part of the rest apparently looked at their work as sheer drudgery.

Workers grumbling about their jobs is certainly not a new phenomenon. What is new is the intensity of their gripes and their increased willingness to do something about it by staying absent from the job, by slowing down the work process, or by just quitting.

Behind this worker rebellion are a number of factors—government growing ever bigger; employees feeling more remote, unimportant, and insecure; and the increasing strains of urban living. But perhaps the most significant factor is the expanding role played by young employees. Two-thirds of the growth in the nation's work force in this decade is expected to take place in the 16-34 age group—a group with better educations and higher expectations for job satisfaction and participation in the decision-making process than their elders had. Job security was something to be treasured by their Depression-scarred parents, but for them there has to be more to a job than just scratching out a living. And, generally speaking, they are not worried about leaving a job; they're confident they'll survive.

Young workers are likely to be more independent, more accustomed to comforts, and less respectful of codes of dress, speech, and personal appearance than are their elders. As noted in an American Management Association book, *Managing the Young Adults*, "Youngsters participate more in decisions that affect them and are taught to become progressively independent from childhood on through their school years. By the time a young potential employee applies for a job, he has been conditioned toward a state of independence for many years . . . as people acquire more education, especially in a permissive climate, their expectations rise with regard to the responsibility they will receive."

Is it possible to join together the work needs of the municipal employer and fulfill the needs of the municipal worker and in the process produce better delivery of municipal services to the residents? The answer from a few dozen city leaders who have experimented with some innovative approaches to improving job satisfaction has been "Yes." They also caution that job content and job schedules can't be revamped in order to erect job ladders for everyone on the payroll; indeed, some workers don't want to change. They like things as they are and look to their job only to provide the necessities so that they can really live it up in their time away from the job.

Traditionally, employers—private and public—have tucked workers into timeworn slots shaped by classification and job evaluation plans, adjusting them a bit as union-management agreements came into being, but always subjecting the job holders to a formidable pyramid of layer upon layer of supervision. If new technology required change, the work assignments were quickly revised. However, if workers needed change in their jobs in order to further their pride and satisfaction in their work, most employers were shaken to the core.

A recent report, *Work in America*, put together by a special task force for the Secretary of Health, Education, and Welfare, warns that significant numbers of American workers are dissatisfied with the quality of their working lives. Dull, repetitive, seemingly meaningless tasks which provide little challenge or autonomy are causing discontent among workers at all occupational levels. This is not because the work itself has greatly changed; indeed, one of the main problems is that work has not changed fast enough to keep up with rapid and widespread changes in worker attitudes, aspirations, and values. A general increase in educational and economic status has placed many American workers in a position in which having an interesting job is now as important as having a job that pays well. Pay is still important. It must support an adequate standard of living and be perceived as equitable, but high pay alone will not lead to job (or life) satisfaction.

There have been some responses to these changes in the nature of the work force, but they have usually been too little and too late. As a result, worker productivity is low—as measured by absenteeism, turnover rates, wildcat strikes, sabotage, poor-quality products, and the alienation of workers from their work tasks. Moreover, a growing body of research suggests that, as the quality of work life decreases, there may be accompanying declines in physical and mental health, family stability, community participation and cohesiveness, and "balanced" sociopolitical attitudes. At the same time, there is an increase in drug and alcohol addiction, aggression, and delinquency.

Job Enrichment

In light of these warnings, the principles of job enrichment and some examples of their application in government should be examined. Until now, industrial engineers have agreed that breaking tasks down to their smallest components is the best way to get the job done. This approach resulted in the assembly line in the auto plant and its white-collar counterpart in the office. Workers rarely saw a project through from start to finish or even to the midway point—fragmentation was the order of the workday.

Today job experts argue that this is no way to develop individuals to their fullest potential. Instead they would consult with groups of employees to broaden modules of work, removing some layers of supervision, and putting more responsibility—and accountability—on the employees themselves. For the worker, this would mean the opportunity to develop and exercise a broader range of skills, to achieve growth and recognition. And motivated workers make for better services, more cheerfully rendered.

Frederick Herzberg of Case Western Reserve University, one of the pioneers in the field, applied this principle to a unit of workers engaged in replying to correspondence—a task well known to local governments. In the reorganization, selected correspondents were appointed as experts in certain subjects, where previously the supervisor had been answering all specialized and difficult questions; correspondents signed their own names to letters, where, before, the supervisor had signed all letters; experienced correspondents did most of their own proofreading, where previously the supervisor did all the inspecting; correspondents were encouraged to answer letters in a more personalized way, rather than the standard form letters; and, finally, each correspondent was held personally responsible for the quality and accuracy of letters.

Few municipal governments have embarked on an organized effort to remodel tasks in this way. But Nassau County, New York, and three towns within its borders have launched a major experiment to redesign jobs through a cooperative effort on the part of public management and public unions aimed at improving productivity. Gains will be shared, and, if the experiment works, other communities should be quick to follow.

There are other routes to increasing job satisfaction. One approach is job rotation, which often provides variety and poses new challenges, useful objectives in themselves. This process also gives workers training which cuts across departmental lines, providing them with a broader view of local government functions. Another is to develop team approaches to problem identification, analysis, and solution, thereby achieving a total effort greater than that of the combined individual efforts. Another has been the introduction of worker participation into decision making, bringing the firsthand insights of workers to this process and helping them better appreciate the obstacles faced by management. Job ladders, reinforced by in-house and outside training, have also been developed. In addition, there has been some experimentation with flexible hours—giving workers a chance to come to work early and leave early or come late and leave late to accommodate their own needs and tastes. A few tentative tryouts of the four-day, and even the three-day, workweek are also under way.

This is not to suggest that change is spreading like wildfire in local governments. It is more like a few candles lit in scattered boroughs, and, in all honesty, some have blown out before sunrise.

Job Rotation

A relatively new city, Simi Valley, California, incorporated in 1969 with a population of 56,000 people, is administered by Bruce Altman, an innovative city manager. He has established the practice of having each department head serve as assistant city manager on a rotating basis, a month at a time. The result, he has said, has been development of "experienced, responsible leadership" for the city, and, perhaps equally important, "each department head gains a profound sensitivity toward city-wide goals and is better able to relate his department's goals and priorities to organizational goals and priorities."

In another thrust, Manager Altman assigned four department managers to other departments as acting heads for a three-month period last year. They retained their usual titles in order to exercise certain functions which could not be legally transferred. Manager Altman considered the program a success and felt it helped achieve not only a widening of capability but a broadening of viewpoint beyond an individual department.

Eugene, Oregon, has a similar program in which various departments "lend" city employees to serve in the offices of the mayor and city manager as the Community Relations Officer of the city for a six-month period. This individual works closely with the two officials, receiving and investigating complaints filed with the city or the Human Rights Commission and working with the news media, as well as carrying out assigned research and general administrative duties. This person thus obtains an overview of municipal operations and an understanding of citizen problems, along with some topside management experience.

Glendale, Arizona, began a job rotation program in 1971 in order to develop an internal manpower pool from which to fill future vacancies and to give employees broader exposure to management problems. Line employees were rotated into the Personnel Department for three months, although their salaries were still paid by their departments. Their tasks included analyzing examinations, redesigning personnel forms, and helping define job specifications. When they returned to their departments, they were a reservoir of information to other employees on a whole range of personnel practices, matters which are important particularly to minority groups who were often uninformed about them.

Claremont, California, has a rotation program involving transfers within departments. In the Police Department, for example, a new recruit will serve as a communications officer for two or three weeks. Patrolmen are rotated through the Detective Division for a month at a time. Patrolmen serve as acting sergeants, and sergeants serve as acting lieutenants, commanding patrols as needs arise.

San Jose, California, gives police officers a chance to designate duty assignment preferences to assist in "career enrichment" as vacancies occur and the Police Chief has to fill them.

An unusual kind of rotation covers secretaries in Placentia, California, who periodically visit their counterparts in other cities and spend the day learning how others perform jobs similar to their own. The City Administrator, Edwin T. Powell, explains that "a majority of our working women have families and are unable to take advantage of educational incentive programs which encourage attendance at local educational institutions. These visits expose them to different, and perhaps better, ways of performing their jobs."

Team Approach

The Urban Institute has identified a number of examples of team policing. San Bruno, California; Dayton, Ohio; and St. Petersburg, Florida, have tried this and reported improved clearance rates, faster responses to calls, and reduced overtime, sick leave, and turnover. The teams provide the whole range of police service in a given area. Some cities—Claremont, California, and Plainfield, New Jersey—have combined police and fire training with subsequent sharing of duties. St. Petersburg, Florida, has a contest among the city's 13 sanitation crews for the "crew of the month." The award is given to the crew achieving the best compaction ratio—the greatest weight of trash hauled per number of trips taken to the dump.

In Dayton, Ohio, management personnel have been organized into various task forces to consider and make recommendations on such issues as the future of the city, racial discrimination, crime, employment, youth services, and housing. Each department head involved is expected to devote as much as half of his time to such assignments. In Tacoma, Washington, a team of department heads was formed in order to analyze how the expected portion of revenue-sharing funds should be allocated. According to Manager William Donaldson, the result was a recommendation for a number of multidepartmental projects, rather than the renewal of the customary projects carried out within individual departments.

Worker Participation

Worker participation in decision making has enabled employees to share their experience and insights with top management on such significant matters as task allocation, scheduling, recruitment, procedure, and policy.

In Vancouver, Washington, a city of 45,000 with 400 municipal employees, proposed changes in city activities are put on the table by the Manager, Allen Harvey, for discussion and consultation by employees. According to Harvey, in matters affecting wages, hours, and conditions of employment in the broadest sense, the local labor coalition also is kept informed.

In Simi Valley, California, the top management team has been expanded to include three lower level employees, each of whom serves in the group for three months at a time. In Scottsdale, Arizona, field staff from the Recreation Department are given a chance to help design and plan new park facilities; custodians have offered suggestions for easier maintenance; and parks repairmen have offered suggestions on the type of lighting fixtures to be used. Washington, D.C., has negotiated a sanitation contract provision which brings together city workers and supervisors for a monthly review of complaints and service problems and ways to solve them.

Other Innovations

Career development through job ladders has been tried in both small and large cities. In Medford, Oregon, a city of 30,000 with a municipal staff of 265, Manager Archie Twitchell has helped a woman employee with a high school education to chart her course from clerk to recorder-treasurer and ultimately, he hopes, up to the post of finance director. He has an open transfer policy, which has already enabled a good building janitor to transfer to a new post in the Park Department. Job requirements for college degrees have been met by giving equivalency examinations. Nonengineers have been tried—and have succeeded—in engineering positions. And a particular success story is that of a planning technician, who, with the help of a reading list and suggested training, has shown "great personal growth in 2-½ years" and now is second in command in the Planning Department.

The city of Los Angeles, California, has developed a series of charts laying out the paths for promotion. This is part of a City Employment Development Program which encourages and offers incentives to personnel. Included are in-service training programs, tuition reimbursement plans for college training, evening classes at the Civic Center jointly sponsored by the city and the East Los Angeles College, and monetary awards for advanced educational achievement.

Experiments with revision of the workweek and workdays have had mixed results. Atlanta, Georgia, and Minnetonka, Minnesota, have been disappointed with their four-day week initiatives. Los Angeles' trial of flexitime, which provided some 60 employees in a part of the Personnel Department with leeway in arriving (between 7 and 9 a.m.) and leaving (4 and 6 p.m.), showed that interdivisional communication was hampered and productivity was reduced. On the other hand, San Diego County, California, permits departments to set hours in a way most agreeable to workers and most conducive to job completion. Various schedules have resulted, including the four-day workweek, and participants enjoy it. In western Europe, flexitime has been a great success for a long time in both the public and private sectors. This is stimulating additional experimentation with it in the United States.

The foregoing compilation is by no means intended to be inclusive. One problem with innovations is that there has been too little sharing of results—good and bad. This article is an effort to overcome this in some measure. In short, the message is "innovate and improve."

Attitudes toward work are changing. It still is an important part of life, but now workers, men and women, black and white, young and old, want to put more into those hours in the offices and shops—and get more out of it than perspiration and a paycheck. There will be many opportunities to develop better ways to do municipal tasks if the best talents of individual workers are identified and challenged. That is the task for modern management in the seventies.

Merrill E. Douglass is Assistant Professor of Management, Graduate School of Business Administration, Emory University, Atlanta, Georgia.

T. Stephen Johnson is Operations Officer with the Trust Company of Georgia.

18
Successful Job Enrichment:
A Case Example

Merrill E. Douglass
T. Stephen Johnson

Performance, productivity, profits—and boredom—are all related to ways in which human resources are utilized. The job enrichment concept provides an effective way to rechannel efforts in this area. It provides a way to recognize and balance structural and psychological aspects of the job. Job enrichment helps demonstrate that what is done with people is often more important than what is done to them.

Job enrichment is basically a strategy for increasing worker motivation in the desired direction. Motivation is considered to be a personal, internal experience determined by the worker's perceptions of the total work environment. The job enrichment strategy deals with changing the work situation in such a way as to bring about changes in job behavior as well as changes in the way a person views the job.

Studies have shown that job dissatisfaction involves factors such as working conditions, salary, status, style of supervision, fringe benefits, and company policies. If these things are inadequate, workers are dissatisfied. If improvements are made, workers are less dissatisfied, but these improvements do not lead to satisfaction.

Satisfaction and increased motivation involve factors which are intrinsic to the job itself. These factors include a sense of achievement, responsibility, opportunity for growth and development, and feelings of importance and personal worth. Improvements in these areas will lead to greater worker satisfaction, motivation, and performance. This is what job enrichment is all about.

The current extension of the early job enrichment theory is the development of concepts and guidelines for job design. These basically fall into concepts affecting either task structure of the job or administrative structure. The administrative structure primarily flows from policy decisions affecting the total organizations. These include salary schedules, fringe benefits, job security, seniority rights, and working conditions.

Task structure concepts are concerned with the work itself and are primarily qualities inherent in the task. For instance:

○ Task integration—vertical and horizontal loading; responsibility and authority.

○ Recognition for achievement—reward contingencies; personal sense of achievement.

○ Co-worker relationships—team building; supervisory style.

○ Feelings of importance—individual contribution; client identity.

○ Opportunity for growth and development—promotional contingencies; challenge.

Many studies have shown the difference between dissatisfaction and satisfaction and the different job concepts related to each. For instance, it has often been assumed that changes in working conditions will provide greater worker satisfaction and therefore greater productivity. On this assumption thousands of rooms have been painted and repainted, music systems installed, and floors carpeted. But working conditions generally fall in the category of administrative structure. Improvement in working conditions prevents dissatisfaction, but these improvements do not lead to satisfaction, and therefore have no motivational impact. This means that boredom and performance are most effectively approached through the task structure concepts.

A typical job enrichment program involves relatively large numbers of people and, consequently, requires greater amounts of resources. Because some of these programs have not been too successful, massive job enrichment efforts have been resisted by the management of some organizations. Other managers have sought concrete evidence, particularly on the adaptability of job enrichment techniques to their particular circumstances, before committing themselves to large programs. If job enrichment concepts are valid, then they can be equally applicable on a small or a large scale.

After carefully considering the potential benefits and possible problems, the management of the Trust Company of Georgia came to the conclusion that job enrichment could be successfully applied to bank jobs. Before undertaking a massive program, however, we decided to conduct a pilot test to determine the applicability of job enrichment procedures. This seemed particularly advisable because many of the potential work groups which were to become involved were small in size.

The method for implementing the job design concepts into a total program was adapted from a model suggested by Richard C. Grote.[1] (See Exhibit 1.)

Exhibit 1: Job Enrichment Model

A. Determine Program Parameters
    1. Establish Job Enrichment Team.
    2. Select the Job Enrichment Project Manager.
    3. Select the Job.
    4. Determine Required Resources.
    5. Determine Attitudinal and Productivity Measures.
    6. Collect Initial Data.

B. Design Change Program
    7. Identify Possible Changes.
    8. Select Changes to Implement.
    9. Plan Implementation.
    10. Implement Planned Changes.

C. Evaluate Change Program
    11. Measure Effectiveness.
    12. Determine Future Implications.

Establishing the Job Enrichment Team: From the outset it was intended that the job enrichment program would become permanent if the pilot project proved successful. If this were to be the case, then a certain amount of stability would be needed in the job enrichment team to facilitate the continuity of effort. The team finally selected consisted of five permanent members.

Three of the permanent team members were line personnel and two were in staff positions. It was felt that including both line and staff personnel on the job enrichment team would allow the best combination of job knowledge, specialized expertise, and authority necessary to assure the success of the program.

The five permanent job enrichment team members were supplemented by additional personnel drawn from the areas under consideration at any particular time. These were always line personnel from the departments where jobs were enriched. For the pilot program the additional membership consisted of three supervisory personnel from the department chosen for the test. These included the department manager, the assistant department manager, and the supervisor in charge of the work unit involved in the test.

One of the first tasks undertaken was the education of each job enrichment team member. It was considered essential for each person on the team to fully understand all aspects of the job enrichment concept. This education was accomplished through reading materials, training seminars, and task force discussion meetings.

Selecting the Job Enrichment Project Manager: If the project is to be successful, someone must provide coordinative management. The project manager was selected simultaneously with the job enrichment team and was the guiding member of the team. Initially his function was to ensure the adequate training of other team members. Beyond that, he assumed daily operational responsibility for the project.

Selecting the Job: The ideal type of job for enrichment was considered to be one in which (1) the work was relatively routine; (2) the job formed a complete work unit; (3) productivity measures could be obtained; (4) implementation of changes could be accomplished at low cost; (5) work attitudes were relatively poor; (6) worker satisfaction was relatively low; and (7) increases in motivation were more likely to result in the greatest relative increase in performance.

One of the keypunch sections within the Special Services Department seemed to be the most appropriate for the initial enrichment program. The Special Services Department processes correspondent bank accounting, payroll accounting for customers, and various odd jobs for other departments within the bank.

The primary task of the keypunch section selected was the processing of correspondent bank accounting transactions. This section consisted of one control clerk and four keypunch operators. The control clerk was responsible for opening and distributing the work, balancing and correcting errors, and routing the completed work. Contact with correspondent banks and with computer division personnel was handled by the control clerk. The operators simply keypunched the work assigned to them.

Determining Required Resources: Very few resources were required for the pilot. Once changes were selected, the primary effort was in necessary skill training needed to implement the plan. No expenditures were made for equipment or space. The development of time budgets was necessary.

Determining Attitudinal and Productivity Measures and Collecting Initial Data: Worker attitudes were measured during a series of in-depth interviews. Discussions were also held to determine what workers liked and disliked about their jobs, as well as to obtain suggestions about how to improve their jobs.

Productivity measures selected included turnover rates, absenteeism rates, error rates, productivity measures, and deadlines met. Historical data on each of these measures were available.

Before determining any job changes, each task in the group was carefully analyzed and flow-charted. These results were matched against task descriptions obtained from the workers.

Identifying Possible Changes: The job enrichment task force met to begin identifying possible changes. They reviewed all of the employee suggestions and the results of the job analyses, flow-charting, and discretionary judgment surveys. The next step involved a brainstorming session of the task force group.

From all of this activity a large number of possible changes were generated. Some were clearly better than others, and implementation of some changes was not feasible. The next job for the task force was to sort through all the possible changes and select the ones most likely to be effective. If at all possible, it was hoped that the workers' suggestions would be included in the selected changes.

Selecting the Changes to Implement: The analysis and sorting proved to be much easier than anticipated. Suggested changes seemed to fall into rather distinct groupings. Changes were selected on the basis of which ones would provide recognition for good accomplishment, help establish a better identification between the worker and the correspondent banks handled, and allow keypunch operators to do a whole task rather than just part of a task.

Five specific changes were finally selected for implementation. The job enrichment team carefully considered comments from the workers in selecting each plan. The changes picked had the support not only of all team members, but the workers as well.

One of the most interesting changes selected required the elimination of the control clerk job. This allowed the promotion of the control clerk to a new supervisory position. Other changes included making each operator responsible for a specific set of accounts; making operators responsible for all aspects of the job, including the distribution of work, balancing, routing completed work, and initiating any necessary contact with the correspondent banks or computer personnel; arranging for operators to physically visit the banks whose work they processed; and providing special recognition for top performance.

Not all changes were implemented simultaneously. Instead, a sequential time plan was worked out to implement each change as rapidly as the work unit could absorb it without creating unnecessary confusion in the work patterns. It was felt that successful adaptation to one step at a time would help ensure the overall success of the job enrichment program.

Planning Implementation of Changes: The job enrichment project manager and key departmental supervisors worked out implementation plans. One interesting development in this phase was that the control clerk whose job was eliminated was one of the most enthusiastic supporters of the change. Since the supervisor had to live with the changes on a daily basis, it was essential that he be sold on the program. This was one of the first priorities undertaken.

As anticipated, the greatest work was involved in training all of the keypunch operators to perform the duties previously handled by the control clerk. Initially this required hiring an additional operator to free the other operators for retraining. New work-flow charts were developed and new job descriptions were written.

Implementing the Changes: When the time came to implement the changes, a new reaction set in. The keypunch operators seemed to be having second thoughts in spite of their earlier enthusiasm for the project. In rethinking the matter their perceptions were that somehow the new jobs would require a great deal more work than the old jobs. This meant more overtime. Several discussions were held with the workers in which management attempted to reassure them that this would not be the case. Even so, as implementation began, workers seemed noticeably downhearted.

Measuring Effectiveness: Research into other job enrichment programs indicated an initial reaction which can be described as a "valley of despair." Satisfaction and productivity frequently decrease. Supervisors were prepared for this effect and cautioned that these decreases would be temporary. It was our belief that many of the job enrichment program failures were the result of managers becoming disillusioned at this point and giving up. We also felt that the "cold feet" of the workers was an indication that our pilot would indeed experience temporary decrements in attitudes and performance. As it turned out, this was the case.

Attitudes of the workers prior to the job enrichment program were primarily negative. All operators had asked for transfers. Not only were attitudes low, but performance measures were also relatively low, as indicated in Exhibit 2.

In any change program a key element involves management

Exhibit 2: Productivity Measures for Keypunch Section

Item	Prior to Changes	Two Months After Changes	Seven Months After Changes
Absenteeism	5.4%	3.1%	1.7%
Error rates	1.3%	.8%	.7%
Unit/Time productivity	21.1 sec.	17.7 sec.	16.8 sec.
Group completion time	181.9 min.	151.0 min.	148.2 min.

attitudes. One of the first positive results in the Trust Company program was the surprise on the part of management. The keypunch operators picked up the new training at a very rapid rate. Managers began reassessing some of the assumptions about workers. The supervisors became excited about the unexpected eagerness which workers displayed in learning the new tasks.

Throughout the planning and implementation of the job enrichment program one of the most positive aspects was the attitude of the line managers. The wholehearted support of all line personnel involved was a key element in the success of the pilot program. Line managers closest to the job were particularly helpful in making innovative suggestions.

Once past the initial letdown, significant changes began to be noticed in workers' attitudes. There was no longer any talk of transfers, and the total atmosphere was more relaxed. Supervisors frequently remarked about changes in workers' attitudes, and changes in supervisors' attitudes and behavior were beginning to be evident. Workers also began perceiving a greater amount of discretionary judgment in their work.

There has been no turnover since the project began. Two keypunch operators will, however, be leaving in the near future. One because she is pregnant, the other because she is being promoted. From an economic standpoint, the reduction in turnover, alone, more than justifies job enrichment programs. It is not unusual for the cost of one turnover to be as high as $1,000, not counting the training costs for the replacement. Multiply this by the number of oeprations personnel turning over each year and the figure becomes staggering. Consider, too, that much of the turnover occurs at various stages throughout the learning curve and the impact of turnover on performance is easily seen.

Has performance changed? The economic pay-off is reflected in Exhibit 2. Improvements have occurred in all the performance measures. And, with improvements in performance, there are corresponding improvements in profitability.

Future Implications: We feel that the pilot job enrichment program has been successful. Improvements have resulted in attitudes, satisfaction, performance, and profits. Managers in other areas of the bank are requesting job enrichment programs for their departments. At the present time plans are being made to expand job enrichment activities to eventually cover all possible areas of the bank's operations.

This project even on a small scale involved changes in each of the task structure concepts. There were no changes required in any of the administrative structure dimensions of the jobs. This is generally the case with most bank jobs. Over the past several years most banks have been improving administrative aspects of the job environment to such an extent that further improvement is probably not required.

The increasing demand for expansion of job enrichment programs deserves a work of caution. The early degree of success in this pilot project has led to the belief that this is a panacea for all problem areas—that all we need to do is "enrich" the problems away. Our concern is that some managers' expectations may be too high relative to the realities of implementing job enrichment. Unrealistic expectations too frequently lead to unwise shortcuts which may seriously impair, or even prevent, the successful outcomes sought.

We do feel that there are better ways to utilize human resources so that everyone comes out a winner. While job enrichment is certainly not a panacea, and while there may be several instances where it may be inappropriate, there are undoubtedly many more situations where job enrichment can result in significant pay-offs for workers, managers, and the company. Furthermore, we have demonstrated that job enrichment efforts need not involve large groups of people to be successful. Motivating employees is an on-going responsibility of management, and job enrichment can be a valuable tool in the motivation program.

---

1. Richard C. Grote, "Implementing Job Enrichment," *California Management Review*, Fall 1972, p. 16.

Pehr Gyllenhammer is President of A B Volvo.

This chapter is taken from an address given at a Conference of the Industrial Participation Association in London, October 23, 1973. It appeared in the Spring 1974 issue of **Industrial Participation,** *London, England, pp. 5-10.*

19
Changing Work
Organization at Volvo

Pehr Gyllenhammar

We have in Sweden, and in Volvo, gone through a number of phases in production planning.

The first phase was quite primitive, it was hardly a planning system at all, we counted numbers of units more or less! The products, and I talk about cars, trucks and buses in our case, were also simple. Foremen were the key to production. They were skilled men who had been promoted. They were asked to, and showed, an authoritarian and paternalistic attitude towards their workers. In the traditional sense morale was high. It was taken for granted that you did a good day's work for your money. Management as such was not really required. You managed the system and you were backed up by the general customs and morale of the country and the corporation. But you did not manage people.

In 1953 we introduced a planning system, methods time measurement, which we brought back from the United States. This became our key planning instrument, and it still is. During this next phase we became heavily mechanized. The human side of planning never had much emphasis because naturally, as in most countries, economic growth was our objective. If you got growth you could pay people more, and they would work hard and be happy. Or so it appeared.

Since the end of the 1960's, the third phase, we have paid more attention to social, sociological and psychological factors. I think we still do so in an amateurish way, as laymen, largely because we have been little helped by research, and I shall come back to that later. We are now looking for new ways of creating a better atmosphere at work and improved efficiency long term, and I want to tell you about some of the alternatives we are developing. But first it is important that you understand why we should go ahead with new production systems and new types of work organization.

Background problems

We have had problems. In 1969 our labour turnover at Volvo reached 52%. At one point absentee rates reached 30% in some plants, and we had to keep one seventh of our labour force in reserve just to plug the gaps on the assembly lines. One year ago turnover of personnel at our Gothenburg plant was 28% and absenteeism 18%. By comparison at our plant in Ghent, Belgium the figures were 7% and 5%.

We are reaching the point in Sweden where people have some choice, not only between different jobs, but how much or how little they want to work. We have a social security system that does not penalize those who stay at home. In the past people often went to work when they were unwell. They could not afford to stay away. In Sweden now everyone who does not feel well stays at home. From a human point of view this is right, but it creates problems for production.

In Sweden today we spend more per capita on education than in any other country in the world, and towards the end of the present decade we estimate that about 90% of our youth will go through college education. It is from these people that we must recruit our labour force. They have different views and different values to the previous generation. Fewer and fewer people actually apply for jobs in industry. It is up to the company to attract people nowadays, and hold them, by the quality of jobs and job satisfaction that you can offer. And many many jobs in the traditional car assembly plant are extremely boring and deadly from a mental point of view. Nobody wants to do them unless they have to. We also find that modern assembly line production isolates people from each other. It is not the noise that makes it impossible to communicate, but the physical distance between jobs. People have no sense of belonging to a group.

It is no wonder that people do not stay in these jobs. In such a situation labour becomes the weakest link in production.

Changing work organization

This then is the background to our activities in the field of work structuring and changing the work organization We have been doing this work now for quite a few years. We think we are getting results, but it is very difficult to prove. It is easier, for example, to recruit today than it was in 1970 and our turnover of personnel has gone down. But it has also gone down for people who have done nothing at all to improve their plants. I can only say that as long as it does not go up, as long as we can increase our productivity and maintain the quality of our product we shall continue. We may never be able to *prove* that a specific step was beneficial, but it is absolutely necessary to have the attitude that change in the sense of creating better jobs for people must be a good way to increase long term productivity and efficiency.

It is also impossible to be flexible in the structuring of work if you do not have a technical design that gives this flexibility. It is also economically impossible on grounds of cost to change the layout of the traditional conveyor belt assembly plant in more than a very limited manner. So job enlargement (increasing the range of operations and responsibilities of job holders) can only come by such means as rotation until you are able to redesign and build a whole new plant layout as we are doing at Kalmar and Skovde — I will come to that in a minute.

Car assembly

In our Gothenburg plant, for example we already have 1,600 operators who are rotating their jobs; some make several changes a day; others change once a week. The numbers are increasing. But the rotation system is not being forced on anyone. We do not in a paternalistic way produce a system and insist that people work it. It is offered and then it is up to the operator whether or not he uses it. People come voluntarily to apply.

I think it is wrong to introduce changes in work organization as if you are making a big contribution to improving the life of your workers. Whenever we have been seen as preaching a doctrine that is "good for others" there has been a boomerang effect. If we are seen as patronizing in our efforts to change the workplace the whole issue will be damned. It is vitally important that many of the suggestions and solutions come from the labour force themselves.

At the Gothenburg plant rotation on the assembly line takes place within teams of 12 to 15 members. A very important part of the deal is that team members decide among themselves how to rotate their jobs and how to meet the team responsibility for the completed job. It is not the foreman who changes people around. In the same plant we have developed joint consultation between foremen and workers who sit down together every two to four weeks to discuss the job and how it can be improved from the technical and quality angles to achieve the economic objectives of the organization. Production engineers who are responsible for introducing technical equipment also take part in these joint consultations.

Trucks and buses

The problems are different in our truck assembly plants. The jobs there are more complex and the movements slower. We can communicate with people because they are in smaller units. Here we have introduced a system of self-controlling groups, each consisting from three to nine people. The groups appoint their own team leader, and rotate this responsibility around the group, each team leader holding the position for about one month. This helps workers to understand the responsibility of managing a group, and the powers needed by a foreman or team boss. Within each group the members agree among themselves what jobs they should have, and how they should be rotated. Some want to specialize in one particular job. Others want increased variety and responsibility. Again, I think that this type of decision is best left to the employees, rather than that management should move in and solve it. So far this system has worked well and increased productivity. Turnover has also dropped dramatically to around 10%, which is extremely low for Swedish standards in an industrial area like Gothenburg. The country average for factory workers is between 20% and 25%.

New design for plant and workplace

I would now like to tell you about the new plants we are building at Kalmar and Skovde.

Kalmar is a car assembly plant, designed with an annual capacity of 30,000 cars and a projected labour force of approximately 600 persons. We want to eliminate the conveyor belt assembly line and to produce a new and more flexible work organization that will increase job satisfaction. We want highly motivated people. The whole conception and the design and arrangement of departments and assembly areas has been the joint creation of management and the unions from the very beginning. And we have not changed our standard demands on efficiency. Rather we have upgraded them for I feel that any solution that lowers efficiency is bad. You cannot afford it in the long run. Secondly if your people are highly motivated it would be very odd if you did not get higher productivity and better quality.

The basic plan for Kalmar was to create work teams of 15 to 20 people, each team having specific responsibility for a particular section of the car. Teams would be specialists — in electrical systems, in instrumentation, in steering and controls, finish, interior and so on. They would then be able to pinpoint their particular contribution, feel responsibility for quality and so identify with the finished product. It was also the plan that each team would have its own separate shop floor area, to help them identify physically with their job in a fairly big plant. Each workshop area would have its own changing rooms and rest rooms, and perhaps its own colour scheme.

The car bodies on which the teams will work will be individually mounted on self-propelled electric carriers. These carriers will transport car bodies both within and between each workshop area. There are to be buffer zones between each workshop containing an accessories depot and space for carrier storage. The buffer zone should always contain at least three units on which work has been completed, ready for the next team. Within this requirement, teams, and individuals within teams, can vary their work pace at will. The idea is that all operators in a team will learn each others' jobs, and they will decide among themselves how to allocate these jobs, and what the pattern of rotation should be. Both management and unions will encourage such a development. The only contract the team makes with management is to deliver a specified number of vehicles each day on which its task has been completed.

Exactly the same considerations guided our thinking and planning in our new Skovde engine plant. This plant has also been planned after full management/worker consultation, the work is based on specialist teams who will control their own work, and again each team will have its own workshop area, rest rooms and changing rooms, etc. This plant will have an initial capacity of some 250,000 engines a year and will employ approximately 600 people.

Need for commitment

We do not think of either of these two new plants as experiments. To me the word experiment implies uncertainty, a lack of determination to go ahead and no commitment. There is no time today to deal with big problems on a miniature scale. We have to deal with them full scale. Our two new plants will have cost the company 10% more than conventional plants of the same capacity. During the last four years we have invested some 17 to 20 million pounds in the job environment, the physical job environment. That is part of the cost to get more hygienic and cleaner surroundings. I feel we must make commitments and these are some of our commitments.

But this does not really give us a better job. It only gives us the conditions in which we can create a better work organization Now we concentrate on the contents of the job rather than wasting too much money on outside things. I feel that the old human relations theory where you build a swimming pool instead of a better workplace is out. The swimming pool is a very nice extra if you have a good place to work in. But it is never a substitute.

I said earlier that we have been little helped by research. We have found very little research which gave real guidance on how to tackle our problems, or which had any realistic appreciation of our time scale. There are plenty of people who would like to study our efforts and come back three years later to tell us where we went wrong! By then you have changed half your workforce and committed yourself to investments in design and layout which you may not be able to alter for 10 or 15 years. That sort of help is useless. I would like to call for dynamic research that comes up with suggestions and solutions for immediate problems based on how industry actually works, and where feedback is rapid enough to influence current planning and developments. However, in spite of the lack of help from research, and the many problems we have had in changing work organization, nothing has defeated us so far, or made us give up.

Works councils

I have several times stressed the importance of consultation with employees and making it possible for them to propose solutions to problems and be in charge of their own activities at the workplace. As a company we have generally a good experience of our works councils. There are those in Sweden who criticize works councils, saying that in them workers lend themselves to an exchange of views, but without gaining any real power. But on the whole both unions and employers recognize them as a good breeding ground for new ideas and a place where any kind of issue can be discussed. I would say it is very much a matter of how management tackles this issue. If management is very open, if it gives full information to the worker, if you really make the works council take decisions, then it is a body that can come to life and play a very important role.

We have another helpful tradition in Sweden. Our unions have a very positive attitude towards rationalization, even when this means getting rid of some jobs. This helped enormously to make organizations more efficient in the fifties and sixties. It also helped to make the jobs "poor", because rationalization meant mechanization, with the object of increased efficiency in the narrow sense. Now of course we are talking about efficiency in the wider sense.

Workers on the board

We have taken another important step in recent years. We now have workers or representatives of the unions on our mother company board. This has been a major issue in most countries — should labour unions accept an invitation to go on the board. In Sweden our unions took a very negative attitude until five or six years ago. The danger they saw was one of bribery, that the unions would become a sort of hostage to the organization and have to back all major decisions and not be able to criticize what was happening. This attitude has softened, primarily I think because the unions think that revolution or drastic change is no longer possible unless we throw the whole present system overboard. If you must cooperate, why not start at the top?

From the company's point of view board representation has been useful. It has demonstrated to employees that there are very few secrets in the board room, that the meetings are very normal, and only extraordinary in the sense that major issues are dealt with. I think this has cleared the atmosphere, and helped to build more confidence in the relationship between employers and employees.

There are those who believe that putting workers on company boards is somehow a political action. I do not agree. I cannot say that there have been drastic changes in our decision-making process because of worker representation on the board. But it has great importance for the whole process of understanding participation throughout the organization. For example the types of issue discussed within the board are new issues to these representatives. And they can bring an entirely new angle or aspect to our work. For the first time in the history of our company the impressions of the labour force are brought directly to the board's attention. These representatives can change the discussion on a variety of subjects where if they are not the experts, they provide the principal input. It is also a learning process for them, where they can influence and change the whole education and training programme throughout the organization. They have their own budget which is financed by their own means, and they also have the company budget which they direct when it comes to training programmes to a very large extent. I think they are starting to focus on new issues because of their participation on the board. So I find it highly useful.

Delegating decisions

When it comes to participation my conviction is that it is not only discussion, it is decision-making powers that you delegate.

I do not believe for one moment that airy talk gets us anywhere. We cooperate at a practical level, and a practical level in my opinion is from the top down. We have delegated responsibility for cleaning up the environment of the plants to local union representatives. This year they have an allocation of 1½ million pounds for this purpose, and they got together a small group to travel around all the plants and then came back with recommendations on how to spend the money. This is outside the individual programmes for each plant.

I gave veto right in Gothenburg to representatives of the workers when it came to the appointment of a new personnel manager. They also have a veto right for the appointment of new company doctors.

Practical cooperation can mean practical problems. I am sometimes asked how long established foremen adjust to the changes brought about by new types of work organization. This group of people is under the greatest pressure. Previously we promoted skilled workers, the best technicians, and suddenly they find they have to manage people. For some of the older ones it is a hard problem. They feel caught between management and labour. But it is also remarkable how many of them, even the older ones, can adjust. We even find that many of them have actually led the way in restructuring work, that we are starting to do now what they have already been doing for some time.

I am also asked whether self-controlling work teams are always fair to their members, whether they may expel those who are in some respect weaker, or do not easily fit into the group. No team is entirely uncontrolled by management. But we have started an internal employment agency within each factory so that workers who have difficulty in adjusting to their group, or to the new work situation, will not necessarily be lost, but may find more suitable or congenial work somewhere else in the plant.

Challenge to unions

Another question of great importance on participation and delegation is that the unions also face the same challenge as management. I repeat that we have never forced anyone to take part in our discussions, or to share in designing new plant and processes with us. But if the unions sought to guide all discussions from the centre, if there was no possibility of shop floor participation, there could be no discussion at all — we would design the whole thing ourselves. We have to operate at a practical level, at a local level. It takes the same strength on the part of the central union to delegate power to local representatives as it does management to delegate labour responsibilities to their foremen. If the unions are unable to delegate in a similar way to the company then nothing can work.

Susan E. Walima is Organizational Development Specialist for Kaiser Aluminum and Chemical Corporation.

This highly personalized approach to job enrichment has been condensed from a larger booklet, **Job Enrichment: An Action Guide,** *published in 1974 by Kaiser Aluminum and Chemical Corporation. Copies are available through the corporation at 300 Lakeside Drive, Oakland, California 94643.*

20
Kaiser Aluminum's Action Guide to Job Enrichment

Susan E. Walima

"In the average company the boys in the mailroom, the president, the vice presidents, and the girls in the steno pool have three things in common: they are docile, they are bored, and they are dull. Trapped in the pigeonholes of organization charts, they've been made slaves to the rules of private and public hierarchies that run mindlessly on and on . . . "

Townsend, *Up the Organization*

Job Enrichment: Who Cares and Why

Job enrichment sometimes sounds too good to be true. After all, how often do you hear about something that can increase profits for the shareholders *and* job satisfaction for employees. (Making *everybody* happy is no simple trick, because no simple trick can be responsive to the complex forces acting on the job environment today.)

Enrichment, however, being far from simple and certainly not a trick, can be responsive to the employee's concerns, management's concerns, and, increasingly, the unions' concerns. Let's look at enrichment from each of those perspectives.

1) Today's employees, first of all, are a changing breed. All of us, whether hourly, salaried, supervisors or managers, apparently want more from our work lives than our predecessors

did. We want more say in the making of decisions that affect us than we have had in the past. We're becoming less willing to perform boring or demeaning work which doesn't use all our skills and knowledge or help us grow and learn as people. We're not as willing to carry out the orders of someone in a chain of command who may not know the job as well as we do. Also, we want to be treated with respect, allowed to exercise our own judgment, and given a chance to see how our efforts fit into the total company picture.

None of this changing work-force picture is new to any of us—particularly to supervisors who recognize that the old hierarchical, autocratic management style no longer works. We realize that tomorrow's successful managers will get there by learning how to tap and develop the resources of his or her own people so that these people, in fact *manage their own jobs.*

2) Management today faces increasing absenteeism, problems in quality control, grievances, pilferage, and even sabotage caused by deepening employee discontent and boredom. Few companies can afford costly strikes or shutdowns, and so have tried to find ways to increase the job satisfaction of their employees. In so doing, they protect the company's ability to continue successful operation. Job enrichment, as one of many participative approaches to managing organizations, can be a way to meet both management and employee needs.

3) But what about the unions? More spokesmen, initially in Europe but increasingly in the United States, are recognizing that job enrichment is becoming an important issue for them because of the potential involvement of hourly people. Initially seen as a management strategy serving management's needs, job enrichment was viewed with some suspicion by union leaders. However, where it has been tried, it has tended to meet employee needs sufficiently that union leaders have opted for involvement. Other spokesmen for labor's point of view argue that the unions have always worked for greater humanization of work and that job enrichment, although a new term, is nothing new to them. These unions are recognizing that job enrichment, as it becomes increasingly attractive to union employees, can be a powerful new bargaining issue which either the unions *or* management could champion to win over the hourly employee. Tomorrow's unions may need to have job enrichment on their side of the bargaining table.

What this means is that job enrichment is becoming a strategy that everyone can support and profit from, provided the management/union/employee relationships are strong enough to handle whatever difficulties might arise in the process of enriching jobs.

Successful Applications.

There's no way to know exactly how many companies have tried job enrichment, or with what degree of success; but a few of the more prominent are:

Alcoa	Kaiser Aluminum
American Airlines	Maytag
AT&T	Monsanto Chemicals
Bankers Trust	Motorola
R. G. Barry	Polaroid
Chrysler Corporation	Proctor & Gamble
Corning Corporation	Saab
Corning Glass	Texas Instruments
Donnelly Mirrors	Travelers Insurance
Ford Motor Company	TRW Systems
General Foods	U.S. Steel
IBM	Volvo
Imperial Chemicals Industries	Western Electric

Obviously, job enrichment is no novelty among the FORTUNE 500 companies—nor is it limited to any one industry. It's been used with technical specialists, assembly line workers, laboratory personnel, insurance agents, production workers, managers; the list goes on and on. Some of the most successful enrichment experiences so far recorded are:

○ *AT&T*, the job enrichment pioneer, has enriched over 10,000 jobs in the last nine years. Their original project in the Shareholder Relations Department brought about a 27 percent reduction in the termination rate and a production cost-savings of $558,000 over a 12-month period. Later, when the jobs of service representatives were enriched in 12 districts, resignations and dismissals dropped by 14 percent. AT&T is one of the few companies to have had a continuous job enrichment effort for so long a time. All but one of their projects have been successful.

○ The *Chrysler Corporation* has several programs underway which significantly involve the worker in decision making. At some plants, assembly workers perform their own quality control by riding through water test booths in cars they just built. In another plant, axle assemblers both assemble and inspect axles; they can reject substandard axles on their own authority. Workers in the parts departments at yet another plant operate without foremen. Chrysler management believes that new attitudes toward work as a result of these programs have reduced corporate turnover from 47 percent in 1969 to 17 percent now, and absenteeism from 7.8 to 5.6 percent.

O *General Motors* is experimenting with a team approach to motor-home assembly. Teams of three to six workers are now building selected coaches from start to finish. At Delco Electronics Division, an individual quality program encourages both hourly and salaried employees to participate in setting departmental and individual goals. Major results have been reduced product repairs, decreased maintenance, and improved attendance.

O A *Kaiser Aluminum & Chemicals* plant has experimented with maintenance work-teams who operate without foremen, fill in their own time-cards, and prioritize and plan maintenance jobs. Machine downtime became almost non-existent as maintenance performance improved. Other Kaiser plants have also experimented with job enrichment.

O At a *Monsanto Chemicals* plant, 50 workers formed task forces to restructure jobs through automation, and eliminate certain "dirty" chores that nobody wanted or did well. In the first year of the change, waste loss dropped to zero and productivity improved by 50 percent.

O Perhaps the most dramatic enrichment project is going on at *General Foods* pet food plant in Topeka, Kansas. Even before it began operations, the plant was designed and staffed to function in a way that would use its human resources to the fullest extent. The employees now work in semi-autonomous teams which select their own team leaders and determine at the start of each shift how to meet production goals, as well as how to divide up the job assignments. Each team member is also trained to do practically any job on the team. The teams interview and hire replacements, as well as train and discipline their own members. As a result, there is an exceptionally high level of worker commitment; absenteeism and turnover are each less than 1 percent; and the production rate is 30 percent higher and quality 80 percent better than in Topeka's sister plant at Kankakee, which operates in the older, traditional fashion.

Observations on Successful Applications

These are a very few of the experiences which have been reported by companies trying job enrichment. (You will find further reports in the reading list attached.) Their total experience allows some generalizations to be made now about the job enrichment process:

☐ No single job enrichment "package" can be applied in every situation. Each company, and each enrichment project within a company, will need to apply enrichment principles in a way that "fits" that particular organization and its technology. This means that an enrichment project team will have to be its own best judge regarding the kinds of job redesign that make sense in its organization.

☐ The most successful projects are long-term, seemingly slow processes. If implementation of job change is hurried or forced, it will almost certainly fail. Recognizing beforehand that the progress will not move fast enough to suit most of those involved can be helpful. Also, there will be unexpected obstacles. The best that can be done to make the job enrichment project go well is to plan thoroughly, using realistic time guidelines.

☐ Production in the early stages of implementation may decrease. Job changes must be tested over a long enough time to allow for adjustments to the changes before results can be fairly measured. How long that adjustment period is depends upon how sweeping the change is, but most enrichment projects seem to require a 6-month to 1-year testing period.

☐ The commitment of first-line supervision seems to be critical to enrichment project success. Since the immediate supervisors of enriched jobs will very likely be giving up some of their former authority, it is important that they not feel threatened or diminished in importance. It will help if they realize that their jobs may be different, but will not be eliminated. More important, their jobs can be similarly enriched if they assume more management responsibility from jobs above them.

Indications for Consideration

To determine if job enrichment is right for your organization, you might as a start consider the following critical factors of work-life:

1) absenteeism;

2) turnover;

3) frequently expressed grievances;

4) evidences of employee dissatisfaction such as strikes, sabotage, or work stoppages;

5) productivity as compared to ability of the people in the organization;

6) degree of apparent boredom with the work;

7) employee suggestions for improving work procedures.

A problem in any of these areas could indicate that the work being performed is boring and unchallenging and well might benefit by job enrichment.

On the other hand, negative indicators aren't absolutely necessary before considering enrichment. Most jobs can be improved in some way—even if only to allow already good employees to grow by learning new tasks, expanding their abilities, and exercising greater authority over their own work.

Perhaps the most important criteria in deciding if it's right for your organization is whether it makes sense to the people who would be involved. Given enough information on job enrichment, they should be able to decide whether to try an enrichment project, and if so, how to proceed.

A word of caution about factors which might later become problems as a result of undertaking a job enrichment program:

1) That the job in question might be automated out of existence;

2) that major organizational change might remove key implementing people;

3) that the people involved might not want it;

4) that management might not be willing to support an enrichment experiment;

5) that management may expect quick results;

6) that the people involved might not be willing to do what would be necessary for successs.

Organizational Effects of Job Enrichment

It would be convenient if successful job enrichment efforts yielded neat, manageable "islands" of satisfied employees, but in reality, they don't. As people in enriched jobs become more autonomous, more risk-taking and more responsible for their own decision-making, problems are created for the nonenriched organizations around them. These problems may be the kind that those organizations haven't faced before.

At the Employee Level

The effect of job enrichment may be so clearly desirable to employees in the non-enriched organizations that many of them ask for such changes to be made in *their* jobs. It's been typical of successful job enrichment that the people in enriched jobs talk about their newly acquired freedoms and responsibilities to their peers in other departments, other functions, and other shifts. And a typical result has been that those peers bid for jobs in the enriched organization at an increasing rate (while turnover in the enriched organization probably decreases—producing fewer openings). Or they may demand that their jobs undergo identical changes, even though such changes would not necessarily constitute the best enrichment strategy for their jobs.

As we said earlier, no enrichment "package" works in every case, and all successful enrichment is a long-term process. That means that each project will require careful guidance and deep involvement by enrichment resource people. So, if the demand for job enrichment projects exceeds the organization's resources to guide them, those employees whose requests for enrichment are not met may be justifiably unhappy. In this event, it will help if you are prepared to explain the reasons for enriching the jobs you did, realistically outlining future plans for enrichment. And, if full enrichment isn't a possibility for other jobs in the near future, it will help, at least, to create more participative management in that organization as an interim measure.

Sometimes these successful job enrichment projects attract considerable publicity. Some managers of highly publicized enrichment projects have been so bombarded with requests for information and on-site visits from people both inside and outside the corporation that they have had little time left to manage. One manager had to have his home telephone number unlisted, and some organizations have even begun to charge a fee for visitor tours. Still others, whose enrichment projects were based on careful joint agreements with unions, fear that the publicity attending a successful project will cause unions to withdraw their support. One company, faced with constant requests for information about its enrichment project, had its corporate public relations staff prepare a handout document describing the project in full. Another company, carrying out the enrichment philosophy of decision making by those affected, has let the enriched work group decide for itself which visitors they will allow and at what times. Other companies have simply avoided the problem by carefully shielding their projects from outside attention or by refusing to acknowledge their existence.

At the Managerial Level

A more serious problem is the transition which must be made by managers of enriched jobs. The more successful the manager is in enriching jobs, the more his or her own job will require reshaping. Managing enriched jobs requires the manager to learn new and more complex skills. These skills are less technical, and more people and planning-oriented. For example, because the work group will be more autonomous after enrichment and less dependent on the manager, he or she may need to develop, and to train the group in conflict-resolution skills so that they can handle their

Basic Managerial Position Before Job Enrichment

own conflict situations. The manager must also shift his or her attention from activities inside the work group to activities outside the work group. After job enrichment, because the work group will have taken over its own direction and control, the manager will need to be free to "manage outward," i.e., to work with and influence other work groups, other managers, and outside forces on the group's behalf. He or she will also need to widen the scope of the job to include long-range strategy planning and anticipating external changes which will affect the work group.

Expanded Managerial Position After Job Enrichment

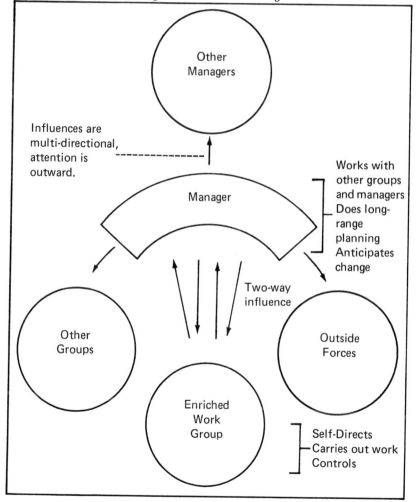

Diagrams of the manager's position before and after enrichment illustrate graphically the extent of this transition. You can see that the manager's job after enrichment is more complex and quite different. Companies with successful job enrichment projects have reported that this management transition is a critical hurdle to overcome and that some managers do not succeed. Regardless of the degree of preparation managers are given, many apparently are still unsettled for a time by a sense of not being needed anymore by their work group. They *are* needed, of course, but in a changed capacity. If their primary contribution has been to direct and control the work group's activities, they will certainly experience a temporary sense of uselessness as the group starts directing and controlling itself. But as the manager learns to "manage outward," his or her sense of being needed will be restored.

When managers fail in this transition, it is probably because they are not comfortable in a new role. We believe this problem might be avoided by:

1) selecting only jobs for enrichment whose managers demonstrate the capability and willingness to take on an enriched job themselves;

2) preparing managers for whatever temporary feelings of uselessness may occur;

3) training managers early in necessary new skills;

4) providing reassurance and support throughout.

If the transition is still too difficult, reassignment (without blame) to a non-enriched work group may be the answer. However, it is important that 1) the move not be seen as punitive, and 2) the enrichment project go on. Ending the project at this point might well be seen as failure of the enriched group rather than a transition problem for the manager in a new role.

At the Corporate Level

Some other far-reaching effects of successful job enrichment have been reported. One company regards its highly successful project as a "monster," at least partly because it has generated so many new "problems" and partly because the enriched operation regularly questions corporate policy. The problems reported have to do with the enriched organization's relationship with other organizations within the company and with the corporate power structure. Since the enriched organization has learned to direct and control itself, it doesn't respond very happily to corporate directives or power strategies used by other parts of the organization. Still, the corporation regards the project itself as a success in spite of the complications which have arisen.

Other companies report that people in enriched jobs have become so growth-oriented that the company can't keep up with their requests for developmental assignments. One line manager of an enriched production function got so "turned on" to enrichment that he requested a leave to practice consulting to other organizations. The company denied the leave, but it is allowing him to spend one-half of his time consulting to other parts of the company.

So, in answer to the question, "Suppose it's successful, what then?", we have to conclude that there will probably be *more* problems. They may be "better" problems, however, in the sense that they'll be symptoms of a healthy, aggressively growing organization rather than those of a sluggish, poor-performance organization. Still, problems are problems; and no matter how indicative of success they are, they will require time, effort, and in this case, ingenuity. The enrichment experimenter who is naive about the consequences of success may be in for some surprises.

Steps for Implementation

Despite all that's been written about job enrichment, not much of the literature deals specifically with the "how to" steps involved; and the companies practicing job enrichment have not, by and large, been generous in reporting exactly what processes they've followed.

Most of them, however, seem to follow a basic process that we can suggest and support. (Even though the steps are listed here in a certain order, they may overlap or differ depending on what fits your organization.) They are:

1) get key management support;

2) decide which jobs to enrich;

3) if union jobs, get union support;

4) select the enrichment project team;

5) hold the enrichment workshop;

6) implement the enrichment plan;

7) follow-up and evaluate.

Taking them one by one, we suggest:

Step 1: Get key management support.
The initial idea to try job enrichment can come from a number of sources. A manager may read or hear about it and want to enrich jobs that he or she manages. Or the employees themselves may express such dissatisfaction with their job routine that line supervision might insist that "*something needs to be done.*" Somebody along the line might suggest job enrichment.

Regardless of where the initiating idea comes from, the first step should be to obtain umbrella-type support from key managers to try job enrichment. To identify who those managers are, decide who, by virtue of their position or influence, could cause a job enrichment project to fail if they were not informed and supportive.

Once identified, you will want to get their support by:

a) holding a face-to-face meeting (allow 1-3 hours);

b) presenting the concept of, and supporting data for, job enrichment (this booklet might be a good source or handout);

c) answering their questions and concerns, and . . .

d) asking for their support (or at least an agreement not to interfere).

Step 2: Decide which jobs to enrich.
You may or may not have had a particular job or jobs in mind when you got management's go-ahead. At this point, however, a specific decision needs to be made.
How do you know which jobs to enrich? Are there some jobs that are more "enrichable" than others? We think so. Here's how you can recognize them:

○ jobs which could (but perhaps currently don't) produce a specific end product which can be measured;

○ jobs which could be organized around a team concept with a group of people taking responsibility for an entire product, from start to finish;

○ jobs which can be redesigned without affecting so many other jobs that an entire work system could be jeopardized;

○ jobs where first-level supervision is currently overloaded with responsibilities;

○ jobs in which the people involved are willing to experiment with changing their ways of working;

○ jobs in which there is troublesome absenteeism, turnover, apparent boredom, grievances, or low production as compared to ability;

○ jobs which currently limit the people in them from growing, learning new skills, or exercising greater responsibility;

○ jobs in which performance can be measured before and after enrichment.

Most enrichment projects involve only one job at a time even though many people may be performing that job. For example, a plant may have seven or eight people performing the same *job* (on different shifts, for different foremen, etc.), but for enrichment purposes it's considered one job.

Step 3: If union jobs, get union support.
If the jobs you've picked are union jobs, it is critically important to get union support and, if possible, involvement early in the job enrichment process. Much has been written about the union's supposed resistance to job enrichment. However, that resistance doesn't need to develop if union leaders are involved early, their questions and concerns answered, and they are given a genuine opportunity to influence the enrichment process.

Generally, the more progressive and enlightened unions tend to realize that enrichment can aid their cause by developing a more skilled and committed employee, who is therefore more secure in his employment and bargaining unit. And as we said earlier, unions are beginning to realize that their continued existence may depend on their assuming control of these new kinds of bargaining issues, before management does.

The union's concern might center around four items:

general unfamiliarity with the job enrichment concept;

fear of job loss for its members;

potential compensation disputes in the redesigned jobs;

jurisdictional and/or seniority concerns.

These are genuine concerns and can only be solved by leveling with the union. It will be helpful for both parties to understand at the outset that the principles and applications of job enrichment are entirely consistent with this company's labor agreements with the unions. Where the job is changed it can be reviewed under the provisions of existing wage agreements, and wage adjustments can be made as appropriate. Job loss for union members is an issue that needn't be troublesome if management makes it clear that reduction of the workforce is *not* its goal in trying job enrichment.

Overall, the more open each party can be, the greater are the chances for a mutually planned and agreed-to enrichment process.

The union leaders' commitment can be sought in the same manner as management's: by holding a face-to-face meeting, presenting the concept of and reasons for job enrichment, answering their questions and concerns, and asking for their support.

Finally, if union-management relations are less than cordial and mutual commitment is difficult to obtain, additional work may be necessary. Such extra effort could range from joint participation in a team-building/problem-solving meeting to a management training program. Another approach might be a negotiated "experiment" with some clearly stipulated goals and criteria for evaluation. In this way, neither party need feel "locked in." Perhaps the overall point to remember is that an open-ended, problem-solving climate maintained by both parties will be more effective in dealing with whatever problems arise than a polarized "win-lose" climate.

Step 4: Select the enrichment project team.
This is the group that will meet offsite to analyze the job, decide how it can be enriched, plan how to implement the job changes, and monitor the implementation process. It might include:

- O 2 or 3 incumbents in the job to be enriched. (They can provide first-hand working knowledge of procedures and tasks.)

- O 2 or 3 people who are one vertical or diagonal level above the job to be enriched. (They can identify higher level decision making which can be moved into the job.)

○ 1 or 2 people two levels above the job to be enriched. (They too, can identify higher level decision making and provide an overall view of the work process the job is a part of.)

○ 1 or 2 people three levels above the job. (They can provide an overall view of the organization and the high level commitment to help implement enrichment changes.)

○ 1 or 2 union leaders or representatives who know the job in question. (They can help raise and resolve union issues.)

○ 1 or 2 industrial relations or personnel specialists. (They can help raise and resolve industrial relations and personnel management issues.)

The specific individuals might be chosen for their knowledge of the job, interest in the project, ability to influence the success or failure of the project, and effectiveness in working with a project team.

The project team will need to decide on a time and place for the enrichment workshop. They might also decide what pre-work needs to be done before the workshop and who should do it. An example of pre-work that can be helpful is to gather data on the job's current tasks, relationship to other jobs, production rates, rejection or re-work rates, absenteeism, etc. This information can be used as input during the workshop, and as a comparison in the before and after measurement of results.

Step 5: Hold the enrichment workshop.
The workshop is typically a 2-4 day meeting which is divided into two parts and "led" by someone outside the immediate group who is trained to conduct enrichment workshops. Holding the workshop away from the work place can prevent interruptions.

The two parts of the meeting are:

1) training in job enrichment concepts and techniques (more detailed information than is included in this booklet), and

2) analysis and planning for enriching the job in question.

The subjects covered in the training are:

> motivating factors in jobs;
>
> maintenance factors in jobs;
>
> complete units of work;
>
> planning, controlling, and "doing" responsibilities;
>
> feedback and performance standards;
>
> diagramming a job;
>
> the "brainstorm" method in group problem solving;
>
> action planning for job enrichment.

The analysis and planning part of the workshop will involve the following activities:

1) review the pre-workshop job data without evaluating;

2) decide on "success criteria" upon which you'll measure your results;

3) Flowchart the current sequence of the job;

4) Brainstorm ("greenlight") ideas for changing the job;

5) Screen the list for purely maintenance items; drop them;

6) For *each* of the remaining items:

    a.   Clearly define the item in detail so everyone has the same understanding. What began as one item may become several. Give the item a number for easy reference.

    b.   List advantages (things that would *result after* the item is implemented).

    c.   List disadvantages (things that would result after the item is implemented). Consider disadvantages of three types:

        1)   risks;

2) negative consequences;

3) impracticalities.

d. Weigh advantages against disadvantages and decide whether to drop, defer, or plan the item now.

e. List the roadblocks (obstacles and hurdles that must be *cleared before implementing*). Decide again whether to drop, defer, or plan now.

f. Plan to minimize the disadvantages listed in Step *c*.

g. Plan to clear the roadblocks listed in Step *e*.

h. Program the item for action:

decide whether it should be broadly or selectively applied to jobs;

plan target dates step by step;

assign individual responsibility;

plan for required approvals.

i. Anticipate individual response and plan to introduce the item to each individual involved if necessary.

j. Plan how, when, and by whom the results of implementing each item will be measured.

The end product of the workshop will be a written action plan describing what changes will be made in the job, who will make them, and when; as well as how, when, and by whom the results will be measured.

Step 6: Implement the enrichment plan.
Although this step can be a fairly straightforward matter of carrying out the plan developed in the workshop, you may also have to be ready to handle setbacks, unplanned-for contingencies, deadlines that prove unrealistic, etc. Some of the implementation problems that other organizations have run into are:

failure to get before and after measures of performance

to use in evaluating their success;

anxiety of middle management who fear their authority is being taken away;

failure to follow up;

desire to move too fast;

unmanageable size of enrichment team;

unwillingness to move roadblocks;

failure to educate managers of enriched jobs;

failure to adjust appraisal criteria to coincide with enrichment changes;

failure to adjust salary plans and wage rates;

failure to build an effective job enrichment team.

Any one of these problems might cause the implementation to fail or become bogged down. If so, the enrichment project team may need to reconvene briefly to map alternate strategies or set new target dates. What will probably be most helpful during this time is a continued shared commitment to carry out the plan in spite of whatever setbacks occur.

Step 7: Follow-up and evaluate.
This step will be the last part of your enrichment action plan. You will already have decided at the workshop what evaluation measurements need to be taken, at what time, and by whom. At this point, you take those measurements and use them to decide whether the enrichment project has been a success.

The criteria for "success" will also have been decided at the workshop. It may be a certain level of increased production, a level of decreased absenteeism or turnover, or more expressed employee satisfaction. These are just examples, and whatever success criteria you set must fit your own organization, its goals and priorities. The important thing is that it is clear, specific, measurable, and useful in making the decision to continue or discontinue your enrichment efforts.

Advisory Resources

At some point in this process you may need help in the form of extra information or assistance. When this happens, you might try the following resources:

your own industrial relations or personnel specialist, either in the plant or division offices;

employee relations specialists in the corporate Industrial Relations and Personnel offices;

the corporate Organization and Management Development staff.

They can probably provide the information or the help you need. The only step which may be impossible to handle completely by yourself the first time is Step 5, conducting the enrichment workshop.

Earlier, we stated that we'd try to outline job enrichment concepts and processes for you. If you'd like, you can check over the following questions to see if you can now answer them.

1.   *What is job enrichment?*

○ *what* is it designed to do?

○ *why* is it important to *organizations* today?

○ *why* is it important to the *unions* today?

○ *which* companies are trying it?

○ how do we know *if it's right* for this organization?

○ how do we know *when it's right* for this organization (and *when it isn't*)?

○ how do we handle the problems *success* might bring?

2.   *How do we do it?*

○ what's the basic process?

○ who should be included, and in what way?

○ what outside help might be needed?

○ what problems might be encountered?

○ how do we measure the results?

If you're *not* satisfied with the information you have so far, you might want to read some of the materials in the list that follows . . . or contact some of the people we mentioned earlier.

If, on the other hand, you're ready to test the potential of job enrichment in your organization, we wish you well.

Kaiser's Recommended Reading List on Job Enrichment

(Editor's note: These materials have been made available from the Organization & Management Development Library.)

Books

Davis, Louis E., and Taylor, James C., eds. *Design of Jobs.* London: Penguin, 1972. 479 pages.

Emanuel, Edward E., and Jaffe, Eugene D., eds. *How to Restore the Will to Work.* Cleveland, Ohio: *Industry Week*, Education Division, 1972. 351 pages.

Ford, Robert N. *Motivation Through the Work Itself.* New York: American Management Association, 1969. 267 pages.

Foulkes, Fred K. *Creating More Meaningful Work.* New York: American Management Association, 1969. 222 pages.

Special Task Force to the Secretary of Health, Education, and Welfare. *Work in America.* Cambridge: MIT Press, 1973. 262 pages.

Articles

Anderson, John W. "The Impact of Technology on Job Enrichment." *Personnel*, September-October 1970, pp. 29-37.

"Assembly Line Cracked; Swedes Tackle Production Boredom by Varying Worker Tasks." *Dayton Daily News*, November 14, 1972, p. 24.

Blum, Albert A.; More, Michael L.; and Fairey, B. Parker. "The Effect of Motivational Programs on Collective Bargaining." *Personnel Journal*, July 1973, pp. 633-641.

Drucker, Peter F. "Beyond Stick and Carrot: Hysteria Over the Work Ethic." *Psychology Today*, November 1973, pp. 87-92.

Ford, Robert N. "Job Enrichment Lessons From AT&T." *Harvard Business Review*, January-February 1973, pp. 96-106.

Fuller, Stephen H. "Employee Development and the Modern Work Force." General Motors publication.

General Foods Corporation. "Organization of a Manufacturing Plant to Fit Business and People's Needs." April 1973.

Gibson, Charles H. "Volvo Increases Productivity Through Job Enrichment." *California Management Review*, Summer 1973, pp. 64-66.

Gomberg, William. "Job Satisfaction: Sorting Out the Nonsense." *AFL-CIO American Federationist*, June 1973, pp. 14-19.

Gooding, Judson. "It Pays to Wake Up the Blue-Collar Worker." *Fortune*, September 1970, pp. 133-135, 162-168.

Harris, Sydney J. "Fatiguing Dead-end Jobs." *San Francisco Chronicle*, July 1, 1973.

Herzberg, Frederick. "One More Time: How Do You Motivate Employees?" *Harvard Business Review*, January-February 1968, pp. 53-62.

Herzberg, Frederick. "Why Bother to Work?" *Industry Week*, July 16, 1973, pp. 46-49.

"How Industry Is Dealing with People Problems on the Line." *American Machinist*, Special Report No. 661, November 12, 1973, pp. 79-91.

"Is Job Enrichment Working?" *Industry Week*, June 19, 1972, pp. 52-59.

Janson, Robert. "Job Enrichment: Challenge of the 70's." *Training and Development Journal*, June 1970, pp. 7-9.

Lawrence, Paul R. "How to Deal with Resistance to Change." *Harvard Business Review*, January-February 1969, pp. 4-12, 166-167.

Mills, Ted. "The Quality of Work Program." National Commission on Productivity, February 1, 1973.

Mills, Ted. "The Thirteenth Dilemma." An address before the National Conference on the Changing Work Ethic, New York, March 27, 1973.

Morse, John J. "A Contingency Look at Job Design." *California Management Review*, Fall 1973, pp. 67-75.

Mossberg, Walter. "A Day's Work—Gene Cafiero Labors to Enhance the Quality of Assembly-Line Life." *The Wall Street Journal*, December 7, 1972.

Myers, M. Scott. "Conditions for Manager Motivation." *Harvard Business Review*, January-February 1966, pp. 58-71.

Myers, M. Scott. "Overcoming Union Opposition to Job Enrichment." *Harvard Business Review*, May-June 1971, pp. 37-62.

Myers, M. Scott. "Who Are Your Motivated Workers?" *Harvard Business Review*, January-February 1964, pp. 73-88.

Norman, Geoffrey. "Blue-Collar Saboteurs." *Playboy*, 1973, pp. 96-194, 250-253.

O'Donnell, Laurence G. "A Day's Work—General Motors' Plan to Increase Efficiency Draws Ire of Unions." *The Wall Street Journal*, December 6, 1972.

Paul, William J., Jr.; Robertson, Keither B.; and Herzberg, Frederick. "Job Enrichment Pays Off." *Harvard Business Review*, March-April 1969, pp. 61-78.

Randall, Robert F. "Job Enrichment Ensures Savings at Travelers." *Management Accounting*, January 1973, pp. 68-69, 72.

Reichard, Birge D. "Implementing Job Enrichment Using O.D. Definition as a Guide." Unpublished presentation paper.

Salpukas, Agis. "Jobs Rotated to Fight Boredom." *The New York Times*, February 5, 1973.

Sirota, David. "Job Enrichment—Is It for Real?" *S.A.M. Advanced Management Journal*, April 1973, pp. 22-27.

"Some Job Enrichment Programs Work; Problem, Terms Ill Defined." *Industry Week*, April 9, 1973, p. 24.

Thompson, Donald B. "Enrichment in Action Convinces Skeptics." *Industry Week*, February 14, 1972, pp. 2-7.

Walters, Roy W. "The Need for Job Enrichment is Urgent." *Industrial Engineering*, July 1972, pp. 14-15.

Walters, Roy W. "Putting Your Best Manager's Foot Forward." *The Personnel Administrator*, May-June 1972.

Walton, Richard E. "How to Counter Alienation in the Plant." *Harvard Business Review*, November-December 1972, pp. 70-81.

Walton, Richard E. "Using Social Psychology to Make Dog Food." Prepared for symposium sponsored by the Social Science Research Council, Majorca, Spain, April 24-27, 1973. 25 pages.

"Who Wants to Work?" *Newsweek*, March 26, 1973, pp. 79-89.

Yorks, Lyle. "Key Elements in Implementing Job Enrichment." *Personnel*, September-October 1973, pp. 45-52.

Zwerdling, Daniel. "Beyond Boredom—A Look at What's New on the Assembly Line." *The Washington Monthly*, July/August 1973, pp. 80-91.